Southern Literary Studies
Louis D. Rubin, Jr., Editor

The Art and Vision of Flannery O'Connor

The Art
& Vision
of Flannery
O'Connor

Robert H. Brinkmeyer, Jr.

LOUISIANA STATE UNIVERSITY PRESS

Baton Rouge and London

Copyright © 1989 by Louisiana State University Press
All rights reserved
Manufactured in the United States of America
First printing
98 97 96 95 94 93 92 91 90 89   5 4 3 2 1
Designer: Patricia Douglas Crowder
Typeface: Linotron 202 Aldus
Typesetter: The Composing Room of Michigan, Inc.

LIBRARY OF CONGRESS CATALOGING-IN-PUBLICATION DATA

Brinkmeyer, Robert H.
    The art and vision of Flannery O'Connor / Robert H. Brinkmeyer,
Jr.
        p. cm. — (Southern literary studies)
    Bibliography: p.
    Includes index.
    ISBN 0-8071-1492-8 (alk. paper)
    1. O'Connor, Flannery—Criticism and interpretation. I. Title.
II. Series.
    PS3565.C57Z587   1989
    813'.54—dc20   89-34063
                                                                            CIP

The author gratefully acknowledges permission to reprint the following excerpts:
Reprinted by permission of Harcourt Brace Jovanovich, Inc.: "A Good Man Is Hard to Find"
from A Good Man Is Hard to Find and Other Stories, copyright 1953 by Flannery O'Connor,
renewed 1981 by Mrs. Regina O'Connor; "Good Country People" from A Good Man Is Hard to
Find and Other Stories, copyright © 1955 by Flannery O'Connor, renewed 1983 by Mrs. Regina
O'Connor; "The Artificial Nigger" from A Good Man Is Hard to Find and Other Stories,
copyright 1954 by Flannery O'Connor, renewed 1982 by Mrs. Regina O'Connor.
Reprinted by permission of Farrar, Straus and Giroux, Inc.: Excerpts from The Complete Stories
by Flannery O'Connor. Copyright © 1962 by Flannery O'Connor. Copyright © 1971 by the
Estate of Mary Flannery O'Connor; excerpts from The Habit of Being by Flannery O'Connor,
edited by Sally Fitzgerald. Copyright © 1979 by Regina O'Connor; excerpts from Mystery and
Manners by Flannery O'Connor. Copyright © 1957, 1961, 1963, 1964, 1966, 1967, 1969 by the
Estate of Mary Flannery O'Connor. Copyright 1962 by Flannery O'Connor; excerpts from The
Violent Bear It Away by Flannery O'Connor. Copyright © 1955, 1960 by Flannery O'Connor;
excerpts from Wise Blood by Flannery O'Connor. Copyright © 1962 by Flannery O'Connor

For Chris and our daughters, Mary, Eliza, and Emma

I think a lot of novels, so-called Catholic novels, American-Catholic novels, are usually Irish Catholic. Some of them are very well done indeed. Like Edwin O'Connor. And then there's Flannery—although she's a Georgia fundamentalist.

Walker Percy, interview with Charles T. Bunting

Contents

Acknowledgments

This book was well under way when a sudden turnaround occurred. While attending a National Endowment for the Humanities Summer Seminar for College Teachers, taught by Giles Gunn on religion and literature, I was introduced to the work of Mikhail Bakhtin. I found myself penciling in the margins of Bakhtin's books comments such as "O'Connor," "Apply to 'A Good Man Is Hard to Find,'" and "O'Connor and her audience?" A pattern was developing; Bakhtin was clearly challenging me to read O'Connor as I had never read her before. By the end of the seminar I knew that my previous work on O'Connor would have to be rethought if not scrapped. I was back to page one.

I thus owe a good deal of thanks for the shape my book has finally taken to Giles Gunn and the National Endowment for the Humanities, together with all the participants in the summer seminar. Three participants deserve special mention—Joe Price, Peter Brown, and Tom Joswick—all of whom were miles ahead of me in their thinking of the interrelations of religion and literature. Their comments were always challenging and insightful, and perhaps more significantly, their examples as inquiring scholars inspired me to enlarge my own perspectives.

At Tulane University I received nothing but encouragement from my colleagues. I thank them for their support, particularly during a period of crisis when two of my original chapters were lost and never recovered. Geoffrey Harpham and Michael Boardman were particularly supportive during that trying time. Of my Tulane friends, Jerry Mulderig gets special thanks; he made a number of judicious comments on parts of the manuscript before I sent it off. Support from

Tulane was also financial, and I thank the Graduate School Committee on Research for a summer fellowship to work on the book.

Others have helped me along the way. Jim Morton frequently helped set things in perspective for me. John May and Louis Rubin have all along been encouraging and supportive, and both provided helpful commentary on my manuscript. At the Louisiana State University Press, Beverly Jarrett, Julie Schorfheide, and Catherine Barton kept a close eye on the manuscript and made valuable suggestions. Mary C. Berry, my copy editor, did a wonderful job polishing up the text. My family, particularly my wife Chris, never flagged in supporting me, even when my work kept me from a number of family activities and duties. Once again, Chris's firm editorial hand helped shape my writing into a manageable manuscript. My thanks and love go especially to her and our wonderful daughters.

Abbreviations

Abbreviations of works commonly cited in the text refer to the following editions:

CFO *Conversations with Flannery O'Connor*. Edited by
     Rosemary M. Magee. Jackson, Miss., 1987.
CS   *The Complete Stories*. New York, 1971.
HB   *The Habit of Being: Letters*. Edited by Sally Fitzgerald. New
     York, 1969.
MM   *Mystery and Manners: Occasional Prose*. Edited by Sally
     Fitzgerald and Robert Fitzgerald. New York, 1969.
PG   *The Presence of Grace and Other Book Reviews by Flannery
     O'Connor*. Compiled by Leo J. Zuber. Edited by Carter W.
     Martin. Athens, Ga., 1983.
VBIA *The Violent Bear It Away*. New York, 1960.
WB   *Wise Blood*. 2d ed. New York, 1962.

The Art and Vision of Flannery O'Connor

Introduction

*A*fter discussing the ideas of martyrdom and purity in her story "A Temple of the Holy Ghost," Flannery O'Connor, in a letter (December 16, 1955) to A., added an emphatic statement of her belief in the transubstantiation. "Understand though," she wrote to her friend, "that, like the child, I believe the Host is actually the body and blood of Christ, not a symbol. If the story grows for you it is because of the mystery of the Eucharist in it." To underscore the significance of the Eucharist to her—and the dismissal of its mystery by the modern mind—O'Connor goes on to tell A. about a dinner she had attended years earlier with Mary McCarthy; McCarthy's husband; and several friends, including Robert Lowell and Elizabeth Hardwick. Given to reticence in social situations anyway, O'Connor was particularly quiet at this gathering, feeling out of place among the group of high-powered intellectuals who, to O'Connor's thinking at least, took themselves and their work—and not much else—quite seriously. (Of McCarthy, O'Connor wrote: "She departed the Church at the age of 15 and is a Big Intellectual.") "We went at eight and at one, I hadn't opened my mouth once, there being nothing for me in such company to say," she wrote to A., adding that she felt as if she were there as the token Catholic (Lowell by this time had left the Church), a role in which she took no comfort. "Having me there was like having a dog present who had been trained to say a few words but overcome with inadequacy had forgotten them," she wrote (*HB*, 124, 125).

O'Connor, however, broke her silence when toward morning the group began discussing the Eucharist. What ignited O'Connor's fury—a fury that propelled her into the conversation—was McCarthy's observing that having left the Church, she now saw the Eucharist as a symbol, and her implying further, in O'Connor's mind and words, "that it was a pretty good one" at that. O'Connor's response was immediate: "I then said, in a very shaky voice, 'Well, if it's a symbol, to hell with it.'" She explained to A. her thoughts then and now about her response, saying that "that was all the defense I was capable of but I realize now that this is all I will ever be able to say about it, outside of a story, except that it is the center of existence for me; all the rest of life is expendable" (*HB*, 125).

O'Connor's narrative about her exchange with McCarthy highlights not only the depth and commitment of her faith but also the absence of sacramental vision in the modern consciousness; it also calls to mind another discussion of the Eucharist, between Martin Luther and Ulrich Zwingli. Erich Heller argues in *The Disinherited Mind: Essays in Modern German Literature and Thought* that this dispute holds large significance in the history of Western thinking. Heller saw this argument, in which Zwingli challenged Luther's contention that the Eucharist was literally the body and blood of Christ with the assertion that it was merely a symbol, as an "articulate climax" ("a mere symptom of a more inarticulate, yet more comprehensive process") of the disruption that occurred during the Reformation of the Western world's prevailing sacramental view of reality. As Heller points out, the nature of the Eucharist had been disputed before in Christian Church history, but never had the challenge generated such widespread attention or gathered such force and authority behind it. The repercussions of the Luther-Zwingli dispute, says Heller, were revolutionary, nothing short of "a radical change in man's idea of reality, in that complex fabric of unconsciously held convictions about what is real and what is not." Before long the realms of the natural and the supernatural stood sundered: "From then onwards the word 'merely' has been attaching itself ever more firmly to the word 'symbol,' soon gathering sufficient strength to bring about a complete alienation between the two spheres. Finally a new order of things emerged. With it the transcendental realm is allotted the highest honours of the spirit, but, at the same time, skillfully deprived of a considerable measure of reality; the mundane, on the other hand, is recompensed for its lowering in spiritual stature by the chance of absorbing all available reality and becoming more 'really' real than before." This radical separation was evidence of the loss of humanity's sacramental vision—a loss that, as Heller observes, looking ahead to the subsequent ages, ultimately comes to mean that "not only the sacraments but the holiness of all that is holy will cease to be 'literally true.'" Heller adds, "Lost will be that unity of word and deed, of picture and thing, of the bread and the glorified body. Body will be merely body, and symbol merely symbol. And as for the refreshing wine, it will be drunk by thirsty souls only when in the very depths of their thirst they are quite sure that it was pressed from real grapes in the mechanic way."[1]

Although O'Connor most likely did not have the Luther-Zwingli dispute in mind when she spoke her terse rebuttal to McCarthy, she certainly shared with Heller many concerns about humanity's loss of the transcendent and the effects of this loss on the modern mind. In fact O'Connor, who read Heller's *Disinherited Mind* in 1959, echoes his observations in her 1963 essay "Novelist and Believer," where she comments on another well-known disputant of the Eucharist, Ralph Waldo Emerson. O'Connor writes that "when Emerson decided, in 1832, that he could no longer celebrate the Lord's Supper unless the bread and wine were removed, an important step in the vaporization of religion was taken, and the spirit of that step has continued apace. When the physical fact is separated from the spiritual reality, the dissolution of belief is eventually inevitable" (*MM*, 161–62).

The loss of the sacramental vision utterly transformed the modern mind. Lewis P. Simpson observes that by the time of the Enlightenment the rational mind had become the model of truth, replacing the authority of revelation and tradition. Accompanying this valorization of rationality was a drastic turn inward that located all value and meaning within the consciousness. "From Descartes on, mind became identified with the introspective, unstructured functions of consciousness—with the processes of cognition," Simpson writes. "Believing solely in its own existence, mind has no knowledge outside

---

1. Erich Heller, *The Disinherited Mind: Essays in Modern German Literature and Thought* (Expanded ed.; New York, 1975), 212, 267, 212, 266, 267.

itself and no reference for action outside its own functioning."[2]

Mikhail Bakhtin also discusses the mind's turn inward, saying that it embodies a destructive monologism that sees all unity within the single self of its own creation. Like Simpson, Bakhtin locates the powerful emergence of such thinking in Enlightenment rationalism and philosophical idealism. At the heart of idealism, Bakhtin suggests, was the transformation of the unity of existence into the unity of consciousness, a transformation that inevitably went one step further, establishing the unity of the single consciousness. Bakhtin writes that by this thinking "a single consciousness and a single mouth are absolutely sufficient for maximally full cognition," and he elaborates on this and its consequences:

All that has the power to mean, all that has value, is everywhere concentrated around one center—the carrier. All ideological creative acts are conceived and perceived as possible expressions of a single consciousness, a single spirit. Even when one is dealing with a collective, with a multiplicity of creating forces, unity is nevertheless illustrated through the image of a single consciousness: the spirit of a nation, the spirit of a people, the spirit of history, and so forth. Everything capable of meaning can be gathered together in one consciousness and subordinated to a unified accent; whatever does not submit to such a reduction is accidental and unessential.

European rationalism, described by Bakhtin as establishing "a cult of a unified and exclusive reason," consolidated and further validated monologic thinking, making it the philosophical foundation of the modern world.[3]

By the twentieth century the isolation of the self in its own subjectivity was total, the consciousness a world unto itself. J. Hillis Miller, in *Poets of Reality: Six Twentieth-Century Writers*, describes the results of this radical subjectification of reality:

Man has killed God by separating his subjectivity from everything but itself. The ego has put everything in doubt, and has defined all outside itself as the object of its thinking power. Cogito ergo sum: the absolute certainty about the self reached by Descartes' hyperbolic doubt leads to the assumption that things exist, for me at least, only because I think them. When everything exists only as reflected in the ego, then man has drunk up the sea. If man is

---

2. Lewis P. Simpson, *The Brazen Face of History: Studies in the Literary Consciousness in America* (Baton Rouge, 1980), 27.

3. Mikhail Bakhtin, *Problems of Dostoevsky's Poetics*, ed. and trans. Caryl Emerson (Minneapolis, 1984), 81–82.

defined as subject, everything else turns into object. This includes God, who now becomes merely the highest object of man's knowledge. God, once the creative sun, the power establishing the horizon where heaven and earth come together, becomes an object of thought like any other. When man drinks up the sea, he also drinks up God, the creator of the sea. In this way man is the murderer of God.

Simpson calls this complete isolation of the self within its own subjectivity the "historicism of consciousness," that is, "mind's willful transference of nature, man, and society—and eventually of God, and finally of mind itself—into itself." Miller's term for it is even starker—nihilism—and by this he means "the nothingness of consciousness when consciousness becomes the foundation of everything."[4]

Modern writers were of course profoundly influenced by the mind's turn into itself, as Heller, Simpson, Bakhtin, and Miller so convincingly show. One of the most significant reactions to the subjectification of experience was the elevation by many writers of their art to the status of religion. Allen Tate's recollections of his literary career in the 1920s, as he himself points out, also speak more generally to the literary environment of the times: "Like most literary men of the twentieth century I have found myself confronted with the dilemma, Religion *or* Literature. This disjunction fifty years ago was widespread, and like most of my contemporaries I went with literature, without trying to think why, because in the nineteen-twenties there was a literary religion without reflection many of us drifted into." For Tate and many other writers, literary creation was a religious act that established the only order possible in a world without transcendent meaning. "Was not the poetic intuition *pure*—free and uncontaminated by ritual and dogma?" Tate remembers wondering in the 1920s.[5] As he points out in an essay written in 1924, "One Escape from the Dilemma," the literary religion was highly individualistic, with each artist striving to achieve an art of pure consciousness—his or her own. Whereas writers before the twentieth century wrote from what Tate called a "community of faith"—that is, a community that shared assumptions about the world's ultimate

4. J. Hillis Miller, *Poets of Reality: Six Twentieth-Century Writers* (Cambridge, Mass., 1965), 3; Simpson, *The Brazen Face of History*, xii.
5. Allen Tate, *Mere Literature and the Lost Traveller* (Nashville, 1969), 3.

meaningfulness and purposefulness—so that they needed merely "to restate the self-evident amenities memorably, those categorical revelations common to all minds, immune to the blighting tentacles of scepticism," the modern writer writes only in a community of self, which is no community at all. In such a situation the writer, says Tate, is "happy only in the obscure by-ways of his own perceptive processes; *a priori* utterance never escapes him. Claude Monet said: 'The chief character in a group portrait is the light.' So the modern poet might tell you that his only possible themes are the manifold projections and tangents of his own perception." Tate adds that the world outside the self is significant merely as a means to project the artist's true subject—the individual consciousness. "The external world is a permanent possibility of sign-posts upon which the poet may hang his attitudes, his sensibility," Tate writes. "Not the world, but consciousness; hence, his difficult abstractness."[6]

Tate, like a number of other southern writers writing in the 1920s and 1930s, remained satisfied with the pursuit of pure consciousness only for a limited time. As I have argued in my previous book, *Three Catholic Writers of the Modern South*, these southern writers frequently were haunted by a sense of meaning and purpose derived from their traditional southern upbringing, and many began to explore in their art the means to reinvigorate their lives with the knowledge borne from southern tradition and community. "What shall we say who have knowledge/Carried to the heart?" asks the poet in Tate's "Ode to the Confederate Dead."[7] This question speaks for a generation of southern writers. The poet's answer is nowhere explicitly stated, but the final lines appear to suggest that he must leave the Confederate graveyard he is standing beside and return to his present life, not forgetting the past but not becoming enslaved by it either, a trap to which he might fall prey if he were to focus his thoughts exclusively on the Confederate war dead and to ignore modern themes and knowledge. Vision, for Tate and other southern writers of his generation, arises from the interplay of the past and the

6. Allen Tate, "One Escape from the Dilemma," *Fugitive*, III (April, 1924), 35.
7. Robert H. Brinkmeyer, Jr., *Three Catholic Writers of the Modern South* (Jackson, Miss., 1985); Allen Tate, *Collected Poems, 1919–1976* (New York, 1977), 22.

present, an interplay usually expressed as the tension between southern traditionalism and modernism.

For southern writers of the next generation (those whose careers began in the late 1940s and 1950s), the interplay of past and present becomes less significant. As Lewis Lawson points out in *Another Generation: Southern Fiction Since World War II*, the southern writer now begins to see the southerner "as a product of present social complexities, not of past philosophic simplicities" and consequently as standing "almost completely deprived of the help of tradition, custom, or community." Cut off from history and tradition, the southerner finds his or her traditional identity shattered. "The southerner's life was once vitalized by his participation in the group, even though it meant sharing the collective guilt of the group," Lawson writes. "Now, however, the Southerner must go it alone, and many of the best recent novels detail the failure of the personality that occurs when one must go it alone."[8] Lawson points out that most southern writers during this period focus less on the disintegration of society than on the disintegration of self, and that what most distinguishes each writer from the others in terms of vision is the mode of survival that each poses.

Flannery O'Connor, whose mature writing career began in 1952 with the publication of *Wise Blood*, belongs in the generation of writers of which Lawson speaks. For her the destruction of the isolated self stems from the self's separation from Christ and the Church and from its failure to embrace a life of Christian commitment. As a widely read student of modern culture, O'Connor was well aware of the process of secularization of modern society and mind that had been under way for several centuries, and she frequently spoke of the consequences in her essays and letters. In

8. Lewis A. Lawson, *Another Generation: Southern Fiction Since World War II* (Jackson, Miss., 1984), 17–18. For further discussion of contemporary southern fiction, see particularly Richard Gray, *Writing the South: Ideas of an American Region* (Cambridge, England, 1986); Louis D. Rubin, Jr., "The Boll Weevil, the Iron Horse, and the End of the Line: Thoughts on the South," in *A Gallery of Southerners* (Baton Rouge, 1982); Lewis P. Simpson, *The Dispossessed Garden: Pastoral and History in Southern Literature* (1975; rpr. Baton Rouge, 1983); Walter Sullivan, *Death by Melancholy: Essays on Modern Southern Fiction* (Baton Rouge, 1972); and Walter Sullivan, *A Requiem for the Renascence* (Athens, Ga., 1976).

"Some Aspects of the Grotesque in Southern Fiction" she writes about the worship of mind and rationality, saying that "for nearly two centuries the popular spirit of each succeeding generation has tended more and more to the view that the mysteries of life will eventually fall before the mind of man." She then goes on to discuss the turn inward to consciousness, particularly by modern writers: "Many modern novelists have been more concerned with the processes of consciousness than with the objective world outside the mind. In twentieth-century fiction it increasingly happens that a meaningless, absurd world impinges upon the sacred consciousness of author or character; author and character seldom now go out to explore and penetrate a world in which the sacred is reflected" (MM, 158).

O'Connor's primary bulwark against the dangers of the isolated self was her Catholic faith; from and with it, she gained strength and purpose to resist any tendency to valorize the individual consciousness.[9] She saw Christ, not herself, at the center of the universe. Nonetheless, O'Connor was also painfully aware that people could become isolated from everyday reality and other people through this faith. Such separation frequently occurred when people embraced their faith with unquestioned enthusiasm, completely ignoring the problems and concerns of the wider world. In a letter (February 19, 1956) to John Lynch, O'Connor characterized this type of faith as "vapid Catholicism," and she said it "can't influence you except to be shut of it. The Catholic influence has to come at a deeper level. I was brought up in the novena-rosary tradition too, but you have to save yourself from it someway or dry up." O'Connor's harsh comments about nuns who teach at Catholic colleges, found in a letter (April 26, 1959) to T. R. Spivey, focus on this very problem; the nuns, she says, though pious and well educated, for the most part "know nothing of the world and have a kind of hot-house innocence which is of very little help to anyone who has to be thrown into the problems of the modern world" (HB, 139, 330).

The ways in which O'Connor in her fiction resisted the tempta-

9. For further discussion of O'Connor in light of Lewis Simpson's ideas on the historicism of consciousness, with a particular emphasis on the significance of memory, see John F. Desmond, *Risen Sons: Flannery O'Connor's Vision of History* (Athens, Ga., 1987), chap. 5.

tions to isolate herself either in a valorized conception of self or in a vapid Catholicism are what we shall be exploring in the coming chapters. As we shall see, O'Connor's fiction arises from pressure and resistance. Genuine discourse, Hayden White argues, is "as *self-critical as it is critical of others*," always challenging the adequacy of its conception and formation.[10] By White's definition, O'Connor's discourse is certainly genuine: Drawing from voices both within and without her self, O'Connor tests and challenges her self-conception and her faith, ultimately enlarging and deepening both, together with her imaginative vision. This openness to critical evaluation of self and vision is, I believe, a crucial characteristic of O'Connor's mind and art, and one heretofore not examined in the depth it deserves.

Much of my approach to O'Connor, which will be discussed in some depth in the first chapter, derives from the work of Mikhail Bakhtin, particularly his ideas on dialogism and dialogic art. But my study is not strictly Bakhtinian—Bakhtin, for instance, has little use for writers whose visions are as forthrightly Christian as O'Connor's. Rather my work attempts to engage Bakhtin in the type of dialogic encounter he so loved, drawing insights from his writings and placing them in dialogue with my own ideas on O'Connor. The result is a quite different view of O'Connor and her fiction, and one that I hope has much depth and insight.

10. Hayden White, "Introduction: Tropology, Discourse, and the Modes of Human Consciousness," in *Tropics of Discourse: Essays in Cultural Criticism* (Baltimore, 1978), 4.

1

Flannery O'Connor and the Dialogic Imagination

In her essay "Reality in Chekhov's Stories," Eudora Welty suggests that one of the most distinctive aspects of Anton Chekhov's imaginative vision is its consistent grounding in the realities of life in the specific human situation. Welty argues that for Chekhov, reality—what she calls "the stuff of life"—is not some general expression, abstracted from living people, of the way things are. Reality in Chekhov's fiction "isn't just *there*," Welty writes, but instead "comes to us through the living human being—and not anonymously. It lives, was born, in the particular—not in the general humanity but in this man, that woman, their child." Matters such as good and evil, love and power, therefore, are never separated from the immediate in Chekhov's world; their significance is found not on the level of idea but in the world of people—in "the particular and personal meaning[s]" they take on "for human beings in the course of their lives." Summing up Chekhov's perspective, Welty writes that "reality is no single pure ray, no beacon against the dark. It might be thought of as a cluster of lesser lights, visible here on earth like the windows of a village at night close together but not *one*—some are bright, some dim, some waywardly flickering. All imply people; there are people there for every light."[1]

Welty sees this multiplicity of perceived reality as lying at the very heart of Chekhov's imaginative life, and she describes his ability to perceive and present in his fiction such a vast number of differing views of reality as perhaps his most extraordinary gift. She stresses

1. Eudora Welty, "Reality in Chekhov's Fiction," in *The Eye of the Story: Selected Essays and Reviews* (New York, 1978), 63.

that he did not impose himself on the reader in his fiction by manipulating characters and their views to express his own beliefs or to illustrate a moral; instead, he strove to present his characters as fully and as deeply as possible. In letting his characters exist as individuals rather than as pieces in a literary game, Chekhov, says Welty, revolutionized the short story. She notes that with Chekhov's work, the "formal pattern imposed on the story by long tradition gave way to a treatment entirely different—something open to human meaning and answerable to that meaning in all its variety." This reworking of the short story, Welty emphasizes, did not destroy its form but reinvigorated it, freeing it from arbitrariness and opening it to the same forces of life that shaped its characters. "By removing the formal plot he did not leave the story structureless," Welty writes; "he endowed it with another kind of structure—one which embodied the principle of growth. And it was one that had no cause to repeat itself; in each and every story, short or long, it was a structure open to human meaning and answerable to that meaning. It took form from within." Elsewhere in this essay, Welty characterizes the Chekhov story as itself a character—"a clear, unselfconscious identity, vigorous, purposeful, ongoing"—that like those identities in his stories is not manipulated or coerced but allowed to grow and take shape by its own will.[2]

Welty's admiration of Chekhov rests squarely on Chekhov's liberation of himself from his own narrow views (which allowed him to take in the myriad other views of reality) and on the liberation of his stories, in terms both of structure and of presentation of character. Only an imaginative vision ultimately comic could achieve such fullness, Welty observes, and further, only a comic vision that at its very heart exhibited a profound respect for all aspects of life. "What but the comic vision could accommodate so much, bring it all in?" Welty writes. "What other frame is generous enough? I think of that vision as an outreach of the artist's compassion—the careful attention to the human scale, a keeping to human proportions. It is the artist's deference, a kind of modesty, a form of ultimate respect, a reverence, for all living things." What Chekhov achieves in his stories is for Welty the ultimate attainment in fiction—the revelation of the mysterious

2. *Ibid.*, 62, 74, 68.

depths of existence. "The very greatest mystery is in unsheathed reality itself," Welty writes. "The realist Chekhov, speaking simply and never otherwise than as an artist and a humane man, showed us in fullness and plenitude the mystery of our own lives." Chekhov's realism, she says in another passage, is a transparency that we look through to see "the blaze of human truth."[3]

Despite the fact that Anton Chekhov and Flannery O'Connor were in many ways quite different writers, I believe that Welty's comments on Chekhov, in several key respects, also speak tellingly to the work of O'Connor. To begin with, O'Connor was, like Chekhov (at least as described by Welty), extremely determined to keep her fiction from becoming abstract and voiceless. As a Roman Catholic writer very much concerned with matters of the spirit, O'Connor was well aware that the only way to portray the spiritual in fiction was to ground her work in the human. "Fiction is the concrete expression of mystery—mystery that is lived," O'Connor wrote in "The Church and the Fiction Writer" (MM, 144). Moreover, it is my contention that much of O'Connor's greatness as a writer results from her ability to embrace the voices and viewpoints of those about and within her— in other words, to give expression to the many realities of which Welty spoke. That O'Connor opened herself to the multi-voiced world, and particularly to those voices of the southern countryside, is evident in every page of fiction she wrote.

If Chekhov and O'Connor shared this openness to the realities of other people—an openness, I would argue, to otherness that ultimately enabled them to free themselves from the limited confines of their own views, thereby enriching their visions—the larger context in which this vision worked in each writer was quite different. Chekhov's ultimate perspective on the world—what Mikhail Bakhtin would call his ideology—is embodied, again according to Welty's observations, precisely in his presentation of the differing realities found in his characters. There is no transcendent, defining order looming behind the interactions of people; there is not one reality, but many, each stemming from a living person. Thus, all meaning and values are located in the interplay of people and their treatment of one another. "Religion, government, science, education, the arts, are not

3. Ibid., 80, 81, 68.

in themselves either moral or immoral, as he had cause to remark in his letters," Welty writes, commenting on Chekhov's ethics. "Peasants, women, schoolteachers, the military, drunks, Turks, persons over forty or under two, revolutionaries, doctors, the raisers of their own gooseberries—none of them are good or evil in so being but in what they do to each other, the ways they treat their fellow human beings."[4] Thus, Chekhov's opening himself up to, and presenting, the multiple realities of the world embodied both his visualization of life and the means for evaluating it; by orienting one's views and actions alongside those of other people's, one gains perspective and insight, which provide the resources for, and the agency of, judgment.

Flannery O'Connor's position was entirely different. Her regnant vision, the organizing center of her thought, was not embodied in her openness to other perspectives, as Chekhov's was, but rather was located squarely in her Catholic faith. To John Lynch, O'Connor wrote (November 6, 1955) of the scope and depth of her Catholic commitment, saying, "I write the way I do because and only because I am a Catholic. I would have no reason to write, no reason to see, no reason ever to feel horrified or even to enjoy anything. I am a born Catholic, went to Catholic schools in my early years, and have never left or wanted to leave the Church" (*HB*, 114). In opening herself and giving voice to other perspectives, O'Connor always remained within the overarching frame of her Catholic faith. It is assuredly one mark of her greatness as an artist that she did not close herself off from the voices of life about her outside the life of the Church; her explorations of what for Chekhov were these other realities deepened both her vision and her faith, testing and pressuring them in ways that challenged their sacred tenets and their limits. Such testing for O'Connor was not a sign of weakness, particularly in terms of religious faith; rather it expressed what she believed most modern people lacked—a commitment to make operable in the natural world a faith in the supernatural.

Welty's observations on Chekhov's imaginative life and vision and my own observations on O'Connor's call to mind Bakhtin's ideas on dialogism and the dialogic imagination. Bakhtin's view of existence is very close to what Welty characterized as Chekhov's—the world is

4. *Ibid.*, 68.

made up of a number of fully realized and independent individuals, each with his or her own system of values and beliefs (what Bakhtin called the individual's ideology and what Welty signified as the individual's reality). The world that Bakhtin finds in Fëdor Dostoevski's novels is also the world he finds at large. *"A plurality of independent and unmerged voices and consciousnesses, a genuine polyphony of fully valid voices is the chief characteristic of Dostoevsky's novels,"* Bakhtin writes. "What unfolds in his works is not a multitude of characters and fates in a single objective world, illuminated by a single consciousness; rather *a plurality of consciousnesses, with equal rights and each with its own world*, combine but are not merged in the unity of the event."[5] Particularly significant here is Bakhtin's observation that, as Welty found in Chekhov, there is not a single objective world but many worlds, one for each individual. When events occur—that is, when people come together in some act—individuals interact with one another, all maintaining their stature and validity as individual consciousnesses, and not merging into some larger group identity or reality.

Bakhtin viewed the individual self much as he did the world—as multi-voiced and multi-centered. He saw the individual consciousness as a collection of many consciousnesses, each with its own voice and ideology and each vying for recognition and authority. For this reason he could declare outright that "no Nirvana is possible for a *single* consciousness. A single consciousness is *contradictio in adjecto*." He added, "Consciousness is in essence multiple. *Pluralia tantum*." Many, if not most, people, Bakhtin believed, lived only by the social self they showed to others—what he at times typified as the hard shell of one's self-image—denying the multiple voices within. This was certainly easier than embracing one's many consciousnesses, for to do that was to engage in a profound experience of alterity that challenged, if not totally destroyed, the secure vision of one's social self. "Consciousness is much more terrifying than any unconscious complexes," Bakhtin wrote, suggesting the frightening otherness that lay at the heart of the self.[6]

As terrifying as that otherness within could be, to affirm the validity and authority of only one's own social self—thereby denying such

5. Bakhtin, *Problems of Dostoevsky's Poetics*, 6.
6. *Ibid.*, 288.

significance both to the other voices of one's self and to those of other individuals—was to close oneself off in a destructive solipsism. Rather than self-sufficiency, Bakhtin asserted the ideal of "nonself-sufficiency, the impossibility of the existence of the single consciousness." He argued that only in our encounters with "others" do we gain understanding, perspective, and growth. "I am conscious of myself and become myself only while revealing myself for another, through another, and with the help of another," Bakhtin wrote in a set of notes. "The most important acts constituting self-consciousness are determined by a relationship toward another consciousness (toward a *thou*). Separation, dissociation, and enclosure within the self [are] the main reason for the loss of one's self." To live by such closure is to practice a radical monologism, and of this ruinous position Bakhtin wrote:

Monologism, at its extreme, denies the existence outside itself of another consciousness with equal rights and equal responsibilities, another *I* with equal rights (*thou*). With a monologic approach (in its extreme or pure form) *another person* remains wholly and merely an *object* of consciousness, and not another consciousness. No response is expected from it that could change everything in the world of my consciousness. Monologue is finalized and deaf to the other's response, does not expect it and does not acknowledge in it any *decisive* force. Monologue manages without the other, and therefore to some degree materializes all reality. Monologue pretends to be the *ultimate word*. It closes down the represented world and represented persons.

From the monologic perspective, the isolated consciousness stands whole and finalized, itself the master of world and self.[7]

Instead of monologue, Bakhtin calls for dialogue, both with the voices within the self and with those of other consciousnesses. "Life by its very nature is dialogic," he argues in his notes for his revised version of *Problems of Dostoevsky's Poetics*. "To live means to participate in dialogue: to ask questions, to heed, to respond, to agree, and so forth." Elsewhere in these notes he expands this idea, writing that "the very being of man (both external and internal) is the *deepest communion. To be* means *to communicate.* . . . To be means to be for another, and through the other, for oneself. A person has no internal sovereign territory, he is wholly and always on the boundary; looking inside himself, he looks *into the eyes of another* or *with the eyes of*

7. Ibid., 287, 292–93.

another."[8] In dialogues with others, meaning and understanding arise on the boundary or threshold between two consciousnesses; to fuse or merge wholly with the other, in contrast, silences dialogue, locking the self within the confines of the other. In one of his early essays, Bakhtin attacks the ultimate value of this type of identification:

In what way will the event be enriched if I succeed in fusing with the other? If instead of two, there is now just one? What do *I* gain by having the other fuse with me? He will know and see but what I know and see, he will but repeat within himself the tragic dimension of my life. Let him rather stay on the outside because from there he can know and see what I cannot see or know from my vantage point, and he can thus enrich essentially the event of my life. In a *mere* fusion with someone else's life, I only deepen its tragic character, literally double it.[9]

In another essay, Bakhtin argues that empathy has value merely in the first stages of understanding, but that true understanding—what he calls creative understanding—occurs only when the observing consciousness does not renounce itself. "The chief matter of understanding," Bakhtin writes, "is the *extopy* of [the staying outside of] the one who does the understanding—in time, space, and culture—in relation to that which he wants to understand creatively."[10]

In opening themselves dialogically to others, people resist the solipsistic tendencies to which they may be given; they come to see that the self is far from the whole and finalized entity it envisions itself as in its self-image. Bakhtin writes in *Problems of Dostoevsky's Poetics* that "the *inner man*[,] 'one's own self,' [is] accessible not to passive self-observation but through an *active dialogic approach to one's own self*" and that this approach "breaks down the outer shell of the self's image, that shell which exists for other people, determining the external assessment of a person (in the eyes of others) and dimming the purity of self-consciousness."[11] Such a dialogic dismantling of the self frees it from the tyranny of its self-image, allowing for the growth and understanding that Bakhtin sees occurring when the self embraces both its own various voices and those of other consciousnesses.

8. *Ibid.*, 293, 287.
9. Quoted in Tzvetan Todorov, *Mikhail Bakhtin: The Dialogical Principle*, trans. Wlad Godzich (Minneapolis, 1984), 108.
10. *Ibid.*, 109.
11. Bakhtin, *Problems of Dostoevsky's Poetics*, 120.

Bakhtin's ideas on human existence bear particular relevance to the artist, for Bakhtin sees artistic creation as the paradigm for self-creation. The artist of the greatest depth—the dialogic artist—for Bakhtin stands on the boundary of the multi-voiced world of his or her work. Although the artist's own vision is on one level the organizing center for the various views expressed in the work, the writer does not impose personal views into the fictional world; these views, in other words, are merely one voice of many in the ongoing dialogue generated by the work. As an active participant in the ongoing dialogues in the work, the author is not closed off from the world of the work, but rather engages the work in interactions that test, probe, and ultimately reveal the dimensions and validity of his or her views. Moreover, through the work the artist enters into a dialogic encounter with the self, because frequently the consciousnesses of the characters created embody voices from within the artist's own consciousness. In creating these fully valid characters, the author thus interacts with internal voices in entirely new situations and contexts, thereby forcing reappraisal and reconceptualization. Likewise, the characters in a dialogic work frequently embody the subjective perspectives by which the author views the world; their creation in fiction thus liberates the author from preconceived ways of seeing. Bakhtin finds this dynamic operating in the work of Dostoevski, the writer he views as the greatest dialogic artist. He writes that Dostoevski "objectifies the entire realm of the author's creative subjectivity which autocratically colors the represented world in a monologic novel, thereby making what was once a form of perception into an object of perception."[12] At some deep level, then, the artist's encounter with the art is an encounter with the otherness of the artist's multi-voiced self.

Monologic artists, in contrast, approach their art quite differently. These artists see themselves as the sole possessor of truth and vision rather than merely one consciousness among many in a multi-voiced world of equal and fully signified consciousnesses. Instead of opening themselves to dialogic encounters with aspects of their fiction, and in the process discovering insights and deepening understanding, monologic artists impose meaning. They finalize everything according to their own preconceived notions of truth—truth found only in their

12. *Ibid.*, 278.

consciousnesses. "A monologic artist does not recognize someone else's thought, someone else's idea, as an object of representation," Bakhtin writes, adding that others' thoughts and ideas in this monologic world are merely affirmed or denied according to whether they fit into the artist's vision or not. This valorization of the artist's consciousness makes dialogic encounters with characters impossible, because "the author's field of vision nowhere intersects or collides dialogically with the characters' fields of vision or attitudes, nowhere does the word of the author encounter resistance from the hero's potential word, a word that might illuminate the same object differently, in its own way—that is, from the vantage point of its own *truth*." Monologic artists do not interact with their characters but manipulate them to illustrate and validate their own visions. Their art expresses not the multi-voiced world but "the unified, monologic world of the author's consciousness."[13]

As a Catholic writer who saw her reading audience and the age itself as predominately secular and without faith, Flannery O'Connor certainly felt the temptation to impose her vision monologically upon others rather than open herself in her art to dialogic encounters that would explore and enlarge her consciousness. At the same time, she was profoundly aware that such monologism was fatal to great art, and indeed she saw much fiction by Catholic writers, particularly American Catholics, as flawed in this way. Time and again in her essays and letters she levels harsh criticism at what she finds the overwhelmingly poor quality of fiction written by Catholics. Much of the problem O'Connor locates in what she sees as the smugness and abstractedness of the typical Catholic mind. "Our Catholic mentality is great on paraphrase, logic, formula, instant and correct answers," she wrote (May 4, 1963) to Sister Mariella Gable. "We judge before we experience and never trust our faith to be subjected to reality, because it is not strong enough" (*HB*, 516). For fiction writers, such a mentality proves disastrous, particularly when Catholic writers are so sure of their faith that they feel no obligation to ground their vision in the here and now. In "Catholic Novelists and Their Readers," O'Connor says that great fiction does not deal with the "Instant Answer"— something with which, she adds, Catholics are much taken—but

13. *Ibid.*, 79, 71, 43.

instead "leaves us, like Job, with a renewed sense of mystery." She explains that writers of fiction must try to achieve something on the order of what Saint Gregory wrote of Scripture—that every time it presents a fact, it also discloses a mystery. "The danger for the writer who is spurred by the religious view of the world is that he will consider this to be two operations instead of one," O'Connor goes on to say. "He will try to enshrine the mystery without the fact, and there will be a further set of separations which are inimical to art." In "Novelist and Believer," O'Connor discusses this tendency in Catholic writers, observing that "the sorry religious novel comes about when the writer supposes that because of his belief, he is somehow dispensed from the obligation to penetrate concrete reality. He will think that the eyes of the Church or of the Bible or of his particular theology have already done the seeing for him, and that his business is to rearrange this essential vision into satisfying patterns, getting himself as little dirty in the process as possible" (*MM*, 184, 163).

O'Connor's observations from "Novelist and Believer" also point to another problem she saw in many Catholic writers: They never subject their vision to any test or challenge from the realities outside the Church. She writes in "The Catholic Novelist in the Protestant South" that poor Catholic fiction usually involves no encounter or engagement with anything outside the writer's Catholic vision; the work, for this reason, usually lacks depth, a solid sense of place, and tension. "It is a novel which doesn't grapple with any particular culture," O'Connor writes. "It may try to make a culture out of the Church, but this is always a mistake because the Church is not a culture. . . . Its action occurs in an abstract setting that could be anywhere or nowhere. This reduces its dimensions drastically and cuts down on those tensions that keep fiction from becoming facile and slick." Becoming entranced with one's faith and enthusiastically displaying it, O'Connor observes in "Catholic Novelists and Their Readers," is fine if a person stops writing fiction. However, she adds, most of the time the person insists on continuing to write, making "the same kind of spectacle of himself that the wolf would have made if, after his meeting with St. Francis, he had started walking on his hind legs" (*MM*, 199, 170).

In part this facile and unchallenged enthusiasm of some Catholic writers results from their belief that fiction must depict Catholic settings—and always in the best light possible. O'Connor, in contrast, found such a premise limiting and even destructive, particularly if a writer wanted to communicate with the general reading public. She understood the designation "Catholic fiction" quite differently than most of her fellow Catholics, who interpreted it as fiction written by, about, and (in many cases) to Catholics. For O'Connor, however, as she wrote in "Catholic Novelists and Their Readers," the Catholic novel (she used the term broadly, signifying all forms of fiction) "is one that represents reality adequately as we see it manifested in this world of things and human relationships" and as such "is not necessarily about a Christianized or Catholicized world, but simply . . . one in which the truth as Christians know it has been used as a light to see the world by. This may or may not be a Catholic world, and it may or may not have been seen by a Catholic." In "The Catholic Novelist in the Protestant South," she outlined the assumptions she saw underpinning Catholic fiction: "It cannot see man as determined; it cannot see him as totally depraved. It will see him as incomplete in himself, as prone to evil, but as redeemable when his own efforts are assisted by grace. And it will see this grace as working through nature, but as entirely transcending it, so that a door is always open to possibility and the unexpected in the human soul. Its center of meaning will be Christ; its center of destruction will be the devil. No matter how this view of life may be fleshed out, these assumptions form its skeleton" (MM, 172, 173, 196–97).

All of this is not to say O'Connor saw writing about Catholic life as a certain way to fail as a writer. But given the secularism of modern readers, she felt that writing about Catholics was an extremely difficult and demanding task. To succeed, the writer had to present Catholics in all their complexity and humanity—the good and the evil— and to tell stories that steered clear of pat, moralistic plots. Because their work achieved both of these things, almost always cutting against the predictable clichés of Catholic piety and faith, O'Connor admired the fiction of J. F. Powers and Graham Greene. O'Connor herself, however, felt more comfortable writing about the very un-Catholic folk of her southern homeland. These were the people she knew best and the ones she could make come most alive—and this was what counted for the novelist. O'Connor believed writing was a vocation, a gift from God, and that writers were obligated to use their talents to the fullest potential, not in explicitly extolling religion but in making their work believable. "Like [Graham] Greene or any other writer," she wrote (May 17, 1963) to Janet McKane, "when I write I do what I have to do with what I can. You are always bounded by what you can make live" (HB, 520).

If O'Connor felt restricted as an artist as to what she could write about—not by the demands of faith but by the limits of her abilities and individual vision—she felt in no way confined or bounded by the Catholic assumptions from which she viewed the world and wrote about it. O'Connor was well aware of the criticism, primarily from those outside the Church, that belief in Catholic dogma limited the freedom and creativity of artists, distorting their vision and limiting imaginative growth. Nonetheless, she felt that her Catholic faith helped both to liberate her vision and to deepen her sense of life's ultimate mysteries. "There is no reason why fixed dogma should fix anything that the writer sees in the world," O'Connor wrote in "Catholic Novelists and Their Readers." "On the contrary, dogma is an instrument for penetrating reality. Christian dogma is about the only thing left in the world that surely guards and respects mystery." A settled belief in dogma, she also believed, actually freed rather than confined the artist's powers of observation. In this same essay, she commented:

The fiction writer is an observer, first, last, and always, but he cannot be an adequate observer unless he is free from uncertainty about what he sees. . . . The Catholic fiction writer is entirely free to observe. He feels no call to take on the duties of God or to create a new universe. He feels perfectly free to look at the one we already have and to show exactly what he sees. He feels no need to apologize for the ways of God to man or to avoid looking at the ways of man to God. For him, to "tidy up reality" is certainly to succumb to the sin of pride. Open and free observation is founded on our ultimate faith that the universe is meaningful, as the Church teaches. (MM, 178)

Such freedom is what Caroline Gordon told O'Connor she discovered after becoming a Catholic. To John Lynch, O'Connor wrote (November 6, 1955) that Gordon had told her that after her conversion "she felt she could use her eyes and accept what she saw for the first time, she didn't have to make a new universe for each book but could take the one she found." This freedom is in all likelihood what prompted her to observe in this same letter, "I feel myself that being a

Catholic has saved me a couple of thousand years in learning to write" (*HB*, 114).

O'Connor's views on the freedom her Catholic faith gave her underscore one of the important ideas that lay behind her conception of artistic freedom—that, as she put it in "The Nature and Aim of Fiction," "the writer's moral sense must coincide with his dramatic sense." For O'Connor, the best writers are those who maintain a balance between their powers of observation and judgment so that judgment becomes integrally involved in the very act of perception and then later in the writer's selection and presentation of details in fiction. "Belief, in my own case anyway, is the engine that makes perception operate," O'Connor says in "On Her Own Work." As she points out in "The Nature and Aim of Fiction," fiction written from such a vision is "a self-contained dramatic unit." She explains that in these works the meaning is contained in the story itself—in its action and characters—and not in "any abstractly expressed compassion or piety or morality" that is tacked on. "When you write fiction," she adds, "you are speaking *with* character and action, not *about* character and action" (*MM*, 76, 109, 75).

O'Connor characterizes this balance between judgment and perception for the Catholic writer as one between two sets of eyes—the individual's and the Church's. Such balance, she notes in "Catholic Novelists and Their Readers," is not without tension; indeed it is fraught with conflict. It is a conflict, she adds, "which we escape at our own peril, one which cannot be settled beforehand by theory or fiat or faith." Achieving an integrated vision means allowing neither the Church's nor one's own individual vision to achieve total mastery; to see with only one set of eyes rather than both is to court artistic disaster, since "to disconnect faith from vision is to do violence to the whole personality, and the whole personality participates in the act of writing." O'Connor notes that when Catholic writers close their own eyes to see only by the Church's, "the result is another addition to that large body of pious trash for which we have so long been famous." To do the opposite (that is, to see only with one's own eyes) is to flatten one's vision, to see in the fashion of a camera, without the extensions of meaning—what O'Connor called "the added dimension"—that a full Christian vision witnesses. O'Connor underscores the difficulty of ever bringing this conflict to rest when she writes that "the tensions of being a Catholic novelist are probably never balanced for the writer until the Church becomes so much a part of his personality that he can forget about her." She adds that "this is the condition we aim for, but one which is seldom achieved in this life, particularly by novelists" (*MM*, 180, 181, 180, 181). Vision for O'Connor thus results from pressure and challenge; a person wholly submits neither to the Church nor to the self, but instead brings these two into contact, allowing each to penetrate and shape the other in an ongoing process of creation.

O'Connor also saw pressure and challenge as crucial for achieving a deep and substantial faith. Although she was a devout Catholic, hers was not a faith without struggle and challenge, and this, she felt, was as it should be. For she believed that embracing religious faith did not mean escape from, and denial of, the problems and challenges of the contemporary world but a fuller experience of the world. Faith was a burden, a bearing of the Cross. She described her own situation in a letter (July 20, 1955) to A.:

I am a Catholic peculiarly possessed of the modern consciousness, that thing Jung describes as unhistorical, solitary, and guilty. To possess this *within* the Church is to bear a burden, the necessary burden for the conscious Catholic. It's to feel the contemporary situation at the ultimate level. I think that the Church is the only thing that is going to make the terrible world we are coming to endurable; the only thing that makes the Church endurable is that it is somehow the body of Christ and that on this we are fed. It seems to be a fact that you have to suffer as much from the Church as for it but if you believe in the divinity of Christ, you have to cherish the world at the same time you struggle to endure it.

To Alfred Corn, a college student who had written her about his religious doubt, O'Connor wrote (May 30, 1962) that in the turbulent modern world a deep religious faith had to be grounded in unbelief; faith, in other words, must never be isolated from its opposite but must be forever speaking to, and struggling with, its challenges and demands (*HB*, 90, 476).

O'Connor was particularly put off by those Catholics who did otherwise, ignoring contemporary affairs and problems by enclosing themselves within their faith. These were the smug and complacent, those who never questioned their faith or struggled with the knotty problems of living their lives in the modern world in full commitment to Christ. In a letter to Cecil Dawkins, O'Connor wrote (July 16, 1957) that she found such Catholics so repulsive because "they don't really have a faith but a kind of false certainty. They operate by the slide rule and the Church for them is the poor man's insurance system. It's never hard for them to believe because actually they never think about it. Faith has to take in all the other possibilities it can" (*HB*, 231). This last sentence is particularly significant, for it points to O'Connor's belief that one's faith must be continually probing and searching out other perspectives of reality—and in turn being pressured and challenged by these—rather than retreating from and ignoring them.

O'Connor called this activity Christian skepticism, and she discussed it in the letter to Alfred Corn cited earlier. Put simply, O'Connor counseled Corn to read as widely as possible and to learn as much as he could, but always to remain skeptical of any ideas that challenged Catholic dogma. In other words, he should not deny these challenges but remain open-minded about them, not seeing them necessarily as absolute answers but as potential aspects of a larger vision of things ultimately Christian. "If you want your faith, you have to work for it," O'Connor wrote Corn, telling him that once a person develops this larger vision, the intellectual problems that provided the challenge to develop this vision no longer seem so wrenching and absolute. O'Connor explained that a problem that at one time gave her great difficulty—reconciling the clashes of the world's various religions—no longer did because after many years she eventually developed a vision that she described as "a sense of the immense sweep of creation, of the evolutionary process in everything, of how incomprehensible God must necessarily be to be the God of heaven and earth." She added, "You can't fit the Almighty into your intellectual categories." This suggested the limits of the intellect before God's mysteries, an idea she returned to near the end of the letter, when she told Corn that a healthy Christian skepticism "will keep you free— not free to do anything you please but free to be formed by something larger than your own intellect or the intellects of those around you" (*HB*, 477, 478).

For O'Connor as artist and believer, the most basic challenges to a Catholic imaginative vision and faith came from the traditions of her southern homeland. O'Connor asserted, much to the surprise of many of her friends, that being a Catholic writer in the overwhelmingly Protestant South was advantageous and nourishing; the pressures of southern life ultimately enlarged her vision through healthy and vibrant tensions and interplay. She wrote in "The Catholic Novelist in the Protestant South" that "the opportunities for the potential Catholic writer in the South are so great as to be intimidating" (*MM*, 208), and she frequently noted what she saw as the healthy interplay between her own southern and Catholic sensibilities. In a letter (September 15, 1955) to Andrew Lytle, she wrote, "To my way of thinking, the only thing that keeps me from being a regional writer is being a Catholic and the only thing that keeps me from being a Catholic writer (in the narrow sense) is being a Southerner" (*HB*, 104). Elsewhere ("The Catholic Novelist in the Protestant South") she said that despite her deep Catholic faith and all of its assumptions about the nature of reality that underpin her vision and fiction, her sensibilities and imaginative life were deeply southern. As she noted, the imaginations of Catholic writers in the South were bound by the influences of the region, influences that begin long before any training in the Church:

The things we see, hear, smell, and touch affect us long before we believe anything at all, and the South impresses its image on us from the moment we are able to distinguish one sound from another. By the time we are able to use our imaginations for fiction, we find that our senses have responded irrevocably to a certain reality. The discovery of being bound through the senses to a particular society and a particular history, to particular sounds and a particular idiom, is for the writer the beginning of a recognition that first puts his work into real human perspective for him. What the Southern Catholic writer is apt to find, when he descends within his imagination, is not Catholic life but the life of his region in which he is both native and alien. He discovers that the imagination is not free, but bound. (*MM*, 197)

To isolate one's fiction from the life of the region—which, O'Connor pointed out, has developed its own life within the artist's sensibilities—is to cut oneself off from the deep springs of inspiration and to flatten one's artistic vision into abstraction.

Specifically, the South had many things to offer the southern Catholic writer, not the least of which were its strong storytelling and literary traditions. Both traditions offered powerful antidotes to the theoretical tendencies of the Catholic mind—a mind, O'Connor said, that was "long on logic, definitions, abstractions, and formulas" (*MM*, 205). Southern storytelling and literature emphasized the significance of narrative and concrete detail for effective communication. "The Southerner knows he can do more justice to reality by telling a story than he can by discussing problems or proposing abstractions," O'Connor said in an interview with C. Ross Mullins, Jr. "We live in a complex region and you have to tell stories if you want to be anyway truthful about it" (*CFO*, 103). The South's profoundly secular literary tradition (and particularly Middle Georgia humor, from which O'Connor herself drew heavily and which will be discussed in some depth in the following chapter) provided the Catholic writer with a strong heritage—and one with little toleration for abstraction—from which to write. O'Connor noted in "The Catholic Novelist in the Protestant South" that in the interplay between the Catholic writer and the South's literary heritage, each side had much to offer and to gain from the other. "In a literature that tends naturally to extremes, as Southern literature does, we need something to protect us against the merely extreme, the merely personal, the merely grotesque, and here the Catholic, with his older tradition and his ability to resist the dissolution of belief, can make his contribution to Southern literature," O'Connor wrote. She added that the South's literary tradition would help the Catholic writer become "less timid as a novelist, more respectful of the concrete, more trustful of the blind imagination" (*MM*, 208).

The South's larger cultural and social heritage also was extremely beneficial to the Catholic writer because it was grounded in concrete thinking and in a profound recognition of human limitation. In "The Regional Writer" O'Connor comments on Walker Percy's response in an interview to the question of why there are so many good southern writers—"Because we lost the War," Percy replied. Percy's answer, O'Connor explains, had less to do with the Civil War's providing southern writers with good source material for their work than it did with the war's effect on the southern psyche. "What he was saying was that we have had our Fall," O'Connor writes. "We have gone into the modern world with an inburnt knowledge of human limitations and with a sense of mystery which could not have developed in our first state of innocence—as it has not sufficiently developed in the rest of the country" (*MM*, 59). Elsewhere O'Connor makes it clear that the southern knowledge of human limitation was profoundly religious. Underpinning the South's social thinking was not the Enlightenment ideal of human perfectibility (characterized by O'Connor in a letter [November 8, 1958] to Cecil Dawkins as the idea "that man has never fallen, never incurred guilt, and is ultimately perfectible by his own efforts") but the biblical awareness of humanity's fallen nature. " 'How far we have fallen' means the fall of Adam, the fall from innocence, from sanctifying grace," O'Connor writes (November 8, 1958) to Dawkins. "The South in other words still believes that man has fallen and that he is only perfectible by God's grace, not by his own unaided efforts" (HB, 302). Such thinking and awareness, she believed, kept the southern mind firmly rooted in the here and now (and not off in some theoretical realm in the pursuit of perfection) and discouraged presumptuous attempts to elevate the individual consciousness into the center of all meaning and values— the sin of gnostic pride.[14]

O'Connor frequently discussed the South's Protestant religious heritage and the advantages it offered Catholic writers. In "Some Aspects of the Grotesque in Southern Fiction," O'Connor says that by and large, people in the South still conceive of humanity in theological terms. "While the South is hardly Christ-centered," she adds, "it is most certainly Christ-haunted. The Southerner, who isn't convinced of it, is very much afraid that he may have been formed in the image and likeness of God." This highly personal, and at times fearful, concern about one's standing with God stems primarily from the South's strong grounding in the Bible. O'Connor notes in "The Catholic Novelist in the Protestant South" that in the South, the Bible Belt, the Bible is read and known by a large cross-section of the population—rich and poor, white and black, educated and uneducated. "Sam Jones' grandma read the Bible thirty-seven times on her knees," O'Connor writes. "And the rural and small-town South, and even a certain level of the city South, is made up of the descendants of

14. Several critics, drawing from Eric Voegelin's ideas on gnosticism, have looked at O'Connor from this perspective. See particularly Desmond, Risen Sons; Marion Montgomery, Why Flannery O'Connor Stayed Home (La Salle, Ill., 1981). Vol. I of Montgomery, The Prophetic Poet and the Spirit of the Age, 3 vols.; and Marion Montgomery, Possum and Other Receits for the Recovery of "Southern" Being (Athens, Ga., 1987).

old ladies like her." Catholics, in contrast, lack this sure grounding in the Bible; it is usually only read, she says, by educated Catholics, and so its stark and powerful vision does not profoundly shape the Catholic consciousness. "The Bible is held sacred in the Church, we hear it read at Mass, bits and pieces are exposed to us in the liturgy," O'Connor writes, "but because we are not totally dependent upon it, it has not penetrated very far into our consciousness nor conditioned our reactions to experience" (*MM*, 44–45, 201–202, 203).

The South's biblical heritage offered writers, Catholic and non-Catholic alike, such profound advantages that O'Connor, in one of her interviews, said that "the fact that the South is the Bible Belt is in great measure responsible for its literary prominence now" (*CFO*, 87). She discussed these advantages in "The Catholic Novelist in the Protestant South," pointing out that great storytellers need standards, rooted not in the everyday affairs of humanity but in something larger and more significant with roots stretching toward eternity, to judge themselves by and measure themselves against. Such standards, she said, are for the most part absent in the modern age, where "men judge themselves now by what they find themselves doing." And she added that these standards cannot be abstract and theoretical, not merely the teachings of the Catholic Church; they must be able to be expressed concretely and must extend into the very heart of the community. O'Connor writes: "For the purposes of fiction, these guides have to exist in a concrete form, known and held sacred by the whole community. They have to exist in the form of stories which affect our image and our judgment of ourselves. Abstractions, formulas, laws will not serve here. We have to have stories in our background. It takes a story to make a story. It takes a story of mythic dimensions, one which belongs to everybody, one in which everybody is able to recognize the hand of God and its descent. In the Protestant South, the Scriptures fill this role" (*MM*, 202).

The entire life of the South, O'Connor asserted, had been conditioned by the Scriptures, particularly in their making absolute matters vivid in the here and now. "Our response to life is different," she wrote, "if we have been taught only a definition of faith than if we have trembled with Abraham as he held the knife over Isaac" (*MM*, 203–204). Seeing everyday affairs by the light of the Scriptures and eternal matters also gave the southern mind a decidedly skeptical bent. The South's biblical vision, O'Connor told a reporter for *Atlanta Magazine*, "gives us a kind of skepticism under God, a refusal to put relative things in the place of the Absolute. It keeps our vision concrete and it forms a sacred heroic background to which we can compare and refer our own actions" (*CFO*, 110).

O'Connor's comment on southern skepticism calls to mind not only her comments on her own "Christian skepticism" but also the work of Herbert N. Schneidau, who, in *Sacred Discontent: The Bible and Western Tradition*, argues that a profoundly skeptical and self-critical approach to reality characterizes the vision of the Bible and its prophets.[15] Schneidau terms this vision *Yahwist* and says its central tenet is that an absolute gulf separates humanity from an all-powerful God. The origins of the Yahwist vision lie in ancient Hebraic culture—a culture whose organizing structure and underlying system of belief were radically different from what Schneidau terms the "mythological" cultures that both predated and existed alongside it. Mythological cultures, Schneidau points out, see their world integrally connected to, and penetrated by, the divine. "Man's culture and the world of the gods," Schneidau writes, "exist in a kind of cosmic continuum with little or no gap between them; the stability of these cultures is reinforced by the interpenetration of the sacred into all areas of life, establishing sanctioned hierarchies and structures." The Hebraic culture, in contrast, saw God as radically other, separated entirely from the human world; as a result, nothing human—not individuals themselves or the institutions they established—possessed inherent sacredness. Before God, humanity and all its works were totally devalued. Schneidau cites an observation of archaeologist Henri Frankfort on this devaluation:

The God of the Hebrews is pure being, unqualified, ineffable. He is *holy*. That means he is *sui generis*. It does not mean that he is taboo or that he is power. It means that all values are ultimately attributes of God alone: Hence, all concrete phenomena are devaluated. It may be true that in Hebrew thought man and nature are not necessarily corrupt; but both are necessarily *valueless* before God. . . . "We are all as an unclean thing, and all our

15. Herbert N. Schneidau, *Sacred Discontent: The Bible and Western Tradition* (Baton Rouge, 1976). For a discussion of Schneidau's work and the Yahwist tradition, see G. Douglas Atkins, *Reading Deconstruction, Deconstructive Reading* (Lexington, Ky., 1983).

righteousness are as filthy rags" [Isa. 64:6]. Even man's righteousness, his highest virtue, is devaluated by comparison with the absolute.

Underscoring the all-encompassing scope and utter omnipotence of Yahweh's presence, Schneidau writes that "his mere being left human pretensions in shambles, in the dust—even the most moral ones, and *a fortiori* those in which man takes most pride: his heroism or riches or wisdom, his mighty armies and empires, his massive building projects, his efficient regimentation of the people."[16]

Because nothing of humanity was sacred and because all value resided in Yahweh, the Hebraic prophets forcefully denounced the strivings and achievements of the individual and society; they probed and called into question the basic structures of thought and belief that guided humanity's life in the everyday world. Schneidau characterizes the thrust behind the prophets' attacks—and indeed the thrust of biblical thought in general—as demythologization, the resistance to all efforts to consolidate and sacralize the social thought and ideology by which a culture defines and perceives itself. He argues that this thrust has become an integral element in Western thinking and tradition. "In their attitude toward the practices of their own culture, and even more in their intolerance of the beliefs of the surrounding nations, to which they ascribed many of the most abominable practices," Schneidau writes, "the Hebrew prophets gave voice to a skeptical, often mocking spirit that has long since pervaded the intellectual life of the Western world, visible in forms that vary from austere revolutions in science's hypotheses to the sensational expose or 'debunking.' " Schneidau sees this skeptical and probing spirit of self-analysis as utterly pervasive in Western culture, with dramatic consequences. "What unites Western culture in all its phases, tying in with the ambivalence that produces the continuity of change, is a series of demythologizings and consequent 'losses of faith'—some gradual, some traumatic," he writes. "Nothing is so characteristic of our traditions, with the result that we can say more truly of Western culture than of almost anything else, *plus ça change, plus c'est la même chose*. The Western world, in short, uses up myth at a tremendous rate, and often has to borrow frantically from other cultures, or to allow the cultural changes and oscillations that 'time and chance'

16. Schneidau, *Sacred Discontent*, 4.

will bring but which mythological societies will manage to dampen effectively."[17]

The Yahwist vision works to decenter and demythologize not only society but also the individual. In the face of Yahweh's omnipotence, the Hebrew prophets were displaced and decentered, alienated not only from those about them but also from their own selves. Whatever significance and value the prophets located in their individual consciousnesses the Yahwist perspective reduced to the empty dreams of vanity and pride; to gain insight into their own insignificance, the prophets, in a sense, stepped free from themselves, seeing themselves from the perspective of the ultimate other—Yahweh. This displacement was an act of radical alienation, and Schneidau sees it, together with the critique of the self it gives rise to, as fundamental to Western thinking. Schneidau suggests that the effort to demythologize the self, leading to one's alienation from the self, ultimately works to transcend the subjectivism and nihilism of the modern consciousness (what J. Hillis Miller characterizes as "the nothingness of consciousness when consciousness becomes the foundation of everything").[18] Such alienation, destroying the valorized self, is the first step to a larger and more enlightened vision. "We have reached out for the apple of self-knowledge, and in doing so have alienated God, nature, and each other," Schneidau writes; "but by pressing our self-awareness to its extreme, where we become alienated from ourselves, we find that this is not the end of the story. The Fall is only the beginning of the Bible. To be thus 'decentered' . . . is the precondition of insight: thus it is a *felix culpa*, good news for modern man of a somewhat unlikely kind."[19]

Schneidau's observations bear significant relevance to the mind and art of Flannery O'Connor, for she, I would argue, was profoundly influenced not only by the searching skepticism Schneidau argues is fundamental to the Western tradition but also by the extreme Yahwist vision that itself engendered this skeptical thinking. Although she remained a devout and committed Catholic, O'Connor nonetheless possessed, primarily through her thorough grounding in the Bible and her enthusiastic southern identity (southern culture's being un-

17. *Ibid.*, 12, 14.
18. Miller, *Poets of Reality*, 3.
19. Schneidau, *Sacred Discontent*, 49.

derpinned by biblical thought), a restless and probing skepticism that critiqued society as well as self. Profoundly influenced by both the spirit of the Bible (its demythologizing thrust) and its theology, O'Connor's skepticism was complex and rich, in many ways resembling the Yahwist vision of the Hebrew prophets. Yet, as we shall see in forthcoming chapters, her skepticism ultimately questioned even that vision, pressuring and challenging it while at the same time allowing its thrust to pressure and challenge her Catholicism.

Perhaps the most striking evidence of O'Connor's ties with Yahwist thinking comes in her own statements asserting her closeness to the fundamentalist preachers of the southern backwoods, themselves striking representatives of modern-day Yahwists. To the confusion and consternation of a good many readers and critics, O'Connor frequently went so far as to align herself, in terms of imaginative vision and commitment to faith, more with southern fundamentalists than with her Catholic brethren (at least with what she saw as the general run of them). In "The Catholic Novelist in the Protestant South," she says that her "underground religious affinities" extend to the fundamentalists and that when she delves into the depths of her imagination she discovers not the life of the Catholic Church but that of the Protestant Bible Belt South, in its most extreme and enthusiastic forms. She elaborates on her ties with the fundamentalists in a passage describing the position of the southern Catholic writer in the Protestant South:

I think he will feel a good deal more kinship with backwoods prophets and shouting fundamentalists than he will with those politer elements for whom the supernatural is an embarrassment and for whom religion has become a department of sociology or culture or personality development. His interest and sympathy may go—as I know my own does—directly to those aspects of Southern life where the religious feeling is most intense and where its outward forms are farthest from the Catholic, and most revealing of a need that only the Church can fill. This is not because, in the felt superiority of orthodoxy, he wishes to subtract one theology from another, but because, descending within himself to find his region, he discovers that it is with these aspects of Southern life that he has a feeling of kinship strong enough to spur him to write. (MM, 207)

So strong were O'Connor's affinities with the fundamentalists that she asserted that she allied herself closely with them not only in their searing commitment to Christ but also in their basic theology. "I am more and more impressed with the amount of Catholicism that fundamentalist Protestants have been able to retain," she wrote (May 11, 1963) to A. "Theologically, our differences with them are on the nature of the Church, not on the nature of God or our obligation to him." To novelist John Hawkes she wrote (September 13, 1959) that southern fundamentalists often get themselves into ridiculous religious predicaments but that she did not view their struggles as merely comic. Unlike most people, the religious fanatics, as O'Connor saw them, wrestled with ultimate matters, and she drove home both the seriousness by which she viewed them and her identification with them when she told Hawkes, "I accept the same fundamental doctrines of sin and redemption that they do" (*HB*, 518, 350).

The primary doctrines of southern fundamentalists that O'Connor speaks of are essentially Yahwist. For southern fundamentalists the powerful presence of God looms above all creation, devaluing all human values and the significance of earthly life. Caroline Gordon, in her novel *The Garden of Adonis*, succinctly captures the fundamentalist spirit in the character Ed Mortimer, a preacher whose sermon focuses on the theme, in his own words, that "this world and all its pleasures. . . . Hit ain't nothin'."[20] The center of all meaning resides for the fundamentalist not in oneself or the world but in Jesus, and how one stands with him is, finally, the only thing that matters. Every person must make a personal choice either to accept Christ into his or her life or to reject him. There is no gray area, no room for compromise: One lives by Christ or the Devil.

Certainly one of the most striking depictions in O'Connor's fiction of a mind given to fundamentalist thinking comes in her story "A Good Man Is Hard to Find." Here The Misfit—no preacher, and indeed an escaped convict who coolly oversees the murder of a helpless family—nonetheless possesses a burning awareness of the fundamentalist imperative to commit oneself for or against Christ. For The Misfit, Christ is the great stumbling block, the one whose presence completely disrupts the order of human life and endeavor. Whereas most people ignore the ultimate matters that the Incarnation and the Resurrection present, The Misfit is wracked by these concerns, his life in utter disarray because he cannot finally bring himself to believe in

---

20. Caroline Gordon, *The Garden of Adonis* (1937; rpr. New York, 1971), 105.

Christ. Too much the literalist, The Misfit says that for him to have given his life to Christ, he would have had to see Christ perform his miracles; and so unable to open himself to Christ, he has closed himself off from him and has embraced a life that is completely without him—a life of waste and destruction, a life embodied, in his own words, of "no pleasure but meanness" (CS, 132).

The rigor demanded by the fundamentalist imperative—the obligation to make a total commitment either for or against Christ—O'Connor found very appealing, and there is no doubt that one part of her, one of the voices of her multi-voiced self, was given to its expression.[21] As we shall see, the fundamentalist perspective is a crucial one in O'Connor's stories; all of her mature work, with varying degrees of intensity, has a narrator profoundly fundamentalist in sympathy, with the result that we find characters and situations sharply colored by the light of a fundamentalist vision. The interplay between the dominant voice of O'Connor's Catholicism and her fundamentalist voice—an interplay expressed most significantly in the relationship between Catholic author and her fundamentalist fiction—is complex, rich, and central to O'Connor's imaginative life.

That O'Connor gave free expression to her fundamentalist voice and to other voices of her self rather than monologically suppressing them is a crucial factor behind her artistic greatness. She believed that the descent into the self through art, where the artist encountered the multi-voiced self, was also a descent into the writer's homeland; thus, to turn within was also, paradoxically, to turn without. The image of the self, on one level, became for O'Connor the image of the South, and it was this image, teeming with heterogeneous voices, that she as artist had to engage and give expression to. "The writer must wrestle with it," O'Connor wrote in "The Catholic Novelist in the Protestant

---

21. For discussions of O'Connor's affinities with Protestantism, see particularly Robert H. Brinkmeyer, Jr., "A Closer Walk with Thee: Flannery O'Connor and Southern Fundamentalists," *Southern Literary Journal*, XVIII (Spring, 1986), 3–13; Robert Milder, "The Protestantism of Flannery O'Connor," *Southern Review*, n.s., XI (1975), 802–19; Louis D. Rubin, Jr., "Flannery O'Connor and the Bible Belt," in Melvin J. Friedman and Lewis A. Lawson (eds.), *The Added Dimension: The Art and Mind of Flannery O'Connor* (New York, 1966), 49–72; and Albert Sonnenfeld, "Flannery O'Connor: The Catholic Writer as Baptist," in Melvin J. Friedman and Beverly Lyon Clark (eds.), *Critical Essays on Flannery O'Connor* (Boston, 1985), 108–19.

South," speaking of the image of the South and also, I would argue, of the image of the self, "like Jacob with the angel, until he has extracted a blessing" (MM, 198). The blessing that the writer discovers is the richness of self and world, the multitudinous others whom the author recognizes and dialogically engages, so freeing him or her from the isolation of the monologic self and opening the consciousness to dialogic growth and understanding.

2

Imaginative Vision and Narrative
Interplay

At some time during her career Flannery O'Connor delivered a lecture (later published in composite form as "The Nature and Aim of Fiction") to a class studying, in the words of the course title, "How the Writer Writes." The course was organized so that each week a different writer addressed the class, and early on in her talk O'Connor commented on the course's format, saying that "the only parallel I can think of to this is having the zoo come to you, one animal at a time; and I suspect what you hear one week from the giraffe is contradicted the next week by the baboon." She went on to attack the idea that there was any such thing as "THE writer," and she admonished those who thought that becoming a successful writer merely entailed "learning certain things about working habits and about markets and about what subjects are currently acceptable" (*MM*, 63, 64). She argued that a writer's "external habits" are insignificant to understanding the artistic process, because they reflect not the artist's imaginative life but his or her personal circumstances and common sense (or, as O'Connor added, the lack of it).

After dismissing the entire thrust of the class's study, O'Connor proceeded to point out what was important to the serious artist: not external habits but, in philosopher Jacques Maritain's words, "the habit of art." She explained that for Maritain *habit* meant "a certain quality or virtue of the mind," and that as such it involved a way of perceiving and understanding the world. "The scientist has the habit of science," she said; "the artist, the habit of art." Elsewhere ("Writing Short Stories") O'Connor said that the accomplished artist always has the story under control, even when the work seems to strike off on its own in haphazard and unpredictable directions. To support her contention, she explained that the creation of art involves the artist's entire personality (including the unconscious mind), and the personality's driving force—its habit—is always at work, perceiving, guiding, creating. "Art is the habit of the artist," she wrote, "and habits have to be rooted deep in the whole personality. They have to be cultivated like any other habit, over a long period of time, by experience. . . . I think this is more than just a discipline, although it is that; I think it is a way of looking at the created world and of using the senses so as to make them find as much meaning as possible in things" (*MM*, 64–65, 101).

At first glance, O'Connor's comments on the habit of art appear to suggest that there is little, if any, dialogic interplay between a writer's vision and his or her art that might foster further growth and insight. By this line of thinking, the writer is more the maker than the seeker of truth—an artist creating an artifact that expresses and communicates an already developed vision that remains virtually rigid and unchallengeable. Art, in other words, does not test or challenge the vision of the artist, because the artist's stance is similar to God's before his handiwork: The artist is the supreme master, detached and often thoroughly ironic, who towers above the art. One thinks in this regard of Stephen Dedalus's musings, in James Joyce's *Portrait of the Artist as a Young Man*, that "the artist, like the God of the creation, remains within or behind or beyond or above his handiwork, invisible, refined out of existence, indifferent, paring his fingernails."[1] As important as this view of the artist was to a number of twentieth-century writers, O'Connor stands outside of this tradition, and her remarks on the habit of art ultimately suggest a quite different understanding of the relationship of the artist to the art. The writer's habit of art was for O'Connor an ordering of self and perception that was not unassailable and unbending but rather in a constant process of growth and development. She suggests, in the words previously cited, that a person's habits develop only "over a long period of time, by experience" (*MM*, 101), and for the writer this means that the habit of art took shape—and continually takes new shape—through the

1. James Joyce, *A Portrait of the Artist as a Young Man* (1916; rpr. New York, 1964), 215.

ongoing interplay with the art. Writing fiction is a means for both embodying a vision of reality and reshaping that vision. Whatever the artist writes, the work on one level probes and pressures the habit that shapes it and initiates (if the artist is not locked in a rigid monologism) its reassessment and reconfiguration.

For O'Connor, then, no matter where the writer appears to stand in relation to the work, he or she on one level is always actively participating in it, responding to its tests and challenges. In this sense writing fiction is an act of self-growth and self-knowledge, a means for probing the depths of the imagination and for pushing those depths deeper into the realm of mystery. O'Connor says in "The Catholic Novelist in the Protestant South" that serious writing "is a kind of personal encounter with the circumstances of the particular writer's imagination, with circumstances which are brought to order only in the actual writing" (MM, 198). The order wrought from one work both tests and is tested by the artist's vision and then itself is undermined and decentered by the order expressed in the work following it. This endless process of building up and breaking down deepens and broadens the artist's habit of art, guaranteeing its ongoing dynamic growth.

In such a way, then, artists create themselves in the very act of writing. Meaning, for O'Connor, was not a moral statement the reader draws from the text—"any abstractly expressed compassion or piety or morality in a piece of fiction is only a statement added to it," she comments in "The Nature and Aim of Fiction"—but was the reader's entire experience with the text. O'Connor's encounters with her own fiction often pressured her into reassessing the views she held before she started writing. In her discussion in "Writing Short Stories" of how she wrote "Good Country People," she begins by saying that she doubts "if many writers know what they are going to do when they start out." She says that when she began her story, she had no idea that a central character would be a woman with a Ph.D. and a wooden leg. In fact, according to O'Connor, she hardly knew anything about where the story would go, both when she started and then later when she was well into it. "I merely found myself one morning writing a description of two women that I knew something about, and before I realized it, I had equipped one of them with a daughter with a wooden leg," she writes. "As the story progressed, I brought in the

Bible salesman, but I had no idea of what I was going to do with him. I didn't know he was going to steal that wooden leg until ten or twelve lines before he did it, but when I found out this was going to happen, I realized that it was inevitable." Although she asserts that on one level her habit of art shaped the story, O'Connor nonetheless admits that the jarring climax of the story stunned her. "This is a story that produces a shock for the reader," she writes, "and I think one reason for this is that it produced a shock for the writer." Clearly O'Connor's own habits—artistic and otherwise—were shaken by the experience of "Good Country People," and at the end of this same essay she suggests that artists must be so jarred if their art is of any merit. "You ought to be able to discover something from your stories," she remarks. "If you don't, probably nobody else will" (*MM*, 75, 100, 106).

On one level that shock that O'Connor describes results from encountering, through literature, intense and heightened experience that suggests the mysterious passage of life on which we are all embarked but to which most of us, locked in our everyday routines, give little thought. O'Connor characterizes our journey through life with the instructions of Saint Cyril of Jerusalem to catechumens: "The dragon sits by the side of the road, watching those who pass. Beware lest he devour you. We go to the Father of Souls, but it is necessary to pass by the dragon." She adds that great fiction describes these encounters with the monster and so proves disturbing to the reader and, by implication, the writer. "No matter what form the dragon may take," she says in "The Fiction Writer and His Country," "it is of this mysterious passage past him, or into his jaws, that stories of any depth will always be concerned to tell, and this being the case, it requires considerable courage at any time, in any country, not to turn away from the storyteller." And, she might have added, considerable courage for the storyteller not to turn away from the story. To experience literature at its deepest levels, O'Connor argues in "The Nature and Aim of Fiction," is not a matter of being educated but rather of having a mind "that is willing to have its sense of mystery deepened by contact with reality, and its sense of reality deepened by contact with mystery" (*MM*, 35, 79).

At another point in "The Nature and Aim of Fiction," O'Connor says that "writing a novel is a terrible experience, during which the hair often falls out and the teeth decay." Her observation here refers not only to the strenuous physical demands of writing—the many long days at the writing table—but also to the intellectual challenges and pressures that the fiction brings to bear upon the writer. Rather than being an escape from reality, as most people believe, writing fiction is instead "a plunge into reality and it's very shocking to the system." It is shocking at the deepest level, because writing engages authors in an experience of otherness: It forces writers outside of themselves to observe and evaluate, from another perspective, their deepest habits of thought and art. "The writer has to judge himself with a stranger's eye and a stranger's severity," O'Connor writes in "The Nature and Aim of Fiction." "The prophet in him must see the freak." Such displacement means that the author's situation in writing is similar to that of the characters in fiction whom O'Connor finds most intriguing: "characters who are forced out [of their everyday existences] to meet evil and grace and who act on a trust beyond themselves—whether they know very clearly what it is they act upon or not." This is not an easy position to be in, and O'Connor frequently characterizes the writing process in terms of battle and conflict. "Like a very doubtful Jacob," she writes in "Catholic Novelists and Their Readers," speaking of the writer, "he confronts what stands in his path and wonders if he will come out of the struggle at all" (*MM*, 77, 78, 81–82, 42, 183).

Ultimately from this struggle the writer reaches an understanding of personal limitations, both as artist and as interpreter of self and world. "He begins to see in the depths of himself," O'Connor comments in "The Teaching of Literature," "and it seems to me that his position there rests on what certainly must be the bedrock of all human experience—the experience of limitation or, if you will, of poverty." This knowledge, in turn, undermines the artist's authoritarian and dominant views, decentering his or her consciousness, so that the self's image of itself is no longer final and whole. In other words, the self no longer coincides with its single dominant voice: That voice, the writer now understands, is not complete but limited, merely one voice among many. That we are all made up of many conflicting voices—in effect, others—is O'Connor's point in her author's note to the second edition of *Wise Blood*, where she says that "free will does not mean one will, but many wills conflicting in one man" (*MM*, 132, 115). Recognizing these other voices is the first step in actively integrating them into one's self through a dialogic interplay whereby voices are not muffled into silence by a dominant voice but allowed their free expression.

O'Connor's convictions about dialogism most likely were influenced heavily by the work of Emmanuel Mounier, the Catholic philosopher known for his concept of personalism. O'Connor was a strong admirer of Mounier and said in her review of his *Character of Man* that "there is little doubt that this book is, as claimed on the jacket, the major work of 'one of the really great men of our time' " (*PG*, 45). Perhaps what she found most absorbing in Mounier's work was his attack on what he called the individualism of modern society. By this, Mounier meant the solipsistic turn inward of the modern mind, an act that led to a destructive isolation and spiritual barrenness. In *Personalism* Mounier writes:

Individualism is a system of morals, feelings, ideas and institutions in which individuals can be organized by their mutual isolation and defence. This was the ideology and the prevailing structure of Western bourgeois society in the 18th and 19th centuries. Man in the abstract, unattached to any natural community, the sovereign lord of a liberty unlimited and undirected; turning towards others with a primary mistrust, calculation and self-vindication; institutions restricted to the assurance that these egoisms should not encroach upon one another, or to their betterment as a purely profitmaking association—such is the rule of civilization now breaking up before our eyes, one of the poorest history has known.[2]

Opposed to individualism, for Mounier, is personalism, a philosophy that stresses that enrichment and growth result not from turning inward to the self but outward to the world and others. "Other persons do not limit [the person]," Mounier writes, "they enable it to be and to grow. The person only exists thus towards others, it only knows itself in knowing others, only finds itself in being known by them. The *thou*, which implies the *we*, is prior to the *I*—or at least accompanies it." In this interaction with the not-self, and particularly in communication with others, a person's rigid conception of isolated being is challenged and undermined. "It shakes me out of my self-

2. Emmanuel Mounier, *Personalism*, trans. Philip Mauret (London, 1952), 18–19.

assurance," says Mounier, "my habits, my egocentric torpor: communication, even when hostile, is the thing that most surely reveals me to myself."[3]

Crucial to one's development as a person—as opposed to an individual—are several steps that call for a radical repositioning of the self. Most fundamental is the necessity of the self to decentralize—that is, to detach the self from itself. This self-dispossession shatters the person's isolating egocentricism, thereby placing the person in a position open to interaction and communication with others. Meaningful communication that leads to new levels of self-awareness and understanding occurs only when a person's detachment from the self is so complete that the person can view that self from the standpoint of others. Understanding, writes Mounier, "is ceasing to see myself from my own point of view. . . . Not looking for myself in someone else chosen for his likeness to me, nor seeking to know another according to some general knowledge (a taste for psychology is not an interest in other persons) but accepting his singularity with my own, in an action that welcomes him, and in an effort that re-centres myself."[4] As Mounier suggests here, a person, in assuming the stance of another, ultimately incorporates those views into himself or herself, thereby recentering the self along new lines of awareness. Recentering, however, does not mean stasis, for in its ongoing encounters and communications with others, the self continually decenters and recenters itself.

Because the central activity of a person is contact with others, unfinalized dialogue is also, for Mounier, the very process that guides our thoughts. Thinking is dialogue, says Mounier, and he asserts that thought cannot be understood (as it usually is said to be) as "the receptivity of the watchful eye, a recording disc, or inversely, as a purely autonomous creator which fabricates objects from its own substance." Rather, Mounier continues, "thought is a constant coming and going between perception and response, assimilation and invention, passivity and activity." In a passage that O'Connor underscored in her copy of The Character of Man, Mounier elaborates on the dialogic nature of thinking: "We never think alone. The unspoken thought is a dialogue with someone who questions, contradicts

3. Ibid., 20, 23.
4. Ibid., 21.

or spurs one on. This inner debate, however complicated and prolonged—it may last a lifetime—is quite different from rumination, which is a wandering around the same spot. . . . It is, in spite of its interiorisation, realistic thought. Its coherence is made of social encounters and solid experience."[5] Frederick Asals points to that passage as a guide to deepen our understanding of O'Connor's inner life, saying that "surely the radical tensions in O'Connor's fiction—its polar images, its extremities of conflicts, its apocalyptic tendencies, its deeply divided heroes, and, not least, its numerous double figures—emerge from just such a creative inner dialogue, a dialogue that indeed seems to have lasted a lifetime."[6] I would go even further: Mounier's observations here and elsewhere on our dialogic existences embody not merely O'Connor's own inner dialogue but the dialogic dynamics that O'Connor saw at the heart of a writer's experience with literature. To engage literature was, for O'Connor, to reach understanding in Mounier's sense: The self is decentered and then later recentered with a fuller conception of its diversity.

For O'Connor as writer, displacement and decentering occurred in her dialogic relationship with three fundamental aspects of her fiction: the narrator, the characters, and the audience. Together these three complex relationships prompted a dynamic process of assimilation and reassimilation that opened up O'Connor to new areas of understanding and propelled her to new realms of growth. Such dialogic interplay was not confined to her conception of the artist; the interplay was both the process of growth (or in its rejection, the process of diminishment) that O'Connor portrayed in the characters of her fiction and the process to which she hoped to open her readers. This work will explore these three areas of O'Connor's art—narration, characters, and audience. The current chapter will finish with a discussion of narration and will be followed (after two chapters exploring the narrative difficulties of specific works) by chapters on the other two topics.

As the creating consciousness of her fiction, Flannery O'Connor stood on the threshold of the various viewpoints expressed and

5. Emmanuel Mounier, *The Character of Man,* trans. Cynthia Rowland (New York, 1956), 252.
6. Frederick Asals, *Flannery O'Connor: The Imagination of Extremity* (Athens, Ga., 1982), 123.

embodied in her fiction. Although her Catholicism was the organizing center of her work—the backdrop that provided the perspective by which characters were assessed and judged—O'Connor refracted this vision by using a narrative consciousness whose perspective was not fundamentally Catholic. With this narrative frame O'Connor achieved several things. To begin with, she was able to assess the views of the narrator (by objectifying the narrator's perspective of the world and manner of organizing plot and structure) to reveal meaning in literature. Bakhtin speaks of this narrative technique in his essay "Discourse in the Novel," saying that "a particular belief system belonging to someone else, a particular point of view on the world belonging to someone else, is used by the author because it is highly productive, that is, it is able on the one hand to show the object of representation in a new light (to reveal new sides or dimensions in it) and on the other hand to illuminate in a new way the 'expected' literary horizon, that horizon against which the particularities of the teller's tale are perceivable."[7] Aleksander Pushkin's narrator Belkin in *Tales of Belkin* is Bakhtin's example in this discussion. In using a prosaic, "unpoetic" character who has no conception of the poetic and romantic conventions of the story he tells, Pushkin undercuts the traditional expectations of romantic stories; and at the same time, by bringing Belkin's views and those underlying the story he tells into tension, he pressures both to reveal their boundaries and limits. O'Connor's use of her narrative consciousness (to be discussed fully shortly) works in a similar fashion. Her employment of a detached and ironic voice to tell stories often intensely violent and wildly comic both distorts the traditional expectations of such dark comedy and tests the limits of the opposing perspectives embodied in the narrator and the story.

Even more significant is O'Connor's use of her narrative consciousness to bring her Catholicism, the central force of her imaginative vision, under assessment and challenge. By refracting her Catholicism through a narrative frame essentially un-Catholic in vision, O'Connor distances herself from the authoritativeness of her defining vision. In a sense she steps free from herself, enabling herself to view

7. Mikhail Bakhtin, "Discourse in the Novel," in *The Dialogic Imagination: Four Essays*, ed. Michael Holquist and trans. Caryl Emerson and Michael Holquist (Austin, 1981), 312–13.

her once-unquestioned Catholic vision from another perspective—
that of the narrative consciousness. By placing her Catholic vision in
this alien context where other voices and perspectives impinge on its
authority, O'Connor tests her vision, pressuring it to respond to life's
multiplicity. O'Connor talks of such interplay, in the larger context of
Catholics' writing in the largely anti-Catholic South, in "The Catholic
Novelist in the Protestant South." She says that when one applies
one's principles in new situations where their authority no longer
goes unquestioned, one is forced not to abandon these principles but,
in her words, "to come up with fresh reactions" (*MM*, 205). From this
act of self-dispossession, and from the fresh reactions that emerge
from stepping free, one gains a fuller knowledge of self and world.

The interplay between the author and the narrator in O'Connor's
fiction is thus extremely complex and stressful. As Bakhtin observes,
the readers of fiction where such author-narrator interaction is at
work must always be aware of what he calls the second story, the story
behind the story. "Behind the narrator's story we read a second story,
the author's story," Bakhtin writes in "Discourse in the Novel"; "he
is the one who tells us how the narrator tells stories, and also tells us
about the narrator himself. We acutely sense two levels at each moment in the story; one, the level of the narrator, a belief system filled
with his objects, meanings and emotional expressions, and the other,
the level of the author, who speaks (albeit in a refracted way) by
means of this story and through this story." Neither level, as Bakhtin
suggests here, is wholly distinct, for each is accented by the other.
Bakhtin continues his discussion by stressing this interpenetration
and by outlining the reader's role in interpretation: "The narrator
himself, with *his* own discourse, enters into this authorial belief system along with what is actually being told. We puzzle out the author's
emphases that overlie the subject of the story, while we puzzle out the
story itself and the figure of the narrator as he is revealed in the
process of telling his tale."[8]

Before puzzling out the structure of O'Connor's fiction in the manner that Bakhtin suggests, I want to explore briefly the literary tradition from which O'Connor primarily writes—that of Middle Georgia
humor—to suggest that much of what I have been saying about the

8. *Ibid.*, 314.

clash of perspectives and the significance of the narrative frame in O'Connor's work derives from this tradition. Middle Georgia humor, typified by such writers as Augustus Baldwin Longstreet, Richard Malcolm Johnston, Johnson Jones Hooper, William Tappan Thompson, and Joel Chandler Harris, has been from its beginnings the most productive and significant tradition of southern literary humor. By and large it is a rough-and-tumble fiction that portrays the escapades and antics of country folk of modest means who, though lacking sophistication, usually possess a zest for life and a down-home shrewdness. A commentator writing in the 1890s, William Malone Baskervill, noted that Middle Georgia humor arose from a people typically southern except in their strong independence and sense of humor. "The Middle Georgians are a simple, healthy, homogeneous folk, resembling for the most part other Southerners of like rank and calling in their manners, customs, and general way of living," wrote Baskervill. "But they have developed a certain manly, vigorous, fearless independence of action, and an ever increasing propensity to take a humorous view of life."[9]

Like most other traditions of American humor, Middle Georgia humor thrives on the clash between two modes of perceiving reality—the genteel and the vernacular. The genteel perspective, as Louis D. Rubin, Jr., points out in his fine essay " 'The Barber Kept on Shaving': The Two Perspectives of American Humor," is theoretical, learned, and cultivated, whereas the vernacular is pragmatic, commonsensical, and realistic.[10] The comic contrasts that arise when these two perspectives run up against each other frequently occur in Middle Georgia humor in the very telling of the tales: Typically, a story of rural life, epitomizing the vernacular mode, is told by a sophisticated observer whose perspective is thoroughly genteel. The extremes in vision can be wrenching. Generally, the genteel view, at least on the surface, is affirmed, with the literate gentleman narrator

---

9. Quoted in Rubin, "Flannery O'Connor's Company of Southerners: Or, 'The Artificial Nigger' Read as Fiction Rather Than Theology," in *A Gallery of Southerners*, 122.

10. Louis D. Rubin, Jr., " 'The Barber Kept on Shaving': The Two Perspectives of American Humor," in Louis D. Rubin, Jr. (ed.), *The Comic Imagination in American Literature* (New Brunswick, N.J., 1973), 385–405.

using the crudeness of the country folk to illustrate a moral about the importance of cultural sophistication and its unfortunate—but humorous—absence in the countryside.

With the better writers, however, the opposition is not resolved so simply. Beneath the surface of their works runs a countercurrent of feeling that finds the country folk worthy of sympathy, if not respect. It is they, rather than the genteel narrator, who appear to be vital and vigorous and to possess a realistic understanding of the here and now. The genteel narrator, in contrast, seems distanced from the world of fact and circumstance by his refinement and cultural standards. In "Flannery O'Connor's Company of Southerners: Or, 'The Artificial Nigger' Read as Fiction Rather Than Theology," Rubin comments on this bias:

Amused and even appalled though the urbane, genteel narrator of the traditional humorous sketches is at the crudeness and vulgarity of the backwoods plain folk, he is also rather impressed at their vigor and their ability to cope with the real world. Indeed, in some instances, the narrator's elegant language, literary diction, and sophisticated syntax are often exaggerated by the author until they seem artificial, and become a device not for confronting the everyday world but for avoiding it and refusing to face it. For Middle Georgia literature, however it pokes fun at the naivete and crudeness of the plain folk, seldom finally demeans the rural white at the expense of more cultivated or wealthy city people. The country man may be discomfited, embarrassed, ridiculed, but the element of integrity is usually his and not the city-dweller's.[11]

This underlying perspective, working against the story's ostensible thrust valorizing the narrator (a thrust embodied in the narrator's position as framer of the tale), pressures, and finally severely undercuts, the narrator's privileged status. Its presence adds a depth and a lively tension to an otherwise simple narrative structure.

Besides exposing the limits of the genteel perspective, the interplay between the vernacular and urbane modes in Middle Georgia humor also suggests that the two modes are not isolated, but interconnected, visions tied together in such a vital way that each one's status in a large sense depends upon the presence of the other. James B. Cox's

---

11. Rubin, "Flannery O'Connor's Company of Southerners," in *A Gallery of Southerners*, 125–26.

brilliant discussion of Augustus Baldwin Longstreet's opening sketch in *Georgia Scenes* reveals this interconnectedness.[12] In this sketch, "Georgia Theatrics," the genteel narrator, a man named Hall, tells of his encounters on a trip through what he calls "The Dark Corner" of Lincoln County. "I believe it took its name from the moral darkness which reigned over that portion of the country at the time of which I am speaking," Hall reports. While riding through the countryside on a beautiful spring day, he suddenly hears an outburst of profane and raucous voices; it sounds as if a number of men are fighting. He rushes to the scene, wondering in his excitement "what band of ruffians has selected this holy season and this heavenly retreat for such pandemonic riots!" As Hall approaches the grove from where the voices come, he sees a man lunge with arms outstretched and thumbs turned out, and he hears an answering cry, "Enough! My eye's out!" The victor rises up, taunting his victim: "Get your owl eye in agin if you can!" With this, Hall approaches the man and berates him for his brutality. The embarrassed youth, "with a taunting curl of the nose," replies to the dumbfounded Hall, "You needn't kick before you're spurr'd. There a'n't nobody there, no ha'n't been nother. I was jist seein' how I could 'a' *fout*." The youth returns to his plowing, and Hall looks down to see two thumb prints "plunged up to the balls in the mellow earth" where the imaginary gouging occurred.[13]

What could have been a simple exposé of the violent, unbridled imagination of a country youth has become much more in the hands of Longstreet. As Cox points out, both the youth and Hall are caught in the act—the youth for his crude game playing and Hall for his overzealous rush to pass judgment before he knows the facts. Hall, indeed, has desired the fight to be real so he could step in and establish his morally superior position. In rushing to help what he thinks is a blinded man, Hall reveals his own blindness to the situation; he tries to cover his own embarrassment, Cox points out, by using exaggerated and self-congratulatory language in his telling of the tale. The joke of "Georgia Theatrics" is thus double-faced, exposing both the

12. James B. Cox, "Humor of the Old Southwest," in Louis D. Rubin, Jr. (ed.), *The Comic Imagination in American Literature* (New Brunswick, N.J., 1973), 101–12.

13. Augustus Baldwin Longstreet, "Georgia Theatrics," in *Georgia Scenes* (New York, 1897), 1, 3, 4, 5.

youth's crudity and Hall's need (and desire) for this crudity in order to establish his morally superior position. Hall's story thus reveals that the opposition between the vernacular and genteel perspectives is characterized by a dynamic tension in which the two modes permeate and pressure each other. Cox correctly observes that the two perspectives "truly depend on and indirectly inform each other."[14]

Like most of the Middle Georgia humorists—and indeed the southwestern humorists—Longstreet was a country gentleman and professional man whose politics were distinctly conservative. The genteel narrators of his sketches clearly are versions of his own perspective. At his worst, Longstreet establishes his narrators as unchallenged— and unchallengeable—paragons who impose meanings upon vernacular life. The genteel perspective, in these works, is authoritarian and monologic, the frame in which it is found being an appropriate metaphor for its dominating aspect—an enclosure to control and dominate the story and the vernacular perspective. At his best, however, as in "Georgia Theatrics," Longstreet uses the genteel narrator to objectify his own perspective and so free himself from its domination. By observing rather than merging with his narrator, Longstreet is able to view his own vision as an outsider would, and to witness— and depict—the constant pressure that the genteel and vernacular perspectives bring upon each other. The narrator in these works still strives to impose meaning and order upon the story, but because the two perspectives are shown to be so dependent upon each other, his efforts ultimately fail. The vernacular mode ultimately breaks through the controlling frame, thereby forcing the narrator to adopt an even more distanced and refined language and perspective in his effort to maintain the facade of his authoritarian position. In the process, the shortcomings of the narrator's mode of vision become readily apparent, both to Longstreet and the reader.

Much of the tension at work in a typical O'Connor story is similar to that found in the sketches and stories of Longstreet and other Middle Georgia humorists. Like their humor, hers frequently centers on the clash between genteel and vernacular perspectives (her bias is more openly with the vernacular perspective, though this allegiance

14. Cox, "Humor of the Old Southwest," in Rubin (ed.), *The Comic Imagination in American Literature*, 105.

often does not become apparent until the climax of the story). Hers also is often a rough-and-tumble humor, with violent acts both setting the tone and embodying a good deal of meaning. O'Connor is particularly adept at manipulating the dichotomies of the genteel and vernacular to set up comic contrasts and to reveal pretense. But of course, as a Catholic writer in the twentieth century, O'Connor was not merely writing Middle Georgia humor; although she drew heavily from this thoroughly secular tradition, O'Connor was aiming toward a good deal more than were her earlier counterparts, and she worked the patterns of the literary tradition in intriguing and challenging ways to express her own unique vision. A close look at several selections from O'Connor's work, drawn from different points in her career, reveals the different ways that O'Connor adapted the conventions of Middle Georgia humor as her artistic vision matured.

O'Connor's early story "The Barber" (*ca.* 1947), one of her first attempts at genuinely comic fiction, represents her initial experiments with the traditions of Middle Georgia humor. "The Barber" is about a liberal intellectual named Rayber who tries to defend to the regular gatherers at the local barbershop—a distinctly uneducated and racist bunch—his support for the nonsegregationist candidate in the Democratic primary. Rayber is confident that with his education and good sense he will be able to overwhelm the group with his views, and he works hard on the speech and on practicing its delivery. In his own mind his speech sounds effective, but as soon as he begins his address in the barbershop he realizes that something is very wrong. The men crowd about him, "their red faces grinning" (and, one gathers, the hair on their red necks bristling), and Rayber feels "as if he were fighting his way out of a net." The words that earlier had rung so powerful and convincing have now, in front of this hostile audience, lost all their effectiveness. Rayber merely mouths, rather than delivers, his speech: "He heard the words drag out—'Well, the way I see it, men elect. . . .' He felt them pull out of his mouth like freight cars, jangling, backing up on each other, grating to a halt, sliding, clinching back, jarring, and then suddenly stopping as roughly as they had begun" (*CS,* 24). The genteel perspective collapses before the vernacular, and Rayber, in his impotent rage, knocks down the barber and rushes from the shop with the barber's bib about his knees and shaving lather dripping inside his collar.

"The Barber" is a relatively straightforward comic story, built almost entirely on the clash between the genteel and vernacular perspectives. The confrontation between the two modes of vision is itself kept free from complexity: The two perspectives are shown to be entirely distinct and utterly incompatible. The humor results from both this stark dichotomy and Rayber's unsuccessful efforts, fueled by his intellectual pride, to bridge the gap separating the two ways of seeing. Rayber clearly gets the worst of it here, not so much because of the rightness of the barbershop bunch but because of his own intellectual pretense. He sees the last line of his speech—"Men who use ideas without measuring them are walking on wind" (*CS*, 21)—as a blasting commentary on the group's bigotry, but as the story turns out, his words ring out as a mocking taunt of his own abstract ideology.

Distinctive here in terms of O'Connor's reworking of the conventions of Middle Georgia humor is not only her heavy-handed undercutting of the genteel perspective at the hands of the vernacular but also her use of a narrative consciousness that offers an alternative vision to the other two. Where the earlier comic writers framed their stories with the commentary and perspective of a gentleman narrator, O'Connor frames "The Barber" with a narrative consciousness (not present as a character) whose perspective stands apart from both the genteel and the vernacular. Although O'Connor does not explicitly identify the narrative consciousness, its language and commentary clearly indicate that it embodies a levelheadedness and general sanity that the other two perspectives in their own ways lack. If Rayber's liberal intellectualism, grounded in an undue faith in the rational and the theoretical, is out of touch with the world of fact, then the more pragmatic perspective of the barbershop crowd, although grounded in the here and now, is nonetheless crude and racist.

In undercutting both the genteel and the vernacular perspectives, O'Connor establishes the narrative consciousness's vision as something apart, an embodiment of generally accepted values and ideals that call into question the other two perspectives. Rubin's observations on one of the significant strains of American humor come close to describing the dynamics of O'Connor's story:

What this approach finds amusing is the inadequacy of the everyday, the ordinary, for it measures the raw fact from the standpoint of genuine culture and absolute value. It assumes that the mere fact of something is not what is important; what is crucial is what one can make of the fact. It is all very well to ridicule the traditional values of culture, knowledge, taste, ethics, but what is to be substituted in their place, if life is to rise above the level of mere getting and spending? What is wrong with the genteel tradition in arts and letters is not that it is overly civilized, but rather it is not civilized enough. It is false, sentimental, pretentious—because it is not sufficiently imaginative, sufficiently knowing, sufficiently beautiful.[15]

Or, as is usually the case in O'Connor's stories, it is not sufficiently religious. Note, however, that in "The Barber" the narrative consciousness's perspective lacks an obvious religious dimension; as suggested earlier, this perspective appears to be one embodying generally accepted values and so is less the voice of O'Connor as Catholic than that of a conventional satirist, whose voice embodies an implied ideal of culture and morality. One senses that in "The Barber" O'Connor is primarily testing her skills, experimenting with comic conventions to see what she can make them do, preparing herself for her greater works, which come with the discovery of her own unique narrative voice.

The narrative consciousness in "The Barber" is significant not only for the values it embodies but also for the position it assumes in relation to both O'Connor as author and the story told. Rather than establishing a clear-cut position behind the narrative consciousness so as to gain a perspective on its position, O'Connor instead merges with the narrative consciousness, thereby validating its authority and judgment and implicitly inviting the reader to share in its point of view. There is then no dialogic challenge of the narrative consciousness, no testing and pressuring of one voice by another, either from O'Connor (since her voice is essentially that of the storyteller's) or from the story itself (since the narrative consciousness's authoritative position is so secure and so far above the action that it remains inviolable). Unchallenged, the narrative consciousness is in complete control, imposing its own meanings and denying the validity of other positions.

O'Connor's use of this unchallenged and "standardized" narrative consciousness is perhaps the most distinctive characteristic of her early fiction. For the most part this early work is fairly conventional,

15. Rubin, " 'The Barber Kept on Shaving,' " in Rubin (ed.), *The Comic Imagination in American Literature*, 393–94.

depicting familiar people in familiar settings with a familiar narrative consciousness. In *The Question of Flannery O'Connor*, Martha Stephens observes that the only striking thing about O'Connor's early stories is how different they are from the later, and Stephens points specifically to the fact that "each one has a warmly conceived central character with whom the reader is closely engaged from the first line to the last and whose mind is laid completely and sympathetically open to the reader at every turn of the story."[16] Although "The Barber" is something of an exception to Stephens's remarks—Rayber is neither warmly conceived nor sympathetically portrayed—nonetheless the thrust of her comments holds true. Absent from O'Connor's early work is the harsh and strident narrative consciousness that in the later work develops wildly comic and often intensely violent characters and situations.

O'Connor's mature fiction begins with *Wise Blood*, when she abandons the familiar narrative consciousness and starts to use her own distinctive voice. Although this voice does not remain entirely consistent in terms of the severity of its ironic vision, it nonetheless is at all times readily identifiable and quite different from the generally tolerant voice of her earlier works. A look at several passages from her early story "The Train" (1948), together with their later versions as revised into the opening chapter of *Wise Blood*, suggests the startling shift in perspective and tone that occurred. Early in "The Train" the narrative consciousness describes the train and Haze:

Now the train was greyflying past instants of trees and quick spaces of field and a motionless sky that sped darkening away in the opposite direction. Haze leaned his head back on the seat and looked out the window, the yellow light of the train lukewarm on him. (*CS*, 54)

In *Wise Blood* the description has become this:

Hazel Motes sat at a forward angle on the green plush train seat, looking one minute at the window as if he might want to jump out of it, and the next down the aisle at the other end of the car. The train was racing through tree tops that fell away at intervals and showed the sun standing, very red, on the edge of the furthest woods. Nearer, the plowed fields curved and faded and the hogs nosing in the furrows looked like large spotted stones. (*WB*, 9)

16. Martha Stephens, *The Question of Flannery O'Connor* (Baton Rouge, 1973), 87.

Most noticeable here is the intensification of the character and description that occurs in the *Wise Blood* selection. Whereas Haze in "The Train" is leaning back in his seat, apparently calmly gazing out the window, in the revised version he appears to be on a knife's edge, leaning forward and feverishly shifting his stares from the window ("as if he might want to jump out of it") to the aisle. The description of the countryside has been transformed, too, from an evening scene that merely hints at any sense of threat ("a motionless sky that sped darkening away in the opposite direction") to one that is as charged as Haze: the enclosing wall of trees, the blazing red sun, the hogs appearing like boulders. The shift from the lukewarm light to the feverish sun itself embodies the change in perspective that occurs in these two passages, from a close and familiar vantage point to one distanced and intense, when situation and description are pushed to extremes and seem, like Haze, about to erupt.

One of the most drastic changes that O'Connor effected when she revised "The Train" into the first chapter of *Wise Blood* was her transformation of Haze. In "The Train" Haze is a fairly nondescript youth from the country, alone and lonely, and we know him fairly well because the narrative consciousness openly reveals his thoughts. We learn, for instance, that Haze's unusual interest in the porter is prompted by his own deep disorientation resulting from the demise of his hometown, from which he has just left. The porter's looks and gait remind him of a black man named Cash whom he knew in his youth, and he conjectures that the porter might even be Cash's son. The porter's resemblance to Cash—and his denial of being from Eastrod—initiate in Haze thoughts of his own dislocation. Lying in his berth, Haze hears the porter approaching, and he thinks:

He was from Eastrod. From Eastrod but he hated it. Cash wouldn't have put any claim on him. He wouldn't have wanted him. He wouldn't have wanted anything that wore a monkey white coat and toted a whisk broom in his pocket. Cash's clothes looked like they'd set a while under a rock; and they smelled like nigger. He thought how Cash smelled, but he smelled the train. No more gulch niggers in Eastrod. In Eastrod. Turning in the road, he saw in the dark, half dark, the store boarded and the barn open with the dark free in it, and the smaller house half carted away, the porch gone and no floor in the hall. (*CS*, 61)

What had appeared as a rather bizarre fascination with the porter has become, once we know Haze's inner thoughts, an understandable, even touching, response to homelessness.

Such passages directly reporting a character's inner thoughts are extremely rare in O'Connor's later fiction, and when they do occur, they are usually so brief and inconsequential as to confound rather than clarify. As Frederick Asals points out, in her mature fiction O'Connor almost always either filters a character's thoughts through the narrative consciousness (who generally reports them with striking imagery and metaphor) or does not present them at all.[17] In the former case, the reader must fathom a character's inner life from the charged, and not unbiased, perspective of the narrative consciousness, and in the latter, from the character's actions (which, as is often the case in O'Connor's fiction, are bizarre if not inexplicable). Thus, in the first chapter of *Wise Blood*, Haze's interest in the porter is intensified into an obsession that is never adequately explained. Rather than engaging the porter, Haze accosts him, accusing him of being from Eastrod despite his numerous denials. What in the short story was a clear connection between the porter's and Haze's own displacement becomes in the novel a disturbing mystery. At one point, after Haze has confronted the porter with his suspicions of his background, Haze's thoughts (as reported by the narrative consciousness) drift to Eastrod: "Eastrod filled his head and then went out beyond and filled the space that stretched from the train across the empty darkening fields. He saw the two houses and the rust-colored road, the few Negro shacks and the one barn and the stall with the red and white CCG snuff ad peeling across the side of it" (*WB*, 12–13). The connections between the porter's and Haze's past go no further than this and in no way explain Haze's mean-spirited verbal attacks on the man.

The narrative consciousness's treatment of Haze and the porter in *Wise Blood* is typical of O'Connor's mature fiction. The narrator describes a character's intense actions from without and/or reveals only bits of his or her mind, so as to deepen rather than dispel the mystery of the action. In both techniques, the narrative consciousness distances us from the character, making us step back, detached and

17. Asals, *Flannery O'Connor*, 19–20.

wary. Such distancing also results from the narrator's other primary technique of exposing—or shrouding—a character's consciousness: reporting the character's thoughts or actions not directly but filtered through the narrative consciousness, thereby shaping them with its judgments and language. These assessments, frequently marked by charged metaphors, generally embody severe and cutting evaluations of the character.

The opening lines of "Good Country People," which characterize a country woman named Mrs. Freeman, are representative of this technique:

Besides the neutral expression that she wore when she was alone, Mrs. Freeman had two others, forward and reverse, that she used for all her human dealings. Her forward expression was steady and driving like the advance of a heavy truck. Her eyes never swerved to left or right but turned as the story turned as if they followed a yellow line down the center of it. She seldom used the other expression because it was not often necessary for her to retract a statement, but when she did, her face came to a complete stop, there was an almost imperceptible movement of her black eyes, during which they seemed to be receding, and then the observer would see that Mrs. Freeman, though she might stand there as real as several grain sacks thrown on top of each other, was no longer there in spirit. (CS, 271)

The narrative consciousness here characterizes Mrs. Freeman's conscious life by her outward expressions, and these the narrative consciousness reduces to three and describes with the metaphor of an automobile transmission—neutral, forward, and reverse. By using the transmission metaphor to suggest Mrs. Freeman's intense willfulness and overriding drive to dominate conversations and discussions (her forward expression is "steady and driving like the advance of a heavy truck"), the narrative consciousness both characterizes and disparages, reducing the complexity of Mrs. Freeman's consciousness and distancing the reader from her. The comic extremes of the metaphor instantly establish the reader's detached and privileged position above her.

In this comic distancing and disparagement, the narrative consciousness works with the tools of the satirist, much as the narrative consciousness of "The Barber" did. But an important shift has occurred. Whereas in her early work O'Connor merged with the narrative consciousness and established this privileged position to be that representing generally accepted values, in her mature fiction she distances herself from the narrative consciousness and assumes an authorial position above and beyond the storyteller, whose values are now neither conventional nor sacrosanct. Not to recognize these profound repositionings is to miss the complexity of O'Connor's fiction and, in all likelihood, to read her works merely as harsh satires on rural southern folk, who often seem pretentious in their apparent ignorance (like Mrs. Freeman), and on modern intellectuals, who likewise seem pretentious in their knowledge (like Rayber). Although in the hands of the narrative consciousness such satire is frequently at work, it is at the same time being criticized and pressured from both the story itself and the author, who observes the narrator imposing satirical judgments.

Central to the development of O'Connor's mature fiction is the profound transformation of the value system of the narrative consciousness. From the conventional values embodied in the narrators of her early work, the perspective of the narrative consciousness emerges in her mature fiction as one akin to the Yahwist vision of the southern fundamentalist. The foundation of this vision, as was discussed in some depth in the previous chapter, is the absolute gulf separating humanity from the all-powerful God Yahweh. To embrace this vision means to be constantly aware of an all-demanding God and to be always under his scrutiny. Armed with this knowledge—this haunting awareness of God's omnipotence and humanity's insignificance—one views the world of human endeavor with detachment and irony. Human pretensions are not merely undercut but utterly destroyed; they are shown to be worthless and insignificant if not terribly evil. Ruby Turpin's vision at the end of "Revelation," revealing to her the presumptuousness of her worldly virtues by the stern standards of God's judgment, embodies just such a Yahwist perspective, and this perspective is essentially that of O'Connor's narrative consciousness throughout her mature fiction. Although the severity of tone and the emphasis differ from story to story, nonetheless the narrative consciousness's basic fundamentalist vision remains almost entirely consistent.

O'Connor's use of a narrative consciousness whose perspective is drastically fundamentalist is one reason why her fiction is both so extreme and so difficult to come to terms with. There is among educated modern readers a great resistance to seeing any validity in a fundamentalist vision, and this resistance includes denying the possibility that O'Connor might be telling her stories from such a perspective. Despite the stark imagery and fierce commentary in the stories, many readers assume that the perspective from which they are told is essentially their own—sophisticated and learned—and focus their attention almost entirely on enjoying, from their elevated position, the wildly comic characters and plots. O'Connor herself may be partly to blame for this overlooking of the narrative consciousness's fundamentalism, because the language of the narrator is distinctly elevated and controlled; it is more the language of a sophisticated intellectual than that of a southern fundamentalist, whose speech has traditionally been closely allied with the vernacular. Mainly through the advice of her friend and fellow writer Caroline Gordon, O'Connor was convinced that for her stories to work she had to maintain an elevated tone, and that entailed having the narrator speak only standard English. Gordon was a convert to Catholicism who was much less sympathetic than O'Connor to the backwoods southern religion (in her novel *The Strange Children,* for instance, Gordon uses the intense faith of a fundamentalist family to underscore the lack of faith of modern intellectuals, but in the end, when the Catholic hero emerges, she cursorily dismisses the family's faith in a way O'Connor never would).[18] She persuaded O'Connor that having the narrative consciousness speak in the vernacular drastically lowered a story's tone. To Ben Griffith, O'Connor wrote (March 3, 1954) that "the omniscient narrator is not properly supposed to use colloquial expressions. I send a good many of my things to Caroline Gordon (Tate) for her criticism and she is always writing me that I mustn't say such things, that the om. nar. never speaks like anyone but Dr. Johnson." O'Connor also spoke on this topic in a letter (August 21, 1955) to A., saying that "in any fiction where the omniscient narrator uses the same language as the characters, there is a loss of tension and a lowering of tone" (*HB*, 69, 95). In both letters she stressed how difficult it was for her to keep the language elevated and free from local idiom.

Not merged with the narrative consciousness but standing apart from it is O'Connor, author and Catholic. Although her Catholicism

18. Caroline Gordon, *The Strange Children* (1951; rpr. New York, 1971).

remains the organizing center of her imaginative vision and her fiction—its dogma the framework underpinning all her endeavors—her fundamentalist sympathies become, in the narrative consciousness, the voice of her stories. In looking at O'Connor's extreme narrative strategy, it is helpful to recall her own observations in "The Catholic Novelist in the Protestant South," cited in the previous chapter, on the deep religious affinities she felt with southern fundamentalists. She writes that the southern Catholic writer's "interest and sympathy may well go—as I know my own does—directly to those aspects of Southern life where the religious feeling is most intense and where its outward forms are farthest from the Catholic, and most revealing of a need that only the Church can fill." She adds that the Catholic writer feels this intense interest not because of a desire to correct the fundamentalist theologically but because "descending within himself to find his region, he discovers that it is with these aspects of Southern life that he has a feeling of kinship strong enough to spur him to write" (*MM*, 207).

In creating a narrative consciousness embodying the fundamentalist perspective with which she felt so keenly in touch, O'Connor sets up a complex interaction between her Catholic faith and her fundamentalist sympathies. To begin with, O'Connor objectifies with the narrative consciousness that part of her own consciousness given to fundamentalist thinking, making it possible for her to detach herself from it and to view it as an outsider would. She achieves what Bakhtin says Dostoevski accomplishes—the objectification of the "realm of the author's creative subjectivity which autocratically colors the represented world in a monologic novel, thereby making what was once a form of perception into the object of perception."[19] By refracting her Catholic vision through this fundamentalist perspective, O'Connor also gains a perspective on her Catholicism and establishes a dynamic interplay between both visions that keeps either from exerting a monologic control over the story or, indeed, over O'Connor herself. Such interplay in part explains the stark power, reverberating in any number of tensions, of O'Connor's fiction.

The insights of Bakhtin help us to understand further the interplay between O'Connor's Catholicism and fundamentalism in her fiction.

19. Bakhtin, *Problems of Dostoevsky's Poetics*, 278.

According to Bakhtin, we are always in the process of assimilating the discourses of others into our own consciousnesses, a process of struggle and displacement that shapes our interior growth. Bakhtin defines two types of discourse—authoritative and internally persuasive—according to how we evaluate the authority of the discourse. Authoritative discourse, as its name suggests, demands allegiance and submission. Bakhtin writes in "Discourse in the Novel":

> The authoritative word demands that we acknowledge it, that we make it our own; it binds us, quite independent of any power it might have to persuade us internally; we encounter it with its authority already fused to it. The authoritative word is located in a distanced zone, organically connected with a past that is felt to be hierarchically higher. It is, so to speak, the word of the fathers. Its authority was already *acknowledged* in the past. It is *prior* discourse. It is therefore not a question of choosing it from among other possible discourses that are its equal. It is given (it sounds) in lofty spheres, not those of familiar contact. Its language is a special (as it were, hieratic) language. It can be profaned. It is akin to taboo, i.e., a name that must not be taken in vain.

Internally persuasive discourse, in contrast, as its name suggests, is significant not because of its authority (in fact, it is denied all privilege) but because of its appeal—it strikes our consciousnesses as being something that matters and that should be taken account of. Rather than submitting to its word, as we do with authoritative discourse, in effect closing ourselves off from growth initiated from within, we experiment with internally persuasive discourse, testing its truth and its limits by bringing it to bear alongside other views and perspectives. Bakhtin describes this as a process of creativity and growth whereby in our applying internally persuasive discourse to new material and conditions, "it enters into interanimating relationships with new contexts" and, even more significantly, "into an intense interaction, a *struggle* with other internally persuasive discourses." Bakhtin continues, "Our ideological development is just such an intense struggle within us for hegemony among various available verbal and ideological points of view, approaches, activities and values. The semantic structure of an internally persuasive discourse is *not finite*, it is *open*; in each of the new contexts that dialogize it, this discourse is able to reveal ever newer *ways to mean*."[20]

20. Bakhtin, "Discourse in the Novel," in *The Dialogic Imagination*, 342, 345–46.

According to Bakhtin, the writer creates art from the struggles with internally persuasive discourse. Artistic creation thus becomes, on one level, a process of resistance and liberation: The writer, in attempting to explore the possibilities and limits of an internally persuasive discourse, resists its growing influence by objectifying it in situations and characters in art. This objectification liberates the author from the discourse so that dialogic interplay can take place. Bakhtin characterizes this interplay as a conversation—but one of a special order—that brings the internally persuasive discourse under intense pressure: "It is questioned, it is put in a new situation in order to expose its weak sides, to get a feel for its boundaries, to experience it physically as an object." Authoritative discourse, in contrast, has no place in the dynamic of artistic creation, because its authority, by the very nature of the discourse, is unchallenged and stifles all other discourse. For this reason authoritative discourse in fiction is generally flat and lifeless, free from dialogic tension and interplay, doomed by what Bakhtin says is "its inertia, its semantic finiteness and calcification, the degree to which it is hard-edged, a thing in its own right, the impermissibility of any free stylistic development in relation to it."[21]

O'Connor's fiction represents an intriguing variation from Bakhtin's model, for her work embodies less a struggle between various internally persuasive discourses (though that is indeed at work) than a struggle between an internally persuasive discourse (her fundamentalism) and her authoritative discourse (her Catholicism). In this way O'Connor's authoritative center does indeed enter into the dynamic of artistic creation without utterly destroying the possibilities of dialogic interplay. So strong is O'Connor's fundamentalist voice that it is not merely dismissed in the face of her Catholicism but instead powerfully challenges her regnant Catholic vision. Itself rooted in a fierce monologism, as its name suggests, O'Connor's fundamentalism does not limit her perspectives, as one might think, but actually opens them up, since through its fierce power it forces O'Connor's Catholicism to respond to its discourse. In this dialogic interaction both discourses are thus pressured, and although her Catholicism remains the ruling force, O'Connor's fundamentalism challenges its

authority, forcing it to take account of this distinctly different discourse. O'Connor's use of a fundamentalist narrative consciousness
thus embodies her struggles with her Catholicism as much as with her
fundamentalism, and indeed on one level her stories can be seen as her
efforts, through dialogic interplay, to test her authoritative voice in
such a way as to make it internally persuasive.

O'Connor sought to pressure her Catholicism because such a struggle lay at the heart of both artistic creation and religious belief. In one
of her interviews, O'Connor attacked the idea of the artist as a lofty
creator who possessed an "untouchable sensibility that ought to be
left to its pleasure." For her, the artist's sensibility matured and
deepened only when it was challenged by situations and perspectives
outside its own. In an interview with C. Ross Mullins, Jr., she said
that the sensibility must wrestle with these challenges and that "it
ought to be a good bone-crunching battle." She continued, "The
sensibility will come out of it marked forever but a winner. What ails
a lot of people is that the writer's so-called sensibility has had nothing
to struggle with, no opposition. Conversely, in the case of some
novels by Catholics, the writer's belief has had nothing to struggle
with. Just as bad a situation" (*CFO*, 105). Likewise, O'Connor believed that religious faith of any depth was founded on doubt and
struggle. "What people don't realize is how much religion costs," she
wrote (undated, 1959) to Louise Abbot. "They think faith is a big
electric blanket, when of course it is the cross." In this same letter she
said that she herself suffered the torments of religious doubt but she
saw it "as the process by which faith is deepened." She added that "a
faith that just accepts is a child's faith and all right for children" but
that a mature faith demanded much more (*HB*, 353–54).

Whereas O'Connor's Catholicism comes under intense pressure in
her fiction, her fundamentalism, seen most forcefully in the narrative
consciousness, is subjected to an even greater challenge. As I suggested earlier, O'Connor's Catholicism remains dominant in the
interaction between her Catholic and fundamentalist discourses;
its values are pressured but not dismantled. In contrast, although
O'Connor's fundamentalism significantly challenges her valorized
Catholicism, it is ultimately pressured to reveal its shortcomings and
limits. In this invoking and then eventual undercutting of her funda-

mentalist voice, O'Connor both acknowledges its profound power and liberates herself from its control.

The fundamentalism of O'Connor's narrative consciousness comes under challenge from both O'Connor's Catholicism and the story itself that the narrator tells. In observing the narrative consciousness tell its story, O'Connor sees that the detached and ironic voice is reductionist as it pigeonholes the immensity and complexity of human experience into a simple ideology that categorizes everything, in stark terms, as being for or against Jesus. Such a perspective makes for wildly comic and satiric fiction that often focuses on bare-bones and dramatic religious dilemmas, yet this harsh and demanding view embodies a turning away from the richness of life and the glories of the here and now. This perspective represents an act of closure rather than growth. Despite O'Connor's keen attraction to this Yahwist vision of the fundamentalists, she ultimately realized, primarily through her Catholicism and her sympathetic understanding of the human situation, that this utterly stark perspective is limiting and not finally acceptable.

O'Connor discussed the dynamics of her fiction in a revealing letter (June 19, 1957) to Cecil Dawkins. In it she said that the standard of judgment in her stories was not based on some pat moral such as "Do unto others"—"That can be found in any ethical culture series," she wrote—but rather on Christ and the Incarnation. "It is the fact of the Word made flesh," she continued. "As the Misfit said, 'He thrown everything off balance and it's nothing for you to do but follow Him or find some meanness.' That is the fulcrum that lifts my particular stories. I'm a Catholic but this is orthodox Protestantism also, though out of context—which makes it grow into grotesque forms. The Catholic, using his own eyes and the eyes of the Church (when he is inclined to open them) is in a most favorable position to recognize the grotesque" (*HB*, 227). As she said here, a Yahwist vision is the fulcrum of her stories, and this vision, without a Catholic perspective, is out of context and thus leads to grotesque characters and situations. Such is the vision of O'Connor's narrator, and it is O'Connor's Catholic vision—as the author behind the work—that provides the perspective that recognizes and judges the grotesqueness of the narrator and the narrator's story. And yet, as I have been suggesting, the interaction is dialogic; the grotesquerie of fundamentalist Protestant-ism pressures O'Connor's Catholicism, bringing it under intense scrutiny and forcing O'Connor to evaluate her vision according to discoveries ushered in by this alien vision. It is this pressuring that O'Connor referred to in her essay "Some Aspects of the Grotesque in Southern Fiction," where she said that the primary quality of gro-tesque characters is not their comic aspect, because they "carry an invisible burden; their fanaticism is a reproach, not merely an eccen-tricity." Elsewhere she wrote that when a writer of any depth por-trays a grotesque fanatic, the writer "is not simply showing us what we are, but what we have been and what we could become. His prophet-freak is an image of himself" (*MM*, 44, 118).

Besides the challenge from O'Connor's Catholicism, the action of the stories also challenges the narrator's fundamentalist perspective, implicitly if not explicitly. Marshall Bruce Gentry, who in his intrigu-ing study *Flannery O'Connor's Religion of the Grotesque* explores the conflict between O'Connor's narrators and the stories they tell, argues that what happens in the stories explicitly challenges the nar-rator's authority. Gentry sees the characters in O'Connor's fiction as participants in an ongoing struggle against authoritarian narrators— the voices of whom embody what Gentry calls a "debased form of religiosity"—to achieve their own salvation.[22] This struggle for sal-vation involves a process whereby characters transform the negative grotesque of the narrator into the positive grotesque of their own doing (drawing from Bakhtin, Gentry sees the positive grotesque as a force that degrades authority and liberates the self). Characters who make this transformation stand free from the narrator and forge for themselves a meaningful and redemptive wholeness. Salvation, in other words, results not from an act of grace but from the working out of powerful psychological forces within us all, primarily those of the unconscious. These internal forces of regeneration and redemption stand opposed to the narrator's disarming and reductive religious vision, and the conflict between these two systems, says Gentry, is the central paradigm of O'Connor's fiction.

Gentry's emphasis on the resistance to narrative authority is re-freshing and insightful, but in the end his analysis undercuts too

22. Marshall Bruce Gentry, *Flannery O'Connor's Religion of the Grotesque* (Jackson, Miss., 1986).

severely the significance and place in O'Connor's work of her Catholicism. He replaces her profound vision of Christ's presence in the world and in our lives with what comes close to psychological determinism. One is reminded here of O'Connor's discussion in "Some Aspects of the Grotesque in Southern Fiction" of mystery in literature. She writes that the writer who "believes that our life is and will remain essentially mysterious" (as O'Connor certainly does, and as opposed to the writer who "believes that actions are predetermined by psychic make-up or the economic situation or some other determinable factor") creates fiction that "will always be pushing its own limits outward toward the limits of mystery, because for this kind of writer, the meaning of a story does not begin except at a depth where adequate motivation and adequate psychology and the various determinations have been exhausted" (*MM*, 41–42). Rather than seeing, as Gentry does, the resistance to the narrator as being located in forces of psychological redemption, I believe that this resistance is less explicit and occurs implicitly in one of the central thematic structures of the story. This structure—which suggests that there is potentially great danger inherent in assuming a superior and judgmental stance toward others—when implicitly applied to the narrative consciousness's position, exposes its shortcomings and undercuts its authority.

A central action in a number of O'Connor's works is the shattering of the pretensions of a character who, because of feelings of superiority, is bent on teaching, often cruelly, some other character (or characters) a lesson about life. These lesson givers are frequently intellectuals who see themselves as clear-minded and self-sufficient possessors of truth. In their relationships with the not-so-intelligent others, these characters assume a detached and ironic stance, one that distances them from any perspective that might undercut their own and that blinds them to the feelings and the worth of their intended victims. Ultimately, however, those out to teach a lesson are the ones so taught. It is their pretensions, rooted in a willful arrogance toward, and a destructive detachment from, others, that are shown up. They, rather than their intended victims, are enlightened by searing truth.

On one level O'Connor's stories that follow this pattern work as I have described them—as stories revealing the pretensions of the pretentious. But on a deeper and more profound level the action of these stories fundamentally challenges and undermines the exalted stance of the narrator. As becomes evident, those characters who seek to expose the pretensions of others and to impose their beliefs upon them assume superior stances (characterized by cruel and unforgiving irony) similar to those taken by O'Connor's narrators. Although the visions of these characters and narrators are generally at opposite extremes (liberal intellectualism versus strict fundamentalism), both outlooks share a willful arrogance and detachment that are crucial for each's valorization. In sharing this similar orientation toward others, O'Connor's lesson givers and her narrators, despite their radical differences in belief, become disturbing doubles of each other. Thus, the fate of O'Connor's pretentious characters implicitly speaks to that of the narrators. When the characters in the stories are finally taken to task (as they always are, as much for the destructive stance they assume as for what they believe), the narrator's sanctified position is also being severely challenged. Ultimately this pressure forces the narrator's authoritative position to deconstruct, and his or her exalted stance—though not necessarily beliefs—is revealed to be as limited and potentially destructive as that of the character (or characters) whom the narrator set out to expose. In the next two chapters we shall explore the dimensions of this narrative dynamic in several of O'Connor's stories, as well as her two novels.

3

Narrator and Narrative: The Stories

This chapter looks at four of O'Connor's stories—"Everything That Rises Must Converge," "The Artificial Nigger," "The Enduring Chill," and "The Lame Shall Enter First"—in order to explore the crucial role that the narrator plays in the dynamic of O'Connor's fiction. As I have suggested in the previous chapter, the narrator is a central figure in O'Connor's stories, and the narrator's relationship with both O'Connor and the story itself is fraught with tension. "Everything That Rises Must Converge" embodies what I see as O'Connor's characteristic dynamic involving the narrator, with the narrator's fundamentalism pressuring, and being pressured by, O'Connor and the story. Ultimately the narrator's severe perspective comes undone; ironically, it is dealt a severe blow by the story itself, a story that was told to validate rather than to deny the narrator's perspective. "The Artificial Nigger," "The Enduring Chill," and "The Lame Shall Enter First" represent variations of this dynamic; in all three of these stories the tension between O'Connor and the narrator is less severe as the two figures come close to sharing perspectives. In "The Artificial Nigger" O'Connor softens the fundamentalism of the narrator, making this narrator less detached from the action and less the evangelist serving an all-demanding God. This shift in perspective reduces the distance between O'Connor and the narrator, making for a fiction less burdened by the crushing tensions of her other work and more affirmative of the human experience. Here her Catholicism is not severely challenged and thus is more decidedly in control. In "The Enduring Chill" O'Connor's Catholicism is more intensely pressured by her fundamentalism, with O'Connor's striving to merge the two visions in the single voice of the narrator. The result is an uneasy balance that embodies the strains involved in any attempt to integrate these two conflicting perspectives. There is little of such integration in "The Lame Shall Enter First." Here the severe fundamentalism of the narrator is so powerful and authoritative that O'Connor herself apparently gives into it. With author and narrator both driven by a fundamentalist rage, "The Lame Shall Enter First" is one of O'Connor's fiercest stories, particularly in its attacks on modern life and liberal intellectualism.

In looking at these four works, I will focus primarily on the stories that the narrators tell, and my approach will be essentially thematic. Although recognizing the limits of such an approach, I also believe that the themes that the narrators develop in the stories ultimately are reversed to critique and undermine their authoritative positions. The fundamentalist narrators, in other words, tell stories meant to assert their visions, but within those stories are the very challenges that undercut their authority and perspectives.

The narrator of "Everything That Rises Must Converge" might be called O'Connor's characteristic narrator—a detached and harshly judgmental storyteller guided by a stern fundamentalist vision. Generally this narrator presents character and situation with an intense irony, frequently heightening and intensifying descriptions and characterizations for both comic and shock effect to drive home a certain religious perspective. The narrator is particularly given to telling stories exposing the pretensions of intellectual and spiritual pride in the face of God's power. It is just such a story that the ironic narrator tells in "Everything That Rises Must Converge."

At the center of the story is a young intellectual named Julian, who because of his conception of his own superiority is determined to teach his mother a lesson about the silliness of her ways. Despite the fact that his mother had scrimped and saved for years to give him every advantage she could, including getting him braces ("her teeth had gone unfilled so that his could be straightened") and sending him to college, Julian has nothing but contempt for her. He believes that he sees his mother with "absolute clarity," and from his perspective her generosity is merely the bumblings of a silly lady who lives in a fantasy world. The guiding tenet of what Julian interprets as her imaginary world "was to sacrifice herself for him after she had first created the necessity to do so by making a mess of things. If he had permitted her sacrifices, it was only because her lack of foresight had made it necessary." Julian finds it amazing that, having been raised by such an incompetent and unperceptive mother, he has turned out so learned and insightful. "In spite of going to only a third rate college, he had on his own initiative, come out with a first-rate education," the narrator reports him thinking; "in spite of growing up dominated by a small mind, he had ended up with a large one; in spite of all her foolish views, he was free of prejudice and unafraid to face facts. Most miraculous of all, instead of being blinded by love for her as she was for him, he had cut himself emotionally free of her and could see her with complete objectivity" (CS, 411, 412).

For Julian this perspective of clarity and objectivity results from his ability to withdraw from the world and to view life from a detached and authoritative perspective. He strives to cut himself off from other people and all their problems and predicaments; such involvement, he believes, would only undercut his impartiality and therefore distort his rational vision. The narrator observes that Julian spends most of his time withdrawn into the world of the rational self—"the inner compartment of his mind." The narrator reports, "This was a kind of mental bubble in which he established himself when he could not bear to be a part of what was going on around him. From it he could see out and judge but in it he was safe from any kind of penetration from without" (CS, 411). Such are the foundations of the monologic consciousness: a solid faith in the superiority of one's own perspective, a total reliance on one's isolated consciousness in discovering truth and passing judgments, and an utter disregard for the perspectives of others.

From this monologic position, Julian critiques what he sees as the emotionalism and racial prejudice of his mother, the latter of which he finds a prime embodiment of her unenlightened views. Rather than recognizing the generosity behind her devotion to him and understanding the roots of her admittedly backward racial views (they express Old South noblesse oblige, and apparently Julian's mother has endorsed them unthinkingly from her socialization; although her views may be ultimately malicious to the blacks who must confront them, Julian's mother does not knowingly act maliciously), Julian dissects his mother's foibles with the cold eye of a clinician. "He studied her coldly," the narrator at one point reports. "Her feet in little pumps dangled like a child's and did not quite reach the floor. She was training on him an exaggerated look of reproach. He felt completely detached from her. At that moment he could with pleasure have slapped her as he would have slapped a particularly obnoxious child in his charge." At another point, after imagining the stunned horror his mother would feel—and express—were he to bring home a black woman as his fiancée, he looks across in his rage to his mother: "His eyes were narrowed and through the indignation he had generated, he saw his mother across the aisle, purple-faced, shrunken to the dwarf-like proportions of her moral nature, sitting like a mummy beneath the ridiculous banner of her hat" (CS, 414–15). In both examples, Julian's gaze is cruelly reductive, distorting his mother into a thoroughly grotesque figure (something it is made clear throughout the story that she is not) devoid of humanity.

So obsessed is Julian with his mother's weaknesses that he constantly looks for the means to teach her a lesson, and a cruel one at that, about her silliness and ignorance. Establishing a relationship with a black woman is one such musing, and there are others—making friends with black professionals, joining civil rights demonstrations, bringing home a black doctor when his mother is ill. On a bus ride with his mother, Julian makes a conscious effort to annoy her by sitting next to a black man. He is joyous when he notices that a black woman on the bus is wearing the same hat as his mother—now, he thinks gleefully, his mother's pettiness and prejudice can be revealed to her. Julian's motives in all this have little to do with what is best for his mother; his actions, as the narrator reports, instead grow from "an evil urge to break her spirit." At one point Julian momentarily senses his cruelty and his mother's essential innocence when, after drawing his mother's attention to the black woman's hat with a taunting chuckle, he notices her eyes have turned a "bruised purple." But such realization is fleeting, for Julian cares less for his mother than he does for the intellectual construct he uses to define his actions as just and meet. So, in the midst of what he sees as a moment of weakness, "principle rescued him. Justice entitled him to laugh. His grin hardened until it said to her as plainly as if he were saying aloud: Your punishment exactly fits your pettiness. This should teach you a permanent lesson" (CS, 409, 416).

Julian's efforts to shatter his mother's spirit intensify after she is knocked down by the black woman. Despite the fact that his mother is clearly in a state of shock and in desperate need of help, Julian sees "no reason to let the lesson she had had go without backing it up with an explanation of its meaning," and he presses home his attack on her. He tells her that the black woman is her "black double" and is the embodiment of the entire black race, which will no longer tolerate her condescension. He tells her further that the black woman's actions embody the collapse of his mother's world. "The old manners are obsolete and your graciousness is not worth a damn," he says, adding shortly thereafter, "From now on you've got to live in a new world and face a few realities for a change." He taunts her, saying, "You aren't who you think you are," and he challenges her to "buck up" and enter the new world that he has announced. "It won't kill you," he tells her (CS, 419–20).

Shortly thereafter Julian's mother collapses to the pavement and (apparently) dies; as much the victim of her son's berating as of the black woman's beating. Julian is stunned by her death, blasted into a new realm of self-awareness. As now becomes clear, it is Julian more than his mother who has been taught a "permanent lesson"; his cruel taunts of her have been turned back upon himself as ironic accusations of his own ignorance and cruelty. "You aren't who you think you are" is precisely what Julian discovers about himself, and his challenge to his mother to prepare herself for entry into a new world is what Julian now faces. With his mother's death, Julian witnesses the collapse of his world of intellectual pride and domination. This leaves him lost and helpless, poised (as the story concludes) at the entrance into "the world of guilt and sorrow" (CS, 420).

Much of the force of "Everything That Rises Must Converge" derives from this stunning turnaround that makes startlingly clear the ironies involved in Julian's treatment of his mother and the lesson he—rather than she—learns. The narrative consciousness has destroyed the pretensions of Julian, utterly chastening him, and on one level the story validates the narrator's authoritative position and power. And yet on a deeper and more profound level, the story delivers a stinging critique of the narrator's position by revealing the similarities between Julian and the narrator. Although they do not share similar beliefs, Julian and the narrator share a monologism that binds them closely together: Both are cynical authority figures who stand in harsh judgment of those about them, and both seek to impose their views on those blind souls who do not see what they do. In their efforts to show people up, both Julian and the narrator distort and demean; they manipulate to teach a lesson, simplifying the complexity of human experience to validate their own—but no one else's— integrity. A central irony of the story lies in this mirroring of Julian and the narrator, for because of their close identification, Julian's downfall implicitly signals the narrator's, even if the narrator remains unaware of it. This dismantling shows that the narrator's authoritative position is as extreme and potentially destructive as Julian's (if for better ends); the narrator's position is indeed integrally bound up in Julian's in that its fundamentalist power in large part depends upon the presence of modern intellectuals like Julian to fuel its ire. The final irony of "Everything That Rises Must Converge" thus becomes the destruction of the narrator's position even as the narrator destroys another's.

By manipulating her own fundamentalist sympathies in the narrator, O'Connor, as author, achieves several things. To begin with, she liberates herself from these strong religious feelings, objectifying them outside herself so that she can view them as another would. From her primarily Catholic authorial perspective, she can see the freakishness of the narrator's voice, a freakishness due in large part to its fierce monologism that lacks an openness to, and essential charity for, others. [1] But she can also see the power and compelling force of the fundamentalist voice, attributes that derive from its searing faith. If O'Connor critiques the fundamentalist voice for its lack of charity, the fundamentalist voice in its rigorous commitment to Christ pressures O'Connor's Catholicism. "Smugness is the Great Catholic Sin," she wrote (January 17, 1956) to A., adding, "I find it in myself and don't dislike it any less" (HB, 131). It is this smugness to which O'Connor's fundamentalism speaks, with its demands for a vigorous and all-consuming religious commitment. In the end, this stern religious voice humbles, but does not undo, the authority of O'Connor's Catholic position. In "Everything That Rises Must Converge"

1. For a discussion of the conflict between O'Connor's Catholicism and fundamentalism, see Rubin, "Flannery O'Connor and the Bible Belt," in Friedman and Lawson (eds.), *The Added Dimension*, 49–72.

(and a number of other O'Connor stories) O'Connor uses the fundamentalist narrator to critique severely that fundamentalist part of herself, and at the same time she uses her fundamentalism to critique her Catholic self. Such a dynamic is taut and tension filled, and its presence in large part explains the great power of much of O'Connor's fiction.

Many but not all of O'Connor's works employ this fierce and dynamic interplay between Catholic author and fundamentalist narrator. O'Connor almost always employs some type of tension between narrator and author, but she sometimes adjusts the outlooks and intensity of belief of one or the other and in so doing creates a fiction different in tone and thrust from what I have described as her characteristic fiction. Such an adjustment occurs in "The Artificial Nigger," where O'Connor softens the voice of the narrator, making it less the raging fundamentalist and more the sympathetic Catholic. In so altering the narrator's perspective, O'Connor reduces the distance between herself and the narrator, creating a calmer, less raging art.

In terms of basic plot structure "The Artificial Nigger" closely resembles "Everything That Rises Must Converge." At the center of the story are two characters, Mr. Head and his grandson Nelson, who are locked in a conflict of wills, with Mr. Head determined to assert his superiority over the boy. Mr. Head conceives himself to be eminently wise, and like Julian with his mother, he wants to teach Nelson a lesson that will reveal to him his ignorance and immaturity. He plans to take Nelson to the city (they live deep in the backwoods) to show him there is nothing special about city life and certainly no cause for feeling any pride in being born there, as Nelson was. He perceives the trip as a "moral mission," one that will chasten Nelson so that he "would at last find out that he was not as smart as he thought he was." The narrative consciousness reports of Mr. Head's plans, "It was to be a lesson that the boy would never forget. He was to find out from it that he had no cause for pride merely because he had been born in a city. He was to find out that the city is not a great place. Mr. Head meant him to see everything there is to see in a city so that he would be content to stay at home for the rest of his life" (*CS*, 251). Ultimately, of course, the tables turn on Mr. Head, and it is he, more than his grandson, who gains a powerful insight into his own ignorance and sinfulness.

Despite sharing this similar plot structure with "Everything That Rises Must Converge," "The Artificial Nigger" differs significantly from this other story, primarily because of the stance of the narrator. While maintaining a distanced and superior perspective, the narrator here is far less cruel and harsh in his or her perspective on the limitations of Mr. Head and Nelson. The narrator pokes fun at the man and the boy, particularly early on, but not with the punishing severity of fundamentalist rage; the narrator uses comic exaggeration to reveal their foibles and to undercut their pretensions but not to berate and demean the two. There is not much cruelty but a good deal of humor, for instance, in the narrator's report that in the moonlight Mr. Head's eyes "had a look of composure and of ancient wisdom as if they belonged to one of the great guides of men. He might have been Vergil summoned in the middle of the night to go to Dante, or better, Raphael awakened by a blast of God's light to fly to the side of Tobias." This is far different from the more characteristic descriptions offered by O'Connor's narrative consciousness, typified by what one critic has called "the imagery of repulsion" that underscores the ugliness and grotesqueness of physical (as opposed to spiritual) existence.[2] The depiction here, while exaggerating for comic effect the pretensions of Mr. Head, nonetheless at the same time establishes the suggestion that he is on one level actually acting out a dignified role such as that of Vergil or Raphael. He is laughed at and yet dignified all at once. Compare this description and its effect to the first description of Mrs. May in "Greenleaf"; this is another character like Mr. Head, and here she is standing in a room late at night: "Green rubber curlers sprouted neatly over her forehead and her face beneath them was as smooth as concrete with egg-white paste that drew wrinkles out while she slept" (CS, 249–50, 311).

Because of the narrator's less severe perspective, "The Artificial Nigger" is not as searing as much of O'Connor's other work; its characters and situations, as well as the polarities underlying the action, are less extreme and charged. The rivalry between Mr. Head and Nelson, for instance, is far less intense than that between Julian and his mother in "Everything That Rises Must Converge." This is in part due to the less intimate relationship (grandfather to grandson

2. Asals, Flannery O'Connor, 50.

rather than mother to son), to Nelson's youth, and to the fact that the primary focus rests on Mr. Head (the figure of authority) and not Nelson (the figure of rebellion); but even more significant is the simple fact that the two rivals genuinely care for and respect each other, and neither is determined to do the other serious harm. Although Nelson chafes under his grandfather's tutelage, he nonetheless takes pride in the way the old man handles himself, and as he realizes early on in their trip, his grandfather is "his only support in the strange place they were approaching. He would be entirely alone in the world if he were ever lost from his grandfather" (CS, 257). For his part, Mr. Head wants to reform Nelson, but not utterly to break his spirit; even when he hides from the sleeping boy in order to scare him into realizing his dependence upon the grandfather, Mr. Head's motives are not anywhere as meanspirited as is Julian's berating of his fallen mother. Mr. Head's later betrayal of Nelson, when Mr. Head denies his relation to the boy after Nelson has knocked the pedestrian down, is done not in belligerence but in weakness.

This betrayal of Nelson shatters whatever pretensions Mr. Head still holds about being the boy's infallible guide and moral superior. Mr. Head's ennobled position has already been made precarious before his denial of the boy, since the day in the city has gone all wrong; most of the time the two have wandered about aimlessly, lost and hungry and at the mercy of the city folk—even the blacks—for direction and guidance. The denial, then, is the final crushing blow to Mr. Head's authority, and it drives home to him the blindness and vanity that lie at the heart of his self-conception. It is he—and not Nelson— who is fulfilling his own prophecy for the boy that "the day is going to come . . . when you'll find you ain't as smart as you think you are." Mr. Head is thoroughly stunned, not only by his loss of authority but even more significantly by the realization that he was capable of betraying the person he loved most deeply when this person was direly in need. Almost immediately, the narrator reports, "Mr. Head began to feel the depth of his denial. His face as they walked on became all hollow and bare ridges" (CS, 250–51, 266).

Mr. Head's betrayal drives the man and boy apart, destroying the ties of kinship and affection that had bound them together. Their rivalry before the denial, though sometimes heated, had ultimately rested on respect and familial love. It had frequently been in the nature of banter and one-upmanship between friends—Nelson's getting the breakfast ready on the day of the trip despite Mr. Head's plans otherwise, Mr. Head's underscoring on the train Nelson's ignorance of blacks. But after the denial the two are thoroughly isolated, each driven into a separate realm of consciousness that dominates their thoughts and redefines their existence. Mr. Head's world contracts into an overwhelming consciousness of guilt and sorrow; wracked by the certainty of his sin, he envisions a life of hopelessness and despair. He sees the world he is now entering as "a black strange place where nothing was like it had ever been before, a long old age without respect and an end that would be welcome because it would be the end." There he experiences the depths of hell: "He felt he knew now what time would be like without seasons and what heat would be like without light and what man would be like without salvation." Nelson, in contrast, is reduced to a consciousness of hate, his mind "frozen around his grandfather's treachery as if he were trying to preserve it intact to present at the final judgment." Nelson's eyes, "triumphantly cold," having "no light in them, no feeling, no interest," pierce Mr. Head "like pitchfork prongs." He now walks mechanically and without purpose. "He was merely there, a small figure, waiting," the narrative consciousness reports. "Home was nothing to him" (CS, 267, 268, 267, 268, 266, 268).

Were the narrator of "The Artificial Nigger" a strident fundamentalist, one might expect the story to end somewhere around here, with Mr. Head staggered by his sudden insight into his sinfulness and expecting, as he does, only "the speed of God's justice." But the God of this story is less the stern and all-demanding Yahweh than the New Testament God of mercy and forgiveness, and it is his mercy that saves Mr. Head and Nelson and reunites them. Their moment of grace comes when they view a yard statue of a black—the "artificial nigger" of the title. The statue is weather-beaten and chipped, so much so that "it was not possible to tell if the artificial Negro were meant to be young or old; he looked too miserable to be either. He was meant to look happy because his mouth was stretched up at the corners but the chipped eye and angle he was cocked at gave him a wild look of misery instead" (CS, 266, 268).

Neither Mr. Head nor Nelson has ever seen such a statue, and for them it carries a significance that stretches far beyond the everyday.

As they stand awestruck before it, the obsessions that have isolated them from each other and the world fade like the mist, and the two come together, physically almost indistinguishable and united once again as grandfather and grandson:

> The two of them stood there with their necks forward at almost the same angle and their shoulders curved in almost exactly the same way and their hands trembling identically in their pockets. Mr. Head looked like an ancient child and Nelson like a miniature old man. They stood gazing at the artificial Negro as if they were faced with some great mystery, some monument to another's victory that brought them together in their common defeat. They could both feel it dissolving their differences like an action of mercy. Mr. Head had never known before what mercy felt like because he had been too good to deserve any, but he felt he knew now. He looked at Nelson and understood that he must say something to the child to show that he was still wise and in the look the boy returned he saw a hungry need for that assurance. Nelson's eyes seemed to implore him to explain once and for all the mystery of existence. (*CS*, 268–69)

On some deep level both Mr. Head and Nelson have come to see that their fate is integrally related not only to this statue of a suffering black man but also to the suffering of all blacks, and even more generally, to that of all fallen humanity.

The scene with the black statue is the culmination of several encounters with blacks by Mr. Head and Nelson, and it represents their coming to full recognition of their own humanity and their places in God's scheme. Throughout the story Mr. Head time and again links his authority to his knowledge of, and superiority to, blacks. Early on he argues his authority over Nelson by pointing out that unlike Nelson, he knows a black when he sees one; on the train he proves his point when several blacks go down the aisle, their racial identity unnoticed by Nelson until Mr. Head points it out. Soon afterward Mr. Head mocks the rules of the diner car at the black waiter's expense, and as he walks out of the car he basks in pride at the laughter he has elicited from the diners and the admiration that he knows Nelson feels for him.

In all of this, Mr. Head seeks to establish that he is different from blacks; rather than seeing them in any way related to him, he sees them as outsiders to his experience, as others. "They rope them off," he tells Nelson when they see in the dining car a table of blacks set off from the rest of the area by a curtain, and his words here suggest what he does in his own perception of blacks—he views them and their experiences as being completely isolated in another world set apart from his own. This separateness from blacks, again, is for Mr. Head an important aspect of his authoritative stature, and it explains why he taunts Nelson when they stand lost in a black section of the city, saying that "this is where you were born—right here with all these niggers." He says a bit later, "Anybody wants to be from this nigger heaven can be from it!" (CS, 260, 261).

Nelson, for his part, likewise does his best to disassociate himself from blacks. In his complete ignorance of blacks and under the strong influence of his grandfather, Nelson sees blacks as alien figures, embodiments of forces standing opposed to himself and his ways. He easily and unjustly transfers the blame for his own frustrations onto blacks (a universal action of prejudice), so after Mr. Head has embarrassed him on the train when he has failed to recognize a black man in passing, Nelson feels "that the Negro had deliberately walked down the aisle in order to make a fool of him and he hated him with a fierce raw fresh hate; and also, he understood now why his grandfather disliked them." The fortune Nelson receives from the weighing machine at the train station—"You have a great destiny ahead of you but beware of dark women" (CS, 255–56, 259)—embodies his by now deep-seated fears of blacks and the belief of grandson and grandfather that their success is bound up with keeping blacks out of their lives.

Being lost in one of the city's black areas is of course extremely unsettling both for Mr. Head and Nelson. In wandering into the "other" side of town, they find their roles reversed: Now they, rather than the blacks, stand apart as alien others, disfranchised of power and authority. To their dismay blacks seem to be everywhere: "There were colored men in their undershirts standing in the doors and colored women rocking on the sagging porches. Colored children played in the gutters and stopped what they were doing to look at them. Before long they began to pass rows of stores with colored customers in them but they didn't pause at the entrances of these. Black eyes in black faces were watching them from every direction" (CS, 260).

Despite their growing alarm, neither Mr. Head nor Nelson, because of their stubborn pride and their determined unwillingness to acknowledge their loss of authority, will at first ask directions. Finally, however, Nelson approaches a black woman whose presence, exuding a fecund sensuality, leaves him reeling with new sensations:

He understood she was making fun of him but he was too paralyzed even to scowl. He stood drinking in every detail of her. His eyes traveled up from her great knees to her forehead and then made a triangular path from the glistening sweat on her neck down and across her tremendous bosom and over her bare arm back to where her fingers lay hidden in her hair. He suddenly wanted her to reach down and pick him up and draw him against her and then he wanted to feel her breath on his face. He wanted to look down and down into her eyes while she held him tighter and tighter. He had never had such a feeling before. He felt as if he were reeling down through a pitchblack tunnel.

Nelson is so overwhelmed by these mysterious feelings that only Mr. Head's grabbing him away keeps him from collapsing at the woman's feet. Frederick Asals astutely suggests that the black woman embodies the emergence of "the dark unacknowledged self" that stands opposed to the proud contemptuousness and stern self-control that Mr. Head and Nelson characteristically live by. "You act like you don't have any sense!" (*CS*, 262), Mr. Head says when he pulls Nelson away.[3] I think that at the center of this hidden self is a generosity of spirit toward others—a form of charity whereby one both gives oneself to others and also takes them into oneself—that ties people of all description in a common bond of humanity. In their drive for power and identity, Mr. Head and Nelson repress such forces of charity to maintain their separate and discrete identities. If the black woman represents this centrifugal force compelling the self outside its hard shell of social identity, the sneering ghosts of themselves that both Mr. Head and Nelson see reflected in the train window represent the centripetal force to hold it in check. As Nelson recovers after his encounter with the black woman, his conscious self reasserting its authority, one of the first things he thinks of is this ghostly figure from the train.

It is this force of generosity and mercy embodied in the black woman—a force that for a moment melts the differences between Nelson and the woman—that ultimately brings Mr. Head and Nelson together again after Mr. Head's betrayal and leads them both to a fuller understanding of the mystery and wonder of life. At one point before the reconciliation, as Nelson walks along, furious at his grand-

3. *Ibid.*, 87.

father's treachery and locked inside himself in a fierce hate, he senses
from within himself the power of mercy that can dissolve his obsession; he feels, "from some remote place inside himself, a black mysterious form reach up as if it would melt his frozen vision in one hot
grasp." But such feelings remain effectively repressed until Nelson
witnesses the "artificial nigger." The black statue touches both
Nelson and Mr. Head (who by this time has been humbled by his
treachery to Nelson) on some level of mystery so profound that their
rivalry becomes insignificant and forgotten. What they see in the
statue is a mirror image of themselves: a figure supposedly happy but
frozen in misery. Indeed, as Mr. Head and Nelson stare at the statue
they themselves become images of it, "their necks forward at almost
the same angle and their shoulders curved in almost exactly the same
way and their hands trembling identically in their pockets. Mr. Head
looked like an ancient child and Nelson like a miniature old man." As
the black woman had earlier profoundly touched the spirit of Nelson,
the black statue so moves both Mr. Head and Nelson, this "monu-
ment to another's victory" bringing them—Mr. Head, Nelson,
blacks, and further, all humanity—"together in their common defeat" (CS, 267, 268–69). What they now understand on some deep
level is that they share with blacks and all people a common identity as
a fallen people and that in this world of common defeat the joy of life
derives from a generosity of spirit and mercy ultimately Christian in
origin. Where Mr. Head and Nelson had earlier, on the train, seen
reflected back at them scowling ghostlike images that seemed to embody their deepest selves, they now understand that these figures
represent not their core identities but their distorted illusions of their
own superiority, and that this devilish tendency blinds them from
seeing the true image of their deepest spiritual life—the suffering
"artificial nigger."

Such knowledge, known as much on an unconscious as a conscious
level, brings Mr. Head and Nelson together again, "dissolving their
differences like an action of mercy." Rather than being two characters
determined to act out their self-sufficiency and claims of authority
over each other, they are now humbled, repentant, and forgiving,
joined together in the bonds of Christian fellowship. On the train
ride home, Mr. Head comes to a full understanding of his—and
humanity's—place in God's creation:

Mr. Head stood very still and felt the action of mercy touch him again but this time he knew that there were no words in the world that could name it. He understood that it grew out of agony, which is not denied to any man and which is given in strange ways to children. He understood it was all a man could carry into death to give his Maker and he suddenly burned with shame that he had so little of it to take with him. He stood appalled, judging himself with the thoroughness of God, while the action of mercy covered his pride like a flame and consumed it. He had never thought himself a great sinner before but he saw now that his true depravity had been hidden from him lest it cause him despair. He realized that he was forgiven for sins from the beginning of time, when he had conceived in his own heart the sin of Adam, until the present, when he had denied poor Nelson. He saw that no sin was too monstrous for him to claim as his own, and since God loved in proportion as He forgave, he felt ready at that instant to enter Paradise. (*CS*, 269–70)

Mr. Head and Nelson return home chastened and alive in a way they never had been before.

The ending of "The Artificial Nigger," with Mr. Head's triumphant (and explicit) Christian vision and the unification of him and Nelson, clearly embodies a profound shift in the position of the narrative consciousness away from the more characteristic fundamentalist perspective of most of O'Connor's other works. Indeed, "The Artificial Nigger" is one of the few O'Connor stories—if not the only one—where the narrative consciousness comes very close to embodying O'Connor's essential Catholic perspective. In contrast to her normal narrative technique of creating a hard-line fundamentalist narrator whose viewpoint contrasts sharply with the Catholicism of her authorial perspective, O'Connor creates here a narrator whose outlook, though not strictly Catholic (the narrator, for instance, makes no claim for the Sacraments or for Mr. Head's or Nelson's entrance into the Church), is nonetheless much closer in spirit to her own Catholic (and catholic) views. Indeed, it is possible, I believe, to view the narrator of "The Artificial Nigger," at least in terms of tone and spirit, as a close embodiment of the authorial perspective that is merely implicit in the other works. The perspective of this more generous narrator, a perspective that recognizes the severe justice of God together with his mercy, thus becomes an expression of the spirit of O'Connor's Catholic faith—one celebrating Christian charity and commitment—that stands opposed to the more severe and individualistic faith of her characteristic fundamentalist narrators. Of significance here is the fact that Mr. Head's and Nelson's strict categorical thinking—judging people according to racial categories (a person is *either* white *or* black)—mirrors the similarly rigid thinking of the fundamentalists (a person is *either* for *or* against Christ), and both lack Christian charity and a deep concern for Christian community. Only when Mr. Head and Nelson discover a larger vision based on charity and mercy, and so transcend their narrow, self-oriented views, do they set out on the path toward salvation. Implied here, I believe, is a similar critique of fundamentalism's rigidity and reductiveness.

O'Connor rarely expressed this vision of charity and mercy explicitly in her stories, but she was much less reticent about it in her letters. To her correspondents she frequently wrote that the way to find Christ was to concern oneself not with one's own sufferings but with those of others. To A. O'Connor wrote (September 15, 1955) that "our salvation is worked out on earth according as we love one another, see Christ in another, etc., by works. This is one reason I am chary of using the word, love, loosely. I prefer to use it in its practical forms, such as prayer, almsgiving, visiting the sick and burying the dead and so forth." To Alfred Corn (May 30, 1962) she cited an anecdote of an exchange between Robert Bridges and Gerard Manley Hopkins to make the point "that God is to be experienced in Charity (in the sense of love for the divine image in human beings)" (*HB*, 102, 476–77).

Although O'Connor came upon Pierre Teilhard de Chardin's work relatively late in her career (she apparently began serious study of him in 1959), she most certainly must have found appealing Teilhard's emphasis on charity as the most active force behind what he saw as humanity's evolutionary convergence with Christ. "To what power is it reserved to burst asunder the envelope in which our individual microcosms tend jealously to isolate themselves and vegetate?" Teilhard asks in *The Divine Milieu: An Essay on the Interior Life*. "To what force is it given to merge and exalt our partial rays into the principal radiance of Christ?" His answer: "To charity, the beginning and the end of all spiritual relationships." Teilhard goes on to say that "Christian charity, which is preached so fervently by the Gospels, is nothing else than the more or less conscious cohesion of souls engendered by their communal convergence *in Christo Jesu*. It is impossible to love Christ without loving others (in proportion as these others are moving towards Christ). And it is impossible to love others (in a spirit of broad human communion) without moving nearer to Christ."[4]

That O'Connor expressed her vision of charity in "The Artificial Nigger" more openly than in any of her other stories probably in large part explains her remarks on several occasions that "The Artificial Nigger" was her favorite story. Unlike her more characteristic stories, there is very little pressure here on her Catholicism, either from the story or the narrator, since both affirm—rather than challenge—her authorial perspective. "The Artificial Nigger" thus possesses a harmony of vision that is generally absent in O'Connor's fiction and so represents a significant departure from her characteristic narrative structure built on wrenching and violent extremes.

Another, and quite different, departure occurs in O'Connor's story "The Enduring Chill." Here O'Connor increases the pressure of her fundamentalist voice so as to bring it into an uneasy balance with her Catholicism. In terms of plot, "The Enduring Chill" is very similar to "Everything That Rises Must Converge"; both stories focus on a young intellectual whose misguided vision and intentions are shockingly revealed in all their ugliness. But a significant change occurs here in the narrative voice. Although the narrators of both stories hold to a severe fundamentalism, the perspective of the narrator in "The Enduring Chill" does not undo itself as it does in "Everything That Rises Must Converge." Rather it is validated, becoming closely allied with a Catholic vision in an unstable and charged balance.

The narrator of "The Enduring Chill" is characteristically O'Connor's—harsh and ironic, detached and sternly religious. Like most of O'Connor's narrators, this one heightens character and situation in order to suggest that more than mere everyday concerns are at stake in the story; the backdrop and meaning of the story, the narrator suggests, stretch into the divine, the realm of ultimate matters. Such a suggestion occurs almost immediately in the opening scene when Asbury steps off the train and gives his impression (as filtered through the narrator) of the landscape: "The sky was a chill gray and a startling white-gold sun, like some strange potentate from the

4. Pierre Teilhard de Chardin, *The Divine Milieu: An Essay on the Interior Life,* trans. Bernard Wall (New York, 1960), 125.

east, was rising beyond the black woods that surrounded Timberboro. It cast a strange light over the single block of one-story brick and wooden shacks. Asbury felt that he was about to witness a majestic transformation, that the flat of roofs might at any moment turn into the mounting turrets of some exotic temple for a god he didn't know." Although the vision is only momentary and Asbury is immediately angered that he had "allowed himself, even for an instant, to see an imaginary temple in the collapsing country junction" (CS, 357, 358), the possibility of this larger perspective is established. In fact, as it turns out, Asbury's vision of a mysterious and threatening temple is a fitting description of the narrator's starkly religious perspective from which he or she tells the story. From this perspective, with God's presence looming above and beyond, the action is fraught with withering irony, aimed particularly at Asbury's pretentiousness.

Asbury is another characteristic O'Connor portrait of an intellectual—a young man who believes his education has lifted him above those around him. He puts his faith entirely within himself and his mind: His gods are his intellect and his art, both of which he feels have been stunted by the ignorance of his mother during his upbringing. As the story opens, Asbury, who is very ill and believes he is dying, is returning home from New York, where he had gone to live the life of a writer. His attempts at writing have failed, and he holds his mother ultimately responsible. While in New York he had written a long letter to her—one similar to Franz Kafka's to his father—that fills two notebooks and that he intends her to read upon his death. Asbury sees his mother as literal minded and blinded by her self-satisfaction, and he believes that only through such a damning letter will she be able to realize the part she has played in his failure as a writer. In the only selection of the letter we see, Asbury writes that he moved to New York "to escape the slave's atmosphere . . . to find freedom, to liberate my imagination." He adds, in words underscored twice: "I have no imagination." Asbury believes his mother's influence has been slow and pernicious; she had not forced her way of life upon him, but "her way had simply been the air he breathed and when at last he had found other air [of superior thinking, of art], he couldn't survive in it." He sees his letter as revealing all this to his mother, leaving "her with an enduring chill and perhaps in time lead[ing] her to see herself as she was" (CS, 364, 365).

Asbury's notions of his own superiority define his relationships with the other characters in the story. He lashes out at those he believes of inferior mind (his mother and sister and Dr. Block) and feels attracted to those who he feels show intellectual breeding and authority, particularly the two priests of the story (Ignatius Vogle, whom Asbury meets in New York, and Father Finn, the Jesuit who visits him at home). The priests intrigue him not because of their Catholicism but because of what he interprets as their superior stance resulting from their learnedness and their certainty of faith. When Asbury first spots Father Vogle in the audience at a lecture on the Vedanta, he notes the priest's "taciturn superior expression," an expression Asbury himself likes to use. Later, at home in Timberboro, Asbury thinks he should have called on the priest, since "he appealed to him as a man of the world, someone who would have understood the unique tragedy of his death, a death whose meaning had been far beyond the twittering group around them." He has his mother call up Father Finn and ask him to visit primarily because he seeks intellectual companionship. (He also knows that consulting a priest will irk his mother, and he delights in this.) "Most of them are very well-educated," Asbury tells his mother when she questions his desire to see a priest, "but Jesuits are foolproof. A Jesuit would be able to discuss something besides the weather." He thinks happily, "He would talk to a man of culture before he died—even in this desert!" (*CS*, 360, 371).

In his identification with the priests Asbury reveals his own pride and blindness. Asbury takes what he interprets as the priests' superiority in their certainty of faith and then projects onto these men his own feelings, making them doubles of himself. To Asbury they are brothers in arms, learned men detached from the general run of humanity and cynical toward it. Of course Asbury is extremely disappointed—and thrown off guard—by Father Finn, who is anything but what Asbury envisioned him. Father Finn will have nothing to do with Asbury's attempts to talk about art and the artist. "I haven't met him," he responds when Asbury asks what he thinks of James Joyce. "Now. Do you say your morning and night prayers?" He continually probes Asbury about his spiritual life and becomes more and more irritated by—and concerned about—the young man as it becomes clear that he cares not at all for the life of his soul. "God is an idea created by man," Asbury says at one point, and at another, when the priest tells him that he must pray, he says, "The artist prays by creating." By the end of their conversation, Father Finn has lost all patience with Asbury, and he roars at him: "How can the Holy Ghost fill your soul when it's full of trash? The Holy Ghost will not come until you see yourself as you are—a lazy ignorant conceited youth!" Asbury is helpless in the face of the priest's words and physical presence, particularly the fierce eye (the priest is blind in the other) he turns on him; the narrator describes Asbury as "mov[ing] his arms and legs helplessly as if he were pinned to the bed by the terrible eye" (CS, 375, 376, 377).

Asbury's failure with Father Finn is mirrored in his interactions with the black farmhands, Randall and Morgan. While writing a play about blacks before he moved to New York, Asbury had for a while worked in his mother's dairy so he could get to know Randall and Morgan. As with the priests, Asbury sees himself in the blacks, but this time in those feelings of resentment for being victimized by his mother and, more generally, by society at large. He tries to engage Randall and Morgan in his resentment, prodding them to break the rules of the dairy by smoking and by drinking unpasteurized milk. "Take the milk," Asbury tells Randall as he holds a glass out to him. "It's not going to hurt my mother to lose two or three glasses of milk a day. We've got to think free if we want to live free!" Asbury's efforts for communion with the blacks in a common bond of victimization, however, are lost on Randall and Morgan. "Howcome he talks so ugly about his ma?" Morgan asks his friend. Randall answers, "She ain't whup him enough when he was little" (CS, 369, 370).

The failures with Father Finn and the blacks are two of the significant turnarounds that Asbury endures in the story. Both, by stripping away illusions rooted deep in Asbury's own self-conception, push him closer to a clearer self-awareness. The most crucial setback, however, occurs when Dr. Block, whom Asbury sees as bumbling and ignorant, discovers that Asbury has undulant fever (apparently from drinking the unpasteurized milk in the dairy) and is not about to die. The news stuns Asbury, for he has conceived of his impending death in heroic terms, as a fitting end to his stunted life. "Death was coming to him legitimately, as a justification, as a gift from life," the narrative consciousness reports him thinking at one point. "That was his greatest triumph." And at another: "He had failed his god, Art, but he had been a faithful servant and Art was sending him Death" (*CS*, 370, 373).

That Asbury fails even in his plans for death, and must now go on living, shocks him into seeing himself as he truly is—vain and pretentious, with no one to blame for his errors except himself. As he looks at himself in the mirror, his eyes "looked shocked clean as if they had been prepared for some awful vision to come down on him." He now realizes that the enduring chill he had envisioned for his mother is to be his own:

The old life in him was exhausted. He awaited the coming of new. It was then that he felt the beginning of a chill, a chill so peculiar, so light, that it was like a warm ripple across a deeper sea of cold. His breath came short. The fierce bird which through the years of his childhood and the days of his illness had been poised over his head, waiting mysteriously, appeared all at once to be in motion. Asbury blanched and the last film of illusion was torn as if by a whirlwind from his eyes. He saw that for the rest of his days, frail, racked, but enduring, he would live in the face of a purifying terror. A feeble cry, a last impossible protest escaped him. But the Holy Ghost, emblazoned in ice instead of fire, continued, implacable, to descend. (*CS*, 382)

Asbury's old way of life is entirely shattered, and Father Finn's observation that the Holy Ghost may be the last thing Asbury gets is proved absolutely true.

The narrator thus brings Asbury to a moment of disturbing self-knowledge through an encounter with self and otherness that shatters Asbury's pretensions. On one level, then, the story validates the narrator's authoritative power; Asbury is chastened, violently, by a narrator whose forceful and judgmental stance is perhaps best embodied in Father Finn's commanding presence. Father Finn's enraged questions—"Do you want your soul to suffer eternal damnation? Do you want to be deprived of God for all eternity? Do you want to suffer the most terrible pain, greater than fire, the pain of loss? Do you want to suffer the pain of loss for all eternity?" (*CS*, 377)—spoken in the spirit of an angry fundamentalist (and also echoing the famous sermon in chapter 3 of Joyce's *Portrait of the Artist as a Young Man*, an ironic reminder of Asbury's interest in Joyce), embody the crushing concerns that guide the narrator.[5] That the narrator's voice appears to sound like Father Finn is significant, for it signals the bringing together of O'Connor's Catholicism and fundamentalism into an uneasy unity, an angry Catholicism. Rather than undercutting the fierce monologism of fundamentalism by associating it with the same evils that it set out to correct (as seen in "Everything That Rises Must Converge"), O'Connor here seems to validate the view by voicing it through a Catholic priest. There is less outward concern for charity here than there is about knowing—and communicating—what is right: God's word. Yet beneath the surface, and suggesting the uneasiness of the Catholic-fundamentalist balance, there is indeed a concern for charity, but it is a charity that is rooted in, and cuts with, a violence.

Such charity, necessitated by the stubbornness and pretentiousness of modern people, is what controls the conversation of Asbury and Father Finn. Although Father Finn begins his conversation with Asbury in a friendly and charitable manner, expressing his pleasure at being asked to visit, he quickly sharpens the tone and topic when Asbury resists his comments on the life of the spirit. Finally, Father Finn is reduced to anger and belligerence to get his message across: There is no other way to break through Asbury's stubborn shell. Although he does not appear so, Father Finn nevertheless ultimately proves to be charitable, for he is attending to the soul of another in the only way he can—with violence that echoes fundamentalist rage. The narrator, joined it seems here with O'Connor as author, operates along the same lines.

In "The Enduring Chill," then, O'Connor brings together her two controlling religious visions, her Catholicism and her fundamentalism, to forge a narrative (and, I would suggest, an authorial) voice that is rooted in both. Yoking together a charitable commitment to others with a severe commitment to an all-demanding God, O'Connor creates a balance that is fragile and fraught with tension, and one that represents one more example of the dialogic interplay in her mind and art between her two interacting religious visions. Here both views

5. For a further discussion of parallels between "The Enduring Chill" and Joyce's *Portrait of the Artist as a Young Man*, see David Aiken, "Flannery O'Connor's Portrait of the Artist as a Young Failure," *Arizona Quarterly*, XXXII (1976), 245–59. See also Desmond, *Risen Sons*, 75–76.

pressure each other in ways that open up a new vision not totally controlled by either and embody a balance rarely achieved in O'Connor's fiction.

Such a balance is not what one finds in "The Lame Shall Enter First," a story embodying the predominance of O'Connor's fundamentalist voice. O'Connor, in this story, intensifies the characteristic fundamentalist perspective of her narrator so that the narrator's voice comes close to losing whatever goodness it might have in its intensity to punish characters in order to assert its vision. John Hawkes, in his significant essay "Flannery O'Connor's Devil," argues that despite O'Connor's professed concern for morality, the driving force behind her work is immoral in that it is "unflagging and unpredictable" and driven by the compulsion to demolish "man's image of himself as a rational creature." Ultimately Hawkes sees the driving force of the immoral creative process as dominating O'Connor's vision so that she becomes less the Catholic than the demonic writer. "The creative process," he writes, "transforms the writer's objective Catholic knowledge of the devil into an authorial attitude in itself in some measure diabolical."[6]

Hawkes of course is equating the narrative voice in O'Connor's fiction with O'Connor's own voice, a move that, as I have been suggesting, distorts the complexity of her fiction, yet his observations are nonetheless suggestive when applied to the narrative consciousness. The voice of O'Connor's fundamentalist narrator, though firmly grounded in a Yahwist vision, nonetheless at times does appear close to being diabolic in its leveling of crushing force against many of the characters. There frequently does indeed seem to be something too fierce, too intense—too demonic, perhaps—in the cruelty and anger of the narrator and the world he or she creates. O'Connor predictably disagreed with Hawkes's analysis. She said in a letter (August 3, 1962) to Robert Fitzgerald that Hawkes's devil was subjective, "an unfallen spirit of some purely literary kind," whereas hers, she wrote to Hawkes (November 28, 1961), was objective (Lucifer), and she did not write with his will. But elsewhere she admitted that she did indeed side with some of the diabolic characters in her fiction. In a letter to Hawkes (June 22, 1961) she wrote that she was all for Singleton (the

6. John Hawkes, "Flannery O'Connor's Devil," *Sewanee Review*, LXX (1962), 397, 401.

man in "The Partridge Festival" whose madness destroys the easy sentimentalism and pretensions of a young couple), "devil though I rightly consider him to be." She characterized him as "one of those devils who go about piercing pretensions, not the devil who goes about like a roaring lion seeking whom he may devour. There is a hierarchy of devils surely." In another letter to Hawkes (April 20, 1961) she wrote that she supposed "the Devil teaches most of the lessons that lead to self-knowledge" (*HB*, 486, 456, 443, 439), again characterizing the demonic as a force that pierces pretensions; and elsewhere she wrote that the intensity of the evil situations in her fiction prepared her characters for their moments of illumination.

In all of this, and particularly in her comments on the role of evil in the process of initiating self-knowledge in the complacent, O'Connor could just as well be characterizing her narrative consciousness. This is not to assert that O'Connor's narrators are devils but to suggest that there is a fine line separating severe fundamentalists like her narrators and those devilish characters who know full well the fundamentalist choice between Christ and the Devil and who have chosen the satanic. Both sets of figures live by extremes, sharing an intensity of conviction and an unflagging zeal that frequently leads to bizarre and violent interactions with others. If Old Tarwater, the prophet figure of *The Violent Bear It Away*, knows the commitment that one must make to Christ, so too does The Misfit in "A Good Man Is Hard to Find," and both wreak violence—for different ends, certainly, and in different ways—on others. Significantly, both also end up helping to propel others—Tarwater in the novel and the grandmother in the story— toward Christian redemption by shattering their lives of complacency and noncommitment; and, of course, Old Tarwater is aided in his mission of making a prophet out of his nephew by the boy's devilish "friend" and his several manifestations. Such intensity and drive are also characteristic of O'Connor's narrators, and though they ground their perspectives in Christian commitment, they nonetheless go about their work, at times at least, using means every bit as fierce as those used by O'Connor's characters who are driven by evil and the Devil.

Is it fair then to say that O'Connor saw her narrators—and more generally, all religious fundamentalists—as demonic Christians? I would not press the point, but I would suggest again that though attracted to the severity of the fundamentalists, O'Connor generally understood (in part through her interaction with the narrators in her fiction) that their vision was limited and reductive. It is also clear that the fundamentalist vision, particularly what I have characterized as its demonic aspects, exerted great pressure on O'Connor. If O'Connor for the most part in her fiction held this pressure in check, there were times when she apparently gave in to it, yielding her more charitable Catholic vision to that of the stridency—or demonism—of fundamentalism. Such demonism, so close to the work of the true Devil, is in all likelihood what O'Connor was referring to when, in a letter to Hawkes (February 6, 1962), she admitted that "the Devil's voice is my own" (*HB*, 464) in her story "The Lame Shall Enter First."

O'Connor's reference to her demonic voice refers, I believe, both to her own authorial voice and to that of her narrative voice. Thus, in contrast to "The Artificial Nigger," where the perspectives of the author and narrator appear close to merging in a charitable vision, in "The Lame Shall Enter First" the two perspectives seem closely tied in their demonism. As a result, this story contains far less tension than usual between the two visions. More given over to her fundamentalist vision than she generally is, O'Connor exerts less pressure on her narrator, and the story becomes more strident and less complex as the demonic voice is more free to hold forth. It is perhaps for this reason that O'Connor felt so uneasy about the story; she spent an especially long time revising it, and then later, once she saw it in galleys, decided it was a failure. At this point she wrote her agent, Elizabeth McKee, that she was going to try to stop the *Sewanee Review* from publishing it, even at this late date. She later wrote to Cecil Dawkins (September 6, 1962), agreeing with Dawkins's dismissal of the story: "I certainly agree that it don't work and never have felt that it did" (*HB*, 490).

"The Lame Shall Enter First" is another story focusing on a liberal intellectual and in many respects resembles "Everything That Rises Must Converge" and "The Enduring Chill." As in these other stories, the intellectual, here a social worker named Sheppard who works at a reformatory, comes under intense attack by the fundamentalist narrator. Ultimately Sheppard's intellectual pride is shattered, the lesson giver being himself taught a rude and shocking lesson. Although the basic plot structure is similar in all three stories, the tone in "The Lame Shall Enter First" is more intense and fierce. Most indicative of this heightened shift are the narrator's more aggressive and dramatic attacks on Sheppard; not only are they fiercer here than in the other three stories but also they appear to work on a more elemental level. In large part this intensity results from the fact that a profound change in the intellectual's primary antagonist has occurred. Where in "Everything That Rises Must Converge" and "The Enduring Chill" Julian and Asbury square off against their rather shallow and religiously complacent (if ultimately good-hearted) mothers, here Sheppard faces a juvenile delinquent named Johnson, one of O'Connor's demonic characters who recognizes Christ's searing reality but who, for the time being at least, has chosen the way of the Devil. Like the narrator, whom on one level he embodies, Johnson possesses a severe fundamentalist vision rooted in the stark either-or choice one must make for Christ or the Devil. He tells Sheppard at one point that if he repents his evil ways he will become a preacher, since "if you're going to do it, it's no sense doing it halfway" (CS, 476), and he continuously reacts with scorn toward Sheppard's liberal ideas and atheism.

With Johnson as a central character, "The Lame Shall Enter First" possesses an obvious and charged religious dimension absent from "Everything That Rises Must Converge" and "The Enduring Chill." Although these other two stories are underpinned by a fierce religiosity in their narrators' visions, "The Lame Shall Enter First" has this fervor as an integral and clearly visible element in the interactions of the characters. In the dueling between Sheppard and Johnson, a commitment—or lack of it—to Christ is the issue on which everything depends.

Sheppard is O'Connor's (and her narrator's) typical intellectual—a person smitten with intellectual pride who believes not in the Lord but in himself and the rationality and potential of the human mind. It is the quality of Johnson's mind—he has an IQ of 140—that attracts Sheppard to him and that inspires Sheppard's effort to reform him while ignoring the needs of his own not-so-gifted son, Norton. During his weekly talks with Johnson at the reformatory, Sheppard attempts to engage him with the mysteries of the created world and the mastery of them by human endeavor. He wants to challenge Johnson's mind: "He talked a little above him to give him something to reach for. He roamed from simple psychology and the dodges of the human mind to astronomy and the space capsules that were whirling around the earth faster than the speed of sound and would soon encircle the stars. Instinctively he concentrated on the stars. He wanted to give the boy something to reach for besides his neighbor's goods. He wanted to stretch his horizons. He wanted him to *see* the universe, to see the darkest parts of it could be penetrated" (*CS*, 451). Later, when Johnson has moved into Sheppard's home, Sheppard buys the boy a telescope and a microscope, two instruments to challenge him further; as symbols of Enlightenment rationality and the scientific method, the telescope and microscope at the same time embody Sheppard's own scientific approach to the world, the self, and others.

In attempting to open up the world for Johnson, Sheppard in a sense assumes the role of lord and master, the savior (and shepherd) of Johnson who will not only feed and clothe him but will also correct his physical and mental defects (or as Benjamin Franklin would call them, his errata). Sheppard plans to buy Johnson a special shoe to even the imbalance from his clubfoot, and he hopes to mold him into a brilliant boy by providing him with the proper environment and the best teaching. He wants to reshape Johnson, to bring about a rebirth of sorts, and there is a good deal of truth in Johnson's stinging comments to Norton about his father: "He thinks he's Jesus Christ!" (*CS*, 459). But if Sheppard sees himself as a Christ figure, it is merely as a secular rather than a spiritual savior. He has in fact no concern for Johnson's spiritual life except in figuring out how to smother it by finding a way to counteract what he sees as the pernicious influence on Johnson of his fundamentalist grandfather.

Sheppard's concerted attacks on Johnson's fundamentalism are of course integrally related to his attempts to prod the boy's rational mind—he wants, in effect, to substitute rationalism for the boy's fundamentalism. Such displacement, Sheppard knows, is crucial for his remolding of Johnson, and he knows too that it will take a great deal of effort. During his first interview with Johnson at the reformatory, Sheppard is brought face to face with Johnson's severe religious vision when the boy says that the reason he has gotten into so much trouble is, simply, "Satan. He has me in his power." The intensity of the boy's faith both burdens and angers Sheppard. "He felt a momentary dull despair as if he were faced with some elemental warping of nature that had happened too long ago to be corrected now," the narrative consciousness reports. "This boy's questions about life had been answered by signs nailed on the pine trees: DOES SATAN HAVE YOU IN HIS POWER? REPENT OR BURN IN HELL. JESUS SAVES. He would know the Bible with or without reading it. His despair gave way to outrage." To Johnson's response about Satan, Sheppard responds, "Rubbish. . . . We're living in the space age! You're too smart to give me an answer like that!" After a year of working with Johnson at the reformatory, however, Sheppard is confident that he has converted him. Sheppard interprets Johnson's continued expressions of Christian belief as merely empty rhetoric said not in faith but in childish resistance to Sheppard's authority. "You don't deceive me," Sheppard tells the boy after he has told Sheppard that only Jesus can save him. "I flushed that out of your head in the reformatory. I saved you from that, at least" (CS, 450–51, 474).

But of course Sheppard has done no such thing, and indeed it is Sheppard's attempts to deny Christ's role in the world that Johnson most deeply resists. Nothing steels the boy's resolve more than Sheppard's expression of his own atheism and what he says must be Johnson's also (Johnson is too intelligent to think otherwise, Sheppard reasons). Johnson gets so angry that he rips a page out of the Bible and eats it. "I've eaten it like Ezekiel," he taunts Sheppard, "and I don't want none of your food after it nor no more ever." By Johnson's interpretation, Sheppard's acts of generosity and goodness are irrelevant to this larger issue of knowing and acknowledging Christ's presence. When Norton says that his father is good ("He helps people"), Johnson's response is immediate and charged: " 'Good!' Johnson said savagely. He thrust his head forward. 'Listen here,' he hissed, 'I don't care if he's good or not. He ain't right!' " (CS, 477, 454).

If Johnson damns Sheppard from a biblical perspective ("The devil has you in his power," he says at one point), Sheppard's acts toward his own son reveal his failure as a man of charity and goodwill. In his enthusiasm to reshape Johnson, Sheppard continually ignores the needs and feelings of Norton, who is wracked with grief over the death of his mother. In the story's opening scene, for instance, Sheppard berates his son for what he sees as his selfishness; he compares all the opportunities Norton has—and wastes—to those that Johnson does not have and would flourish with if he did. He interprets Norton's extended grief for his mother as merely selfishness, an overly indulgent concern for himself and not others. "If you stop thinking about yourself and think of what you can do for somebody else," Sheppard says to Norton, "then you'll stop missing your mother" (*CS*, 478, 448). Eventually, after Sheppard levels further accusations of the boy's lack of goodwill, Norton vomits his breakfast. Later, during Johnson's stay, Sheppard continues to overlook his child's needs and to misread his signals for help and understanding; compared with Johnson, Norton appears to Sheppard mediocre and petty, and Sheppard turns his attention away from the son in whom he is so disappointed to the boy for whom he has such high hopes.

Johnson's intense challenges of Sheppard ultimately reveal to him the errors of his ways. The first major setback in Sheppard's plans to reform Johnson, and one that severely tests Sheppard's commitment and motives, occurs when Johnson is apprehended by the police as a suspect for a break-in. Before taking the boy to the station, the police bring him to Sheppard's house, where he appeals to Sheppard to stand up for him. Sheppard does not do it, feeling personally injured that Johnson has failed—failed him, Sheppard, rather than failed himself. "You made out like you had all this confidence in me," the boy says to him before he is taken away. "I did have," Sheppard answers in irritation. When the police and boy leave, Sheppard "summon[s] his compassion" and decides he will go to the station the next day to help Johnson. "The night in jail would not hurt him and the experience would teach him that he could not treat with impunity someone who had shown him nothing but kindness," the narrative consciousness reports him thinking (*CS*, 465).

Throughout this scene, Sheppard's declared commitment to Johnson seems less a commitment to the boy than to Sheppard's own intellectual plan to reform him—a plan whose success or failure is inextricably tied to Sheppard's intellectual pride. Sheppard receives a stinging rebuke for his loyalty to his plan rather than to Johnson when the next day Johnson is released after someone else is accused of the crime. When he receives the news, Sheppard feels sick, with "the ugliness of what he had done bor[ing] in upon him with a sudden dull intensity." But significantly Sheppard still sees his betrayal largely in terms of how it affects his efforts to save Johnson and not in terms of loyalty and commitment to another person. Now he judges himself, rather than Johnson, as a failure because he has fouled up his own plans: "He [Sheppard] had failed him at just the point he might have turned him once and for all in the right direction" (CS, 466).

An even more severe test and rebuke of Sheppard occurs when the police return on another day to question Johnson about having been seen looking in a window of a home. This time Sheppard vouches for the boy, saying he had been with him all evening. He feels elated that he has been given the opportunity to win back Johnson's trust, but his feelings are shattered when Johnson hints that he may indeed have sneaked out earlier and have been at the house. Just as the police seek to entrap Johnson by saying they saw his footprints around the house ("There wasn't any tracks," Johnson later tells Sheppard. "That whole place is concreted in the back and my feet were dry"), so here Johnson entraps Sheppard, pressuring him to examine himself and his plan in a severe and threatening situation. Sheppard is both physically and mentally staggered. As he grips a sofa cushion and stares at the shoe on Johnson's clubfoot, which "appeared to grin at him with Johnson's own face," he is overcome with hatred: "He hated the shoe, hated the foot, hated the boy. His face paled. Hatred choked him. He was aghast at himself." Sheppard attempts to recover, vowing that his resolve is not shaken and that he is stronger than Johnson and will yet save him. But Johnson continues to taunt Sheppard, and the boy's fierce look deals another blow to the already reeling Sheppard: "The boy's eyes were like distorting mirrors in which he saw himself made hideous and grotesque" (CS, 473, 474). Seeing himself from the boy's fundamentalist perspective is too much for Sheppard; he now understands the failure of his compassion and his plan for the boy's reformation, and he only wishes that Johnson would pick up and move out.

The final crushing blow of self-knowledge comes when the police return yet again, this time having caught and arrested Johnson for another break-in. Johnson's taunts of Sheppard are at their most fierce. He says he allowed himself to get caught "to show up that big tin Jesus!" and continues: "He thinks he's God. I'd rather be in the reformatory than in his house, I'd rather be in the pen! The Devil has him in his power." Sheppard is once again staggered and desperately continues to argue that he has nothing with which to reproach himself. "I did everything I knew how for him," he tells the police. "I did more for him than I did for my own child. I hoped to save him and I failed, but it was an honorable failure." After the police have taken Johnson away, Sheppard keeps repeating to himself the sentence that he did more for Johnson than for Norton, until suddenly he is struck with a revelation of his actions:

The sentence echoed in his mind, each syllable like a dull blow. His mouth twisted and he closed his eyes against the revelation. Norton's face rose before him, empty, forlorn, his left eye listing almost imperceptively toward the outer rim as if it could not bear a full view of grief. His heart constricted with a repulsion for himself so clear and intense that he gasped for breath. He had stuffed his own emptiness with good works like a glutton. He had ignored his own child to feed his vision of himself. He saw the clear-eyed Devil, the sounder of hearts, leering at him from the eyes of Johnson. His image of himself shrivelled until everything was black before him. He sat there paralyzed, aghast. (*CS*, 480, 481)

Sheppard, ready to start a new life with Norton, rushes upstairs to find him. Norton, however, has already hanged himself, a step in the quest to join his mother in heaven.

Once again, then, we find in "The Lame Shall Enter First" a character out to teach a lesson being instead taught one himself. Sheppard's finding selfishness in Norton is exactly what he does not see in himself, and the narrator tells a severe story that reveals this to him and the reader. In this telling, the narrator zeroes in on the evil and destruction wrought by Sheppard's intellectual pride and his monologic efforts to impose his will upon others. But an important shift in the narrative dynamic has occurred. Whereas in "Everything That Rises Must Converge" the intellectual's downfall on one level signals the narrator's (both mirroring each other in their willfulness), here that correspondence is much weakened, since it is Johnson, not Sheppard, who stands as a double to the narrator. Indeed Johnson is a fitting embodiment of that demonic voice that O'Connor said was hers (and, as I have suggested, was also the narrator's) in the story— in the words from Sheppard's revelation, that "clear-eyed Devil, the sounder of hearts," whose penetrating stare completely undoes Sheppard. Johnson's actions that test and challenge Sheppard work out dramatically what the narrator is also doing in telling the story— wreaking violence on Sheppard and stopping at no extreme to achieve the purpose of showing up his falsity. Even Johnson's deliberate commission of crimes to strike out at Sheppard is in a sense the method of the narrator, who acts cruelly and fiercely, distorting character and situation to make points. Although such a narrative stance is similar to that of the narrators in "Everything That Rises Must Converge" and "The Enduring Chill," in this story Johnson's presence deflects such criticism. As Johnson tells Sheppard, good intentions and actions are irrelevant in the face of rightness and truth, and clearly being right means being one with Christ. Such logic also extends to the opposite situation: Evil intentions and acts are irrelevant in the larger struggle of Christian commitment.

This is a severe and demanding vision, and one that O'Connor was drawn to—as we can see in her narrative consciousness—throughout her career. Generally O'Connor invokes this vision in the stories but ultimately undercuts it, though as I have suggested not without effort, pressure, and struggle. In a few stories, such as "The Artificial Nigger," this voice is softened, its severity replaced by O'Connor's more charitable Catholicism. In a few others, including "The Lame Shall Enter First," her fierce voice is openly in control, so much so that as O'Connor herself admitted, she as author was given over to it. The great power of the fundamentalist voice is also keenly felt in O'Connor's two novels, to which we now turn.

4

Narrator and Narrative: The Novels

O'Connor's novels represent a significant shift in focus: Where the stories generally center on everyday people in everyday situations who are ultimately propelled out of what Walker Percy would call their "everydayness" into the realm of the absolute, the novels turn their attention to backwoods religious fanatics, the kind of people who possess a fundamentalist vision similar to that of O'Connor's characteristic narrator. But the fanatic characters here are those resisting their calling—those who are aware of the fundamentalist choice of giving all or nothing to Christ, with no room for any compromise, but have chosen to go the way without Christ. Their efforts at renunciation, however, are not so simply carried out or easily achieved, for these characters are haunted by Christ's fierce presence and ultimately find themselves driven to a consuming commitment to him despite their most intense efforts to do just the opposite.

This profound shift from the stories, in terms of subject matter and plotting, also entails an intensification of the narrator's perspective; here the narrator tells the stories of characters who, in their intensity and commitment to deny Christ, represent a strong challenge to the narrator's authority. And because the subject matter is more openly religious, with matters clearly hinging on the fundamentalist choice, the stories possess a more charged religious tone and tension. In this stark religious landscape the narrator is more fiercely fundamentalist, more willing to bend and distort to drive home the significance of the religious underpinning of the story, and more eager to assert a fundamentalist and narrative authority.

The narrators of the novels are quite similar to the narrator of "The

Lame Shall Enter First." They are demonic in the sense that John Hawkes used the word to describe O'Connor—destroyers of humanity's rational pretensions. These narrators exert extreme pressure on O'Connor's Catholic vision, and one senses that, as in "The Lame Shall Enter First," O'Connor gives herself over nearly or completely to the radical fundamentalism that drives the plot and underlies the narrator's perspective. O'Connor frequently complained about how little she enjoyed writing novels, particularly because it took so long to come up with a finished product; her unease probably also reflects the discomforting pressure that her vision of charity underwent when she was writing her longer works.

Despite the overwhelming power of the narrators' fundamentalism, however, in both *Wise Blood* and *The Violent Bear It Away* there is a counterforce to the narrators' authority. As in the stories, this implicit challenge ironically is located in the very stories the narrators tell—stories meant to affirm rather than to deny the narrator's fundamentalist vision. The challenge centers on the dangers and limits of the monologism that underpins the fundamentalist perspective. This challenge is particularly intense in *Wise Blood*, where the novel's final chapter threatens to undo the entire thrust of the narrator's attempt to celebrate the victory of Haze's fundamentalism. Less intense is the challenge in *The Violent Bear It Away*; there the narrator's authoritative force seems to carry the day, and the final chapter, written in some of O'Connor's most exalted prose, openly champions the birth of the fundamentalist prophet. Whatever counterforce exists to the fundamentalist affirmation is overwhelmed by the novel's authoritative close.

O'Connor's first novel, *Wise Blood* (1952), is certainly one of her harshest and most stark works, and it marks the starting point of her mature fiction. O'Connor began work on the novel when she was a graduate student at the University of Iowa, and on the strength of the chapters she completed there she won the Rinehart-Iowa Fiction Award, which gave her a cash prize and gave Rinehart first option on the novel. After leaving Iowa for New York she continued work on the novel, completing new chapters and revising what she had already done. As we saw in chapter 2 in the brief comparison of a selection from "The Train" and its revised version in *Wise Blood*, her revisions were quite radical. Most profound was her shift from a familiar and sympathetic narrative consciousness to one that was strident and de-tached. In place of being sympathetic, this narrator distorted and intensified character and situation with severe irony. It was, as O'Connor noted in letters from this period, a move away from the conventional style of her early work. So dramatic was the change that her editor at Rinehart, John Selby, balked at accepting the novel when O'Connor sent him drafts of the first nine chapters, and he sent her a list of criticisms that zeroed in on what O'Connor considered the book's strengths. Angry and upset, she quickly fired off a letter to Selby (February 18, 1949): "Whatever virtues the novel may have are very much connected with the limitations you mention. I am not writing a conventional novel, and I think that the quality of the novel I write will derive precisely from the peculiarity or aloneness, if you will, of the experience I write from." To make it clear that she was not about to write the type of novel Selby was suggesting, she added: "The finished book, though I hope less angular, will be just as odd if not odder than the nine chapters you have now. The question is: is Rinehart interested in publishing this kind of novel?" They were not (Selby in his release described O'Connor as "stiff-necked, uncoopera-tive and unethical" [*HB*, 10, 17]), and eventually Harcourt, Brace brought out the novel.

The response from John Selby at Rinehart underscores the radical nature of O'Connor's revisions and prefigures much of the shock and misunderstanding that would later greet *Wise Blood* and much of O'Connor's other published work. In any event, *Wise Blood* signals the beginning of O'Connor's mature art; moving away from conven-tional satire and humor, O'Connor now uses a harsh and strident narrator whose detached and ironic voice creates a fiction of an en-tirely different sort—one based on exaggeration, distortion, wrench-ing extremes, and violence. Perhaps fittingly, in terms of making the shift in O'Connor's artistic vision, the narrator of *Wise Blood* is one of the fiercest that we encounter in O'Connor's fiction.

The world created by this narrator is one of grotesque exaggeration and nightmarish colorings and extremes. As Frederick Asals, the most penetrating commentator on the novel, observes, "the entire treat-ment of action and landscape denies the daylight world. As in a ter-rifying dream, characters assume strange and distorted shapes, ap-pearing and disappearing in defiance of waking probability; the familiar landscape of the modern city turns foreign and forbidding; and objects and gestures shimmer with symbolic resonance." Asals with good reason uses *Wise Blood* to illustrate what he calls O'Connor's "imagery of repulsion"—embodying a repulsion of the physical world—and he points to the narrator's frequently employed tactics of describing humans with mechanical and animal metaphors and of ascribing human capabilities to animals and objects.[1] Any number of examples could be cited, but I give here only one, a sentence describing Haze that uses both types of metaphors pointed out by Asals: "His black hat sat on his head with a careful, placed expression and his face had a fragile look as if it might have been broken and stuck together again, or like a gun no one knows is loaded" (*WB*, 68). Building on the observations of Asals and others on animal imagery in the novel, William Rodney Allen further observes that O'Connor— but I would argue the narrator— fuses animal imagery with that of confinement to intensify what Allen sees as the novel's overriding theme: "that the world, without its spiritual dimension, is merely a prison for an odd collection of inmates—a zoo for the human animal." Allen sees Haze's death as "his final liberation from the cage of matter."[2]

This fiercely reductive narrative vision discussed by Asals and Allen is rooted not in a nihilistic outlook on the emptiness of existence, literal and beyond, but in a severe fundamentalism that sees the world and all its undertakings as thoroughly worthless and insignificant before the all-consuming and all-demanding presence of God. This presence is indicated by signs—literally by the signs along the rural highways warning of God's justice, and figuratively in the arching sky that looms over Taulkinham. Both kinds of signs enlarge the perspective of the novel by suggesting the divine dimensions with which the action resonates. The highway signs remind Haze of the God that he is trying to deny, and they seem divinely sent, placed down along the road to speak specifically to Haze. When Haze first takes his Essex out

1. Asals, *Flannery O'Connor*, 48–49. See also William Rodney Allen, "The Cage of Matter: The World as Zoo in Flannery O'Connor's *Wise Blood*," *American Literature*, LVIII (1986), 256–70; Margaret Peller Feeley, "Flannery O'Connor's *Wise Blood*: The Negative Way," *Southern Quarterly*, XVII (1979), 104–22; and Daniel R. Littlefield, Jr., "Flannery O'Connor's *Wise Blood*," *Mississippi Quarterly*, XXIII (1970), 121–33.
2. Allen, "The Cage of Matter," 257, 269.

onto the highway, for instance, his car stops before a sign that could well be a fundamentalist's response to all Haze has been doing in the novel: "WOE TO THE BLASPHEMER AND WHOREMONGER! WILL HELL SWALLOW YOU UP?" Beneath these words is the fundamentalist's answer to humanity's sinful condition: "Jesus saves." On his final journey from Taulkinham, before the policeman pushes his car over an embankment, Haze sees a sign—"Jesus Died for YOU" (*WB*, 75, 207)—that perhaps signals what Haze contemplates before he blinds himself.

Likewise, the overarching sky, ignored by the people of Taulkinham and pondered by Haze before his blinding, suggests God's looming presence and the larger spiritual dimension that frames everyone's actions in the novel. Early on, the narrator suggests the universal backdrop to what occurs in Taulkinham in a description of the night sky: "The black sky was underpinned with long silver streaks that looked like scaffolding and depth on depth behind it were thousands of stars that all seemed to be moving very slowly as if they were about some vast construction work that involved the whole order of the universe and would take all time to complete." The narrator adds, "No one was paying any attention to the sky," and later in the novel, in one of his blasphemous sermons, Haze declares that there is no reason to look to the sky for meaning and purpose. "You needn't to look at the sky because it's not going to open up and show no place behind it," he says (*WB*, 37, 165), adding that all significance resides only in one place—within oneself.

But it is the sky, with its sweeping vistas that underscore the insignificance of human endeavor and its divine signs that point to the supernatural alternative, that haunts Haze, as when on another of his trips outside town in his Essex there looms above him a single cloud, "a large blinding one with curls and a beard." As Haze later drives back toward Taulkinham to resume his rebellion against God, the narrator describes what is happening above: "The blinding white cloud had turned into a bird with thin long wings and was disappearing in the opposite direction." Even more significant, it is the vista of the sky—and the meaning residing therein that stretches into eternity—that Haze ponders after his car is destroyed by the patrolman. The narrator describes Haze during his reflections: "His face seemed to reflect the entire distance across the clearing and on beyond, the entire distance that extended from his eyes to the blank gray sky that went on, depth after depth, into space" (*WB*, 117, 127, 209).

From this large perspective of existence, and coupled with a deep awareness of God's searing presence in human history, the narrator relates the novel. The narrator's perspective is embodied in the two figures who haunt Haze: his mother and his grandfather, both rigid fundamentalists. His mother, as revealed in the scene when Haze as a boy returns from the carnival after having gone into the "hooch" tent, inspires in him not merely guilt for any sinful act he commits but a larger "nameless unplaced guilt" that as a fallen creature he always carries with him. "Jesus died to redeem you," his mother says as she spanks him across the legs, and despite his momentary rebellion ("I never ast him," Haze answers), Haze the next day seeks atonement by walking several miles with rock-filled shoes. His grandfather, a circuit-riding preacher described by the narrator as "a waspish old man who had ridden over three counties with Jesus in his head like a stinger," even more searchingly embodies the narrator's fundamentalist position. Indeed the grandfather's sermon, as related by the narrator, not only on one level presents the narrator's severe religious position but also on a broad level defines the issues and thrust of the novel itself:

People gathered around his Ford because he seemed to dare them to. He would climb up on the nose of it and preach from there and sometimes he would climb onto the top of it and shout down at them. They were like stones! he would shout. But Jesus had died to redeem them! Jesus was so soul-hungry that He had died, one death for all, but He would have died every soul's death for one! Did they understand that? Did they understand that for each stone soul, He would have died ten million deaths, had His arms and legs stretched on the cross and nailed ten million times for one of them? (The old man would point to this grandson, Haze. He had a particular disrespect for him because his own face was repeated almost exactly in the child's and seemed to mock him.) Did they know that even for that boy there, for that mean sinful unthinking boy standing there with his dirty hands clenching and unclenching at his sides, Jesus would die ten million deaths before He would let him lose his soul? He would chase him over the waters of sin! Did they doubt Jesus could walk on the waters of sin? That boy had been redeemed and Jesus wasn't going to leave him ever. Jesus would never let him forget he was redeemed. What did the sinner think there was to be gained? Jesus would have him in the end! (*WB*, 63, 20, 21–22)

Although the narrator is clearly going to be more cagey in putting forth personal views—the narrator is telling a story, not preaching a sermon—nonetheless it is the theology of Haze's mother and grandfather that underpins the narrator's story.

This story is designed to validate the narrator's fundamentalist vision, and it centers on Haze's attempts to free himself from bondage to Christ by denying his own fundamentalist awareness of Jesus' presence. Haze is deeply aware of the fundamentalist choice of being totally committed for or against Christ, and he has chosen to go against him, as the name of his church—the Church without Christ—makes so abundantly clear. Haze preaches his religion with a fundamentalist zeal and rage, asserting the validity of the here and now, the only realm in which one can believe. At one point he tells a boy that "it was not right to believe anything you couldn't see or hold in your hands or test with your teeth," and at another point he says that his is the "church where the blind don't see and the lame don't walk and what's dead stays that way." This literalism reduces all truth to the realm of individual experience. From atop his Essex, Haze proclaims his truth:

"I preach there are all kinds of truth, your truth and somebody else's, but behind all of them, there's only one truth and that is that there's no truth," he called. "No truth behind all truths is what I and this church preach! Where you come from is gone, where you thought you were going to never was there, and where you are is no good unless you can get away from it. Where is there a place for you to be? No place."

"In yourself right now is all the place you've got. If there was any Fall, look there, if there was any Redemption, look there, and if you expect any Judgment, look there, because they all three will have to be in your time and your body and where in your time and your body can they be?"

At the center of his church, Haze says, is a new type of Jesus, "one that can't waste his blood redeeming people with it, because he's all man and ain't got any God in him" (*WB*, 206, 105, 165, 166, 121).

At its fundamental level, Haze's rebellion is an attempt to suppress the knowledge of his "wise blood"—that is, an elemental awareness of Christ's divinity. It is this knowledge that haunts and infuriates Haze; in spite of all his attempts to deny Christ and to live a life entirely without him, Jesus remains an active voice in his consciousness, moving "from tree to tree in the back of his mind, a wild ragged figure motioning him to turn around and come off into the dark where he was not sure of his footing, where he might be walking on water and not know it and then suddenly know it and drown." As his fears suggest, Haze sees Christ as the disrupter of the natural order, as a figure who draws people away from everyday reality into a mysterious unknown. Haze, in contrast, strives to center all meaning in the interactions of the individual consciousness with the world about it, a world he sees empty of order and transcendent meaning. "I don't have to run from anything because I don't believe in anything," he says at one point (WB, 22, 76).

Throughout the novel, Haze strives to live the life he preaches—a life entirely of sense and pleasure. Despite his zeal and tenacity, however, it is clear that Haze has not freed himself from Christ; almost everyone he meets comments on his "Jesus look," with Sabbath Lilly perhaps putting it most forcefully: "I seen you wouldn't never have no fun or let anybody else because you didn't want nothing but Jesus!" Sabbath Lilly also correctly points out the difference between her and Haze, saying that they are both rotten and filthy but that "I like being that way and he don't. Yes sir!" (WB, 188, 169).

Sabbath Lilly, as her words suggest, embodies the type of person Haze's preaching calls for—one given entirely to sense and pleasure, with no concern for any higher law or spiritual fulfillment. Her presence—and that of the other doubles to Haze—puts Haze's preaching and acts into a larger perspective, refracting his views through the lives of others to test and reveal the dimensions of his faith. The most obvious and significant of Haze's doubles is Enoch Emery, who as Haze's disciple dramatically acts out the dogma of Haze's church (he, like Sabbath Lilly, is a person entirely sensual) and brings to Haze the "new jesus" ("One that's all man, without blood to waste, and . . . one that don't look like any other man so you'll look at him," Haze preaches [WB, 140–41]) that Haze says his church needs—a sawdust-filled mummy of a shrunken man.

Haze and Enoch are clearly reverse images of each other. Like Haze, Enoch is driven by a mysterious compulsion, his wise blood, but Enoch's is not of the spirit but of the animal, and it dehumanizes him in what some have called a process of "reverse evolution."[3] The narrator observes that Enoch's consciousness is split into two parts, one his blood sense and the other his social self. "The part in communication with his blood did the figuring but it never said anything in words," the narrator observes. "The other part was stocked up with all kinds of words and phrases" (WB, 87). Ultimately Enoch sheds his social self to embrace his wise blood, donning a gorilla suit that signals his entry into the animal world. Likewise Haze eventually follows the compulsion of his wise blood, renouncing the material world by blinding himself and striving to live a life of pure spirit. The opposite directions taken by Haze and Enoch—one toward the spirit, the other toward matter—starkly portray the all-or-nothing fundamentalist choice of being for or against Christ.

In Haze's physical destruction and spiritual rebirth, the narrator means to celebrate Haze's emergence as a fundamentalist hero—as one given entirely to Christ. But also at work in Haze's story are dynamics that call into question the fundamentalism underlying Haze and the narrator, particularly the limits and rage of the monologism that underpins their visions. Two parallel scenes in the novel—Haze's murder of Solace Layfield and the patrolman's destruction of Haze's car—reveal the disturbing ties that link Haze and the narrator and that ultimately point to the narrator's undoing.

When Haze murders Solace Layfield he kills a disturbing double of himself, a man who physically resembles Haze in body and dress and one who preaches the same message. In seeing himself in Layfield, Haze undergoes a profound experience of otherness: He views himself from outside himself, seeing himself as others see him. "He had never pictured himself that way before," the narrative consciousness reports Haze's thinking, and this perspective disturbs Haze not only because he sees his own physical deterioration in Layfield's ("He was so struck with how gaunt and thin he looked in the illusion that he stopped preaching," the narrative consciousness reports) but also because he instinctively senses his own falseness in his double's. It is Layfield's falseness—that he believes in Christ while preaching

3. See discussions *ibid.*, 256, Asals, *Flannery O'Connor*, 248–50, and Stuart L. Burns, "The Evolution of *Wise Blood*," *Modern Fiction Studies*, XVI (1970), 147–62.

otherwise—that most enrages Haze and drives him to murder his impostor. (Interestingly, Haze instinctively sees that Layfield is a follower of Christ, just as other characters see this in Haze.) "You ain't true," Haze accuses Layfield before he runs him down with his car. "What do you get up on top of a car and say you don't believe in what you do believe in for?" And a short while later, with Layfield lying on the road near death, Haze pokes him with his foot and says, "Two things I can't stand—a man that ain't true and one that mocks what is. You shouldn't ever have tampered with me if you didn't want what you got" (WB, 167, 203, 204).

Layfield's falseness, of course, mirrors Haze's, for Haze, though he does his best to resist it, has a burning awareness of Christ's presence in human history. Haze's questions to, and taunts of, Layfield therefore speak crucially to his own situation, calling to mind his own efforts to smother that part of him haunted by Christ. Haze recognizes almost immediately that Layfield, as a mirror image of himself and thus a disturbing reminder of the vision of Christ that underlies his own blasphemous preaching, poses a serious threat to his efforts to free himself from his fundamentalist vision. Rather than engaging this challenge in an interplay that would pressure him to open himself to other perspectives besides that of his own rage against Christ, Haze instead strikes out to silence the challenge by murdering Layfield. Haze's approach to others who challenge him in any serious way is embodied in this cold-blooded deed.

In his murder of Layfield, Haze assumes a position of dominance similar to that of the narrator, and indeed on one level becomes a disturbing double of the narrator. Both Haze and the narrator (with different ends, of course) are fired by a vision that embraces the fundamentalist imperative, and both use violent and extreme means to deliver their messages. Voices that call this vision into question are suppressed if not totally destroyed, and those unsettling doubles that threaten to reveal the true dimensions of the monologic visions of both figures come under particularly harsh attack. As a double to the narrator, Haze thus poses a significant threat, his rage and violence mirroring the narrator's and thus casting the narrator's vision into a new perspective. As Haze does with Layfield, so the narrator does with Haze: The narrator destroys what is seen as the false prophet—

"a man," in Haze's words, "that ain't true and one that mocks what is" (*WB*, 204), and a disturbing double of the narrator.

Haze's encounter with the policeman as he drives away from Taulkinham embodies the narrator's monologic attacks on Haze and on others who threaten the narrative vision. As an embodiment of the narrator, the patrolman polices the limits to which Haze may go, and he ultimately destroys Haze's attempt to flee from Christ. Ironically, the patrolman's actions clearly parallel those of Haze toward Layfield (both pursuers claim unquestioned authority over their unsuspecting victims, destroy their cars—the pulpits from which they preach— and drive them to violent confrontations with Christ), and this fact only intensifies the disturbing pressure that Haze exerts on the narrator.

In mirroring the narrator's monologic stance, Haze, like Julian in "Everything That Rises Must Converge," undermines the narrator's authoritative position and on one level turns the narrator's attacks back on the narrator. Haze's threat to the narrator thus arises more from this monologism than from his nihilism. Ironically, then, as the narrator's efforts to crush Haze intensify in order to affirm the fundamentalist vision and to become free of Haze's disturbing presence— one thinks in this regard of Haze's comment on Layfield's threat to him, "If you don't hunt it down and kill it, it'll hunt you down and kill you" (*WB*, 168)—so too the pressure and challenge on the narrator's authority intensify.

The narrator's efforts to affirm a Yahwist vision culminate in the novel's final chapter, after Haze has blinded himself and turned to Christ. On the obvious level of plot, the ending underscores the evil and misguided intentions of Haze's rebellion from Christ, showing him disavowing his old life and turning, with a vengeance, to Jesus. At Mrs. Flood's boarding house he lives an ascetic life of total commitment to Christ, including walking with glass- and rock-filled shoes and wearing barbed wire around his chest in an effort to atone for his sins. As he progressively withdraws from the world, Haze finds the basic needs of modern life—money, food, shelter—of little matter to him. He throws away any extra money he has at the end of the month from his government check, he eats little and cares not what, and he goes for his walks no matter how bad the weather and how poor his physical condition. The only thing that interests him is his intense interior search for Christ, a quest that eventually consumes his every thought and act. When Mrs. Flood suggests that he begin preaching again, Haze responds simply, "I don't have time" (*WB*, 221).

In all this the narrator portrays Haze as the fundamentalist hero— a person entirely given over to the life of Jesus, having abandoned the natural world. But here, too, the narrator's efforts are undermined by the very story told. In the final chapter of the novel, which relates Haze's life after his blinding, the narrator makes a bold step. The point of view shifts away from Haze (until now the point of view had essentially been one of limited omniscience, alternating between Haze and Enoch) to Haze's landlady, Mrs. Flood, who is until this point a very minor character. By transferring the point of view and thereby denying the reader access to Haze's mind, the narrator intensifies the mystery surrounding Haze and his self-mutilation. The narrator underscores the shocking force of Haze's blinding by keeping Haze silent about it, and instead turns the story over to Mrs. Flood, surely the most normal person in the novel; her efforts to understand the mystery of Haze and her emerging spiritual growth will ultimately reveal, the narrator hopes, the profound dimensions of Haze's religious self.

Mrs. Flood's relationship with Haze undergoes a dramatic deepening during his stay with her. At first their relationship is entirely economic—landlady and tenant—and Mrs. Flood's initial response to Haze's blinding is to evict him because he will not wear dark glasses over his disfigured eye sockets; she changes her mind when he offers to pay extra rent. Despite the fact that she wrings as much money from Haze as possible—she raises his room and board after she steams open one of his letters containing his monthly disability checks, and she picks up money that he drops—she nonetheless is nagged by the suspicion that he is cheating her. She is convinced that Haze blinded himself because he had some secret plan that promised great earthly reward, and she is determined to find out what that plan is. "Why had he destroyed his eyes and saved himself unless he had some plan, unless he saw something that he couldn't get without being blind to everything else?" the narrative consciousness reports her thinking. "She meant to find out everything she could about him" (*WB*, 216).

Mrs. Flood, however, can discover precious little about Haze, for he rarely speaks, and when he does his words frequently make no sense to her; they work on a level entirely alien to her own. When Haze, for instance, tells her he is not clean, Mrs. Flood responds by telling him to get a washwoman for his laundry. "That's not the kind of clean," Haze snaps back. Haze's bizarre habits further frustrate Mrs. Flood's probings. Yet in spite of her frustration (indeed, in part, because of it), Mrs. Flood finds herself mysteriously drawn to Haze, even to looking at his emasculated eyes, something she tells herself she does not like to do. At first Mrs. Flood resists her compulsion to study Haze's face—"If she didn't keep her mind going on something else when he was near her," the narrative consciousness reports, "she would find herself leaning forward, staring into his face as if she expected to see something she hadn't seen before"—but it is not long before she is spending most of her time on the front porch with Haze, occasionally talking to him (he remains for the most part silent) and always carefully observing him. "Watching his face had become a habit with her," the narrator writes; "she wanted to penetrate the darkness behind it and see for herself what was there" (*WB*, 224, 213, 225).

As the narrator's words suggest, Mrs. Flood has come to see, through her everyday dealings with Haze, that behind his bizarre acts and beneath his stony look there is less a drive for profit and fame (as she first had suspected) than a realm of unfathomable mystery that challenges and pressures her way of seeing things. Mrs. Flood prides herself on her common sense and literalism; she likes to see things clearly and unambiguously, without any shadows of complexity and without any extensions of meaning stretching beyond the here and now. "She liked the clear light of day," the narrative consciousness writes. "She liked to see things." The things that she sees and the life that she lives she evaluates entirely pragmatically, and she resists any system of order or belief that does otherwise. After telling Haze that he ought to try preaching again—a blind preacher with a Seeing Eye dog would really attract a good crowd, she says—she adds that she herself is not the religious sort. "I believe that what's right today is wrong tomorrow and that the time to enjoy yourself is now so long as you let others do the same," she says (*WB*, 218, 221).

But despite the strength of Mrs. Flood's will, Haze's presence jars her from her set ways, propelling her into a profound experience of otherness. Blindness suddenly becomes a terrifying reality, and she begins to ponder not only how Haze lives without sight but also how she would. At one point the narrative consciousness describes her thoughts:

She could not make up her mind what would be inside his head and what out. She thought of her own head as a switchbox where she controlled from; but with him, she could only imagine the outside in, the whole black world in his head and his head bigger than the world, his head big enough to include the sky and planets and whatever was or had been or would be. How would he know if time was going backwards or forwards or if he was going with it? She imagined it was like you were walking in a tunnel and all you could see was a pin point of light. She had to imagine the pin point of light; she couldn't think of it at all without that. She saw it as some kind of a star, like the star on Christmas cards. She saw him going backwards to Bethlehem and she had to laugh.

Her fascination with Haze grows as her probings—and her disorientation resulting from them—intensify. Soon she becomes entirely focused on Haze, ignoring everything else so that she can spend as much time as possible with him. Despite his rebuffs, she begins caring for him as she had not before—preparing him special meals, showing concern for his health and future, accompanying him on his walks. Finally she suggests that they get married; she is driven not only by her affection for him ("I've got a place for you in my heart, Mr. Motes," she tells him) but also by her deepening awareness, itself initiated by her relationship with Haze, of the emptiness of her life and the world. "If we don't help each other, Mr. Motes, there's nobody to help us," she says to Haze. "Nobody. The world is an empty place" (WB, 218–19, 227).

Haze rebuffs Mrs. Flood's offer for he knows that there is indeed somebody else to help—Jesus—and he has given his life entirely over to him. Like The Misfit in "A Good Man Is Hard to Find," Haze knows the fundamentalist imperative: One must choose either Christ or the Devil, and in selecting Christ one must give up all else. Haze is characteristically enigmatic with Mrs. Flood, not explaining his thoughts to her, and when he goes out for his walk, she is angry and hurt, and tells him he is no longer welcome in her house. But Mrs. Flood has changed too much to return to her old way of living without Haze, and she is terribly concerned when by that evening a driving storm rages and Haze has still not returned. She wants him back, and she wants to join him on his journey; she imagines finding him in the storm and telling him, "Mr. Motes, Mr. Motes, you can stay here forever, or the two of us will go where you're going, the two of us will go" (*WB*, 229).

Although she still does not know what drives Haze, Mrs. Flood now, more than ever, feels a need to be with him. So strong is her compulsion to share his life that she in a real sense becomes his double, pacing the floor as he had done and pondering blindness, a fate she now envisions for herself. As Haze was driven by his wise blood to seek Christ, so too Mrs. Flood is driven by hers to seek Haze. "If she was going to be blind when she was dead, who better to guide her than a blind man?" the narrative consciousness reports her thinking. "Who better to lead the blind than the blind, who knew what it was like?" Later, when Haze is brought back by the two policemen, Mrs. Flood, who does not realize that he is dead, stares into his face, where "the deep burned eye sockets seemed to lead into the dark tunnel where he had disappeared." She wants to understand Haze's mystery and to understand if indeed she has been cheated of anything (her old self here reasserting itself), but as she stares into his eyes, into the dark tunnel, she cannot see anything. In turning within by closing her eyes and (at least momentarily) becoming blind like Haze, however, she comes to a deeper understanding of Haze's—and perhaps her own—journey "backwards to Bethlehem": "She shut her eyes and saw the pin point of light but so far away that she could not hold it steady in her mind. She felt as if she were blocked at the entrance of something. She sat staring with her eyes shut, into his eyes, and felt as if she had finally got to the beginning of something she couldn't begin, and she saw him moving farther and farther away, farther and farther into the darkness until he was the pin point of light." The narrative consciousness has here brought Mrs. Flood if not to revelation, then to a point where the process leading to revelation may begin. Mrs. Flood now sees Haze as the pinpoint of light at the end of the tunnel of humanity's blind journey through life (recalling her earlier thoughts on blindness, where the point of light was like "some kind of a star, like the star on Christmas cards" [*WB*, 229, 231, 231–32, 219]). Haze, in other words, is the guiding light, the way to Bethlehem and redemption, and if Mrs. Flood feels "blocked at the entrance of something" and at "the beginning of something she couldn't begin," it is because she is not capable—at least at this point—of making the type of all-or-nothing commitment to Christ that Haze has made. She sees the way, but her selfish self, as has been noted, is still with her, and for the journey to begin she must leave it behind.

Wise Blood ends here, with Haze revealed as the guiding light of salvation (as O'Connor noted in a letter [July 9, 1955] to Ben Griffith, Haze finally emerges as "a kind of saint" [*HB*, 89]) and with Mrs. Flood's standing on the frontier between a life of selfish worldliness and one of Christian commitment. The narrative consciousness has in this final chapter celebrated Haze's fundamentalism without openly preaching it and has pointed the way for others to follow through the struggles of Mrs. Flood. On this surface level the novel thus affirms the stark fundamentalism from which the narrator has told the story and resolves the action within a framework of meaning marked most tellingly by the necessity of Christian commitment.

And yet the novel does not end so simply and neatly, for on one level the story of Mrs. Flood drastically undercuts the narrator's fundamentalism by ushering in an opposing religious viewpoint, one based not on the either-or choice for Christ or the Devil but on Christian charity. This view, as I have suggested earlier, is an integral component of O'Connor's Catholic vision, and one that frequently in her fiction goes head-to-head with her fundamentalism. Such a confrontation is what occurs in the final chapter of *Wise Blood*, for if Hazel Motes becomes a fundamentalist saint in his renunciation of the world for Christ, Mrs. Flood becomes his follower through Christian charity. At the heart of Mrs. Flood's progressive awareness of Haze's significance are both the compelling force of Haze's commitment and her growing charity toward him. Her commitment to Haze on one level parallels Haze's to Christ, yet it is also quite different, for hers is marked by a charitable concern for others in this world, whereas Haze has renounced this world and all its citizens for the next. While Mrs. Flood becomes more and more committed to Haze, Haze progressively cuts himself off from her, showing no concern for her spiritual welfare. Significantly, Mrs. Flood's final vision comes only after her betrayal of Haze—her telling him he is no longer welcome—has revealed to her the cruelty of that action and has opened the way for the growth of true charity. Charity, in other words, leads to vision and religious growth.

From this perspective, Mrs. Flood's final vision takes on new significance. Unlike Haze, who progressively cuts himself off from the here and now, Mrs. Flood remains in and of this world. Although she stands, as the narrator suggests, at "the beginning of something she couldn't begin"—that is, the fundamentalist religious commitment sworn to by Haze that carries him away from the everyday world and "farther and farther into the darkness" (*WB*, 232)—she nonetheless appears to be moving toward a religious commitment of an altogether different sort, less a withdrawal from than a reaching out to others. Her burgeoning charity that brings her to her final vision of Haze thus stands as an alternative to Haze's fundamentalism and severely undercuts its affirmation. The very structure of the novel supports this undoing, for it is Mrs. Flood's story as much as Haze's that ends the book, and it is she who survives and whose vision we last see. Haze may have become a star to lead the blind, but as Mrs. Flood's example suggests, he leads the blind not to a fundamentalist rejection of the world but to a charitable commitment to it.

Ultimately, then, the narrator's story of Mrs. Flood, meant to affirm Haze's and, by extension, the narrator's fundamentalism, actually undermines both. As in several of the stories already examined, the very action of the story pressures the authority of the narrator and calls the narrator's perspective into question. Interestingly, *Wise Blood*, generally accepted to be the work with O'Connor's harshest and fiercest narrative voice, also contains in its story some of the most severe criticism of that voice. For O'Connor, at this early stage in her career, such dynamics were particularly significant for artistic growth. Her use of a severe fundamentalist narrator allowed her to orient herself and her art, both grounded in her Catholic faith, around tension and dialogue with other perspectives rather than write from a rigidly monologic perspective that affirmed her Catholicism and suppressed all other voices. In this first attempt at using this narrative voice, O'Connor seems almost mesmerized by its force and power—a fact, I believe, that in part explains the narrator's ferocity. Yet as the author witnessing the narrator telling the story, O'Connor could also see the great pressure the story was exerting on the narrator, a pressure exposing the limits of the narrator's vision and testing his or her theology; and O'Connor could further see the redeeming powers of charity embodied in Mrs. Flood. Spurred to a higher level of awareness by her interactions with Haze, Mrs. Flood points the way to the dialogic growth that O'Connor would experience in her art, particularly in her interplays with her narrators, who, like Haze at the end of the novel, are driven by a rigid fundamentalism that shatters smugness and complacency.

Published eight years after *Wise Blood*, *The Violent Bear It Away* is very similar to it, particularly in terms of plot. Once again there is a central character, here the boy Tarwater, resisting a deeply felt and ingrained religious identity passed on to him during his upbringing. Like Haze, Tarwater is driven to violent extremes, including murder, to act out his rebellion; and like Haze, Tarwater, after a violent chastisement, eventually realizes his errors and wholeheartedly accepts his religious calling. Both novels, moreover, have a significant subplot that mirrors the main one: in *Wise Blood*, Enoch's devolution to his gorilla identity and in *The Violent Bear It Away*, Rayber's resistance to the religious seed both he and Tarwater carry in their deepest selves. Finally, the action of both novels, at least from the narrator's point of view, is meant to celebrate the emergence of the fundamentalist hero, the person who forsakes all else in a commitment to Christ.

The narrators of the two novels are also very similar, although there are some differences in terms of tone and emphasis. As in *Wise Blood*, the narrator of *The Violent Bear It Away* possesses a severe fundamentalist vision, one that creates in the novel a world where, in the words of the child evangelist Lucette Carmody, "the Word of God is a burning Word to burn you clean." Lucette's fierce sermon—"Are you deaf to the Lord's Word? The Word of God is a burning Word to burn you clean, burns man and child, man and child the same, you people! Be saved in the Lord's fire or perish in your own!" she shrieks—embodies the narrator's own perspective, as does the vision of Old Tarwater, the backwoods prophet who raises Tarwater. Just as the preaching of Haze's grandfather in *Wise Blood* defined the larger issues of the novel and, on a broad level, even sketched out its plot, so too, in *The Violent Bear It Away*, Old Tarwater's frenzied exhortations play the same role:

"Ignore the Lord Jesus as long as you can! Spit out the bread of life and sicken on honey. Whom work beckons, to work! Whom blood to blood! Whom lust to lust! Make haste, make haste. Fly faster and faster. Spin yourselves in a frenzy, the time is short! The Lord is preparing a prophet. The Lord is preparing a prophet with fire in his hand and eye and the prophet is moving toward the city with his warning. The prophet is coming with the Lord's message. 'Go warn the children of God,' saith the Lord, 'of the terrible speed of justice.' Who will be left? Who will be left when the Lord's mercy strikes?" (*VBIA*, 134, 134–35, 60)

Old Tarwater may keep a still, but like the whiskey priests in Graham Greene's fiction, he is nonetheless one of God's chosen, a "prophet" and "a natural Catholic" (*HB*, 407), as O'Connor wrote in a letter (September 13, 1960) to William Sessions. Old Tarwater's voice, as mirrored in, and spoken by, the narrator, tells the story and constructs the meanings of the novel. Even O'Connor, the Catholic author, was won over by the old man. "Old Tarwater is the hero of *The Violent Bear It Away*," O'Connor told Granville Hicks, "and I'm right behind him 100 per cent" (*CFO*, 83).

Although *Wise Blood* and *The Violent Bear It Away* share similar fundamentalist narrators, the two storytellers nonetheless use somewhat different techniques to get across their fundamentalist messages. The narrator in the second novel uses means, at least in terms of surface effects, that are less fierce and extreme and employs more familiar narrative conventions. Frederick Asals observes that *The Violent Bear It Away* is "a less wild, less totally dislocating and estranging work than its predecessor. The flat, external, and dehumanizing treatment of the characters and the starkly dramatized presentness of scene that marked the earlier book are gone; flashback, the stylized rendering of internal perception, and the shifting centers of consciousness place us in a more familiar fictional mode."[4] Yet this familiarity of narrative technique can be deceptive, for the fundamentalist vision underpinning *The Violent Bear It Away* is every bit as fierce as that of *Wise Blood*, and further, as I hope to show, there is in the end much less undercutting in O'Connor's second novel of this vision's force and power.

As in almost all of O'Connor's works, the action of *The Violent*

4. Asals, *Flannery O'Connor*, 162.

Bear It Away hinges on the fundamentalist choice demanding a commitment to Christ or the Devil. Both Tarwater's and Rayber's struggles center on this choice, but the choice has been significantly altered (until the end of the novel, that is, when it becomes clear that it has been operating all along)—here it is not Christ or the Devil, but Christ or the individual self, a choice much more modern in scope and emphasis. This restating of the fundamentalist imperative, though inherent in the action of the novel, occurs explicitly in the first chapter during one of Tarwater's conversations with his "friend," that strange voice that prods him to live guided solely by his own lights:

> The way I see it, he [Tarwater's friend] said, you can do one of two things. One of them not both. Nobody can do both things without straining themselves. You can do one thing or you can do the opposite.
>
> Jesus or the devil, the boy said.
>
> No no no, the stranger said, there ain't no such thing as a devil. I can tell you that from my own self-experience. I know that for a fact. It ain't Jesus or the devil. It's Jesus or *you*.

This crucial shift in terms defines the dilemmas that both Tarwater and Rayber see themselves facing: a life of commitment to Christ or one of individual freedom and self-sufficiency. Indeed the concept of freedom is crucial to the novel, with two basic interpretations of the term defining the choices facing Tarwater and Rayber. On the one hand there is personal freedom, the freedom to act on one's own and to do what one wants; on the other there is Old Tarwater's type of freedom—to be free in Christ and thus free from the grasp of the Devil. Old Tarwater articulates this choice to his nephew: "You were born into bondage and baptized into freedom, into the death of the Lord, into the death of the Lord Jesus Christ" (*VBIA*, 39, 20). Around this conflict the narrator creates the story—a story meant to reveal the destructive evil of personal freedom and the constructive necessity of freedom in Christ—focusing on the struggles of Rayber and Tarwater. Through describing their efforts to achieve "freedom," the narrator means to reveal the utter worthlessness of everything except one's relationship to Christ, and in the end to celebrate the fundamentalist hero and his vision.

Both Tarwater and Rayber came under the strong fundamentalist influence of Old Tarwater during their childhoods, and both are later haunted by his vision—to be free in Christ, not from Christ—when they set out in life on their own. Tarwater's education by his great-uncle has been complete, for he has spent his entire childhood living with Old Tarwater deep in the backwoods. Besides teaching the boy the fundamentals of reading, writing, and arithmetic, Old Tarwater has instilled in him a fundamentalist understanding of the world and history, "beginning with Adam expelled from the Garden and going on down through the presidents to Herbert Hoover and on in speculation toward the Second Coming and the Day of Judgment." More significant, he has raised the boy to be a prophet and has schooled him accordingly: "The old man, who said he was a prophet, had raised the boy to expect the Lord's call himself and to be prepared for the day he would hear it. He had schooled him in the evils that befall prophets; in those that come from the world, which are trifling, and those that come from the Lord and burn the prophet clean; for he himself had been burned clean and burned clean again. He had learned by fire." Tarwater sees it as a sure sign of his election that while other children suffer through school ("herded together in a room to cut out paper pumpkins under the direction of a woman," the narrative consciousness reports him thinking), he is "left free for the pursuit of wisdom, the companions of his spirit Abel and Enoch and Noah and Job, Abraham and Moses, King David and Solomon, and all the prophets, from Elijah who escaped death, to John whose severed head struck terror from a dish" (*VBIA*, 4, 5, 17).

Rayber's education by Old Tarwater was much briefer, but nonetheless significant. When Rayber was seven, Old Tarwater took him from his parents to his backwoods home, Powderhead, where he baptized him and instructed him in God's ways. Old Tarwater made sure that Rayber learned what he needed to in the four days the boy was with him. "He made him understand that his true father was the Lord and not the simpleton in town and that he would have to lead a secret life in Jesus until the day came when he would be able to bring the rest of his family around to repentance," the narrator writes. "He had made him understand that on the last day it would be his destiny to rise in glory in the Lord Jesus" (*VBIA*, 64).

Living with the knowledge instilled by Old Tarwater is no simple task, for it requires the fundamentalist commitment that devalues all else, and not surprisingly both Rayber and Tarwater rebel from his teaching. Rayber asserts his rebellion when he is fourteen, returning to Powderhead to tell Old Tarwater that none of what he had taught him was true. Yet, as becomes clear, Rayber still is, and will continue to be as an adult, haunted by his uncle's teachings; what Old Tarwater tells Tarwater about Rayber is absolutely true: "I planted the seed in him and it was there for good. Whether anybody liked it or not." Rayber puts it differently, in words addressed to Old Tarwater: "You pushed me out of the real world and I stayed out of it until I didn't know which was which. You infected me with your idiot hopes, your foolish violence" (*VBIA*, 67, 73).

To be free of his uncle—and of Christ—Rayber embraces a rationalism as fierce as his uncle's faith. Rayber's commitment is to modern-day Enlightenment thinking, particularly that concerning individual integrity and self-improvement. At the core of his thinking is a faith in the power and freedom of the individual will. At one point Rayber tells Old Tarwater that he has cured himself of the evils his uncle bore upon him. "I've straightened the tangle you made," he tells him. "Straightened it by pure will power. I've made myself straight." It is this celebration of the individual self and its self-sufficiency that leads Rayber to declare that the self must be its own savior. He tells Old Tarwater at one point to stay away from his retarded son, Bishop, because he is going to raise the boy his way. "He's going to be brought up to expect exactly what he can do for himself," he tells his uncle. "He's going to be his own saviour. He's going to be free!" At another point he likewise challenges his uncle to save himself. "You've got to be born again, Uncle," Rayber advises, "by your own efforts, back to the real world where there's no saviour but yourself." So, too, does Rayber challenge Tarwater, telling him, after Old Tarwater's death, that now, living with Rayber, he has "a chance to develop into a useful man" and to live a life of his own making and not of his great-uncle's, "whatever idiocy it was." Elsewhere he tells Tarwater that he should choose the way he himself has chosen: "It's the way you take as a result of being born again the natural way—through your own efforts. Your intelligence" (*VBIA*, 73, 70, 76, 92, 195).

For Rayber freedom means control—controlling one's emotions and actions and controlling other people, by bringing everything to bear under the fierce rule of rational thinking. To keep in check what he sees as an irrational love for creation and its divine creator—a burden he sees passed on to him by Old Tarwater—he lives a life of severe discipline that, as the narrator observes, is rigidly ascetic: "He did not look at anything too long, he denied his senses unnecessary satisfactions. He slept in a narrow iron bed, worked sitting in a straight-backed chair, ate frugally, spoke little, and cultivated the dullest for friends. At his high school he was the expert on testing. All his professional decisions were prefabricated and did not involve his participation. He was not deceived that this was a whole or a full life, he only knew that it was the way his life had to be lived if it were going to have any dignity at all." Keeping his rationalism intact by smothering all other voices from within and without is for Rayber to be free; it is a freedom that, as the previous citation suggests, comes at a dear cost. Its driving force is a rigid monologism that celebrates the rational self above all else and so closes Rayber off from the multiplicity of his own interior life and that of the world around him. "To feel nothing was peace," the narrator reports him thinking, and "this indifference was the most that human dignity could achieve" (*VBIA*, 114, 200).

Rayber's monologism is clearly evident in his interaction with others. Rayber has little concern for other people except in how he can engineer their lives to be like his—lives of rationalism. Guided by his own insights into human psychology, he believes he thoroughly understands all others. Not long after Tarwater shows up at his house, Rayber already is completely confident that he knows the boy's dilemmas: "He understood that the boy was held in bondage by his great-uncle, that he suffered a terrible false guilt for burning and not burying him, and he saw that he was engaged in a desperate heroic struggle to free himself from the old man's ghostly grasp." He tells Tarwater later, "You're eaten up with false guilt. I can read you like a book!" Rayber had years earlier also believed he could read Old Tarwater, and under the pretense of charity had invited him to live at his home so he could observe him and write an article about what he saw as his religious fixation. Of Old Tarwater he wrote: "His fixation of being called by the Lord had its origin in insecurity. He needed the assurance of a call, and so he called himself" (*VBIA*, 106, 174, 19).

Rayber's reductive psychology embodies his own monologic stance: Because he possesses so much wisdom, others have nothing to offer him and are of no significance except as problems to be solved. In this respect he resembles Sheppard in "The Lame Shall Enter First" in that both men see themselves as modern-day Christ figures, shepherds not of humanity's spiritual life but of its social and psychological well-being. Such efforts at control can be seen in Rayber's interactions with both Old Tarwater and Tarwater, as well as in the engineering of the relationship of his sister and her lover, a relationship that ends with her death in an accident and his suicide. Ultimately these efforts represent Rayber's profound attempt at subjectifying all reality. He wants to signify and evaluate all experience according to his own subjective vision; he wants, in other words, to draw in and enclose all experience within his own rational mind. Such domination is what Old Tarwater experiences when he reads the article about himself written by Rayber: "He felt he was tied hand and foot inside the schoolteacher's head, a space as bare and neat as the cell in the asylum, and was shrinking, drying up to fit it. His eyeballs swerved from side to side as if he were pinned in a straight jacket again. Jonah, Ezekiel, Daniel, he was at that moment all of them—the swallowed, the lowered, the enclosed." This domination by Rayber is what Old Tarwater warns young Tarwater about, telling him that if he were to go live with Rayber, "the first thing he would do would be to test your head and tell you what you were thinking and howcome you were thinking it and what you ought to be thinking instead. And before long you wouldn't belong to your self no more, you would belong to him" (VBIA, 76, 56).

Although Rayber portrays himself as confident and sure in his rationalism, he is wracked by the fundamentalist knowledge given to him by Old Tarwater, a knowledge he considers utterly irrational and destructive. Through his asceticism, Rayber strives to keep this in-burnt knowledge suppressed, for when it surfaces, as it occasionally and unexpectedly does (often stemming from his feelings for Bishop, his retarded son), his life tumbles into disorder. The fundamentalist vision that then wracks him is an all-consuming and all-demanding love for creation:

It was love without reason, love for something futureless, love that appeared to exist only to be itself, imperious and all demanding, the kind that would cause him to make a fool of himself in an instant. And it only began with Bishop. It began with Bishop and then like an avalanche covered everything his reason hated. He always felt with it a rush of longing to have the old man's eyes—insane, fish-coloured, violent with their impossible vision of a world transfigured—turned on him once again. The longing was like an undertow in his blood dragging him backwards to what he knew to be madness.

Maintaining his stability, Rayber knows, depends on keeping Bishop with him, for, as the narrative consciousness tells us, "he could control his terrifying love as long as it had its focus in Bishop, but if anything happened to the child, he would have to face it in itself. The whole world would become his idiot child" (*VBIA*, 113–114, 182). Rayber, in simple terms, sees his mind split into two parts—the rational and the violent—and he does everything in his power to bring the violence of his fundamentalism under rational control. His struggles are not unlike those of Hazel Motes in *Wise Blood*.

Tarwater's struggles against his great-uncle's fundamentalism are every bit as intense as Rayber's. When Old Tarwater dies, Tarwater finds himself in a position wholly new in that he is now on his own and can live however he wants. He is pulled in two directions, toward a life of freedom in Christ and a life of individual freedom. His dilemma focuses on Old Tarwater's demands on him: Raised as the prophet to take over after Old Tarwater's death, Tarwater has been given the responsibility of baptizing Bishop. Tarwater is perfectly aware of the life that awaits him should he take up his calling:

He only knew, with a certainty sunk in despair, that he was expected to baptize the child he saw and begin the life his great-uncle had prepared him for. He knew that he was called to be a prophet and that the ways of prophecy would not be remarkable. His black pupils, glassy and still, reflected depth on depth his own stricken image of himself, trudging into the distance in the bleeding stinking mad shadow of Jesus, until at last he received his reward, a broken fish, a multiplied loaf. The Lord out of dust had created him, had made him blood and nerve and mind, had made him to bleed and weep and think, and set him in a world of loss and fire all to baptize one idiot child that He need not have created in the first place and to cry out a gospel just as foolish.

As the final words indicate, a part of Tarwater keenly resists his prophetic calling. He knows, as the narrative consciousness reports elsewhere, that "in the darkest, most private part of his soul, hanging upsidedown like a sleeping bat, was the certain undeniable knowledge that he was not hungry for the bread of life" (*VBIA*, 91–92, 21).

Tarwater initiates his rebellion from his great-uncle not long after his death; goaded on by his "friend" or "stranger," a voice that counsels him to get out from the yoke of Old Tarwater and be himself, Tarwater does not finish burying his great-uncle, burns down the farmhouse, and lights out for the city. So begins his quest for self-fulfillment, a quest that will take him to Rayber's house and then back to Powderhead. His struggle is similar to Rayber's in that he strives to silence the voice of Old Tarwater, but he opposes the old man's fundamentalism less with modern rationalism than with a fierce breed of American individualism, the kind lived by Huckleberry Finn, a figure Tarwater in many respects closely resembles. Along the way Tarwater encounters a number of people offering him advice on how he should go about living, and it is in large part from his interactions with these others—who challenge and pressure him—that the boy gains the perspective finally to solve his central dilemma.

One of the people Tarwater must contend with is Rayber, who, as I have said, counsels him to forget all that Old Tarwater taught him and instead to be his own savior. Another figure who offers Tarwater similar advice is the voice that begins counseling Tarwater immediately after his great-uncle's death. The central thrust of this voice's thinking is a celebration of complete individual freedom, with the self free from all constraints and control by others. "Be like me young fellow," the voice tells him at one point, "don't let no jackasses tell you what to do." And early on in the first conversation with Tarwater, as I pointed out earlier, the voice changes the fundamentalist imperative of choosing Christ or the Devil to that of choosing Christ or the individual. Tarwater immediately picks up on the stranger's spirit, muttering to himself in its voice as he digs Old Tarwater's grave and thinks about his great-uncle's demands for burial: "You can't be any poorer than dead. He'll have to take what he gets. Nobody to bother me, he thought. Ever. No hand uplifted to hinder me from anything; except the Lord's and He ain't said anything. He ain't even noticed me yet" (*VBIA*, 166, 24).

Most spirited are the voice's attacks on Old Tarwater and his stance as prophet. The stranger speaks of Old Tarwater as utterly foolish, even crazy, and he says that as a prophet, all Old Tarwater did was condemn the faults of others while ignoring his own. "That's all a prophet is good for—to admit somebody else is an ass or a whore," he tells the boy, and a bit later he lashes out at Old Tarwater's own eccentric life: "A prophet with a still! He's the only prophet I ever heard of making liquor for a living." The voice tells Tarwater that he was tricked by his great-uncle, that the only reason Old Tarwater brought him to Powderhead was so there would be somebody around to give him a proper burial. The voice adds that Tarwater's life has been thoroughly stunted by his living in the backwoods alone for fourteen years with a fanatic. "You could have been a city slicker for the last fourteen years," he says to the boy (*VBIA*, 40, 45, 46).

According to the stranger, Old Tarwater's death gives Tarwater the opportunity to achieve his personal liberation, and he urges the boy to leave Powderhead and forget his great-uncle's teachings. During Tarwater's stay with Rayber, the voice continually calls into question Tarwater's own religious calling; using a starkly literalist, show-me attitude, he challenges Tarwater on the certainty of God's plans for the boy. "The Lord speaks to prophets personally and He's never spoke to you," the voice says to Tarwater, "never lifted a finger, never dropped a gesture." He suggests that the boy demand a sign from God—not any sign, but "an unmistakable sign, not a pang of hunger or a reflection of himself in a store window, but an unmistakable sign, clear and suitable—water bursting forth from a rock, for instance, fire sweeping down at his command and destroying some site he would point to, such as the tabernacle he had gone to spit on" (*VBIA*, 161, 162). Throughout Tarwater's struggles the stranger urges the boy not to baptize Bishop, and at the lake he goads Tarwater to drown him.

The other significant character offering advice and perspective to Tarwater—though not spoken to him specifically—is the child evangelist Lucette Carmody. Lucette burns with fundamentalist rage, and her message and zeal echo Old Tarwater's (and the narrator's). For Tarwater, seeing and hearing Lucette is particularly significant because her role as child prophet mirrors his own potential vocation. Seeing her is thus seeing a version of himself—the version that Old Tarwater meant him to be. Tarwater is clearly shaken by Lucette, as is Rayber, who also sees himself in her (although from his perspective he and the girl are both child victims of religious fanatics).

Like Rayber, Tarwater focuses most of his energies into resisting the fundamentalist imperative—for him, the specific task of baptizing Bishop. Besides the vision of his great-uncle and the presence of

Lucette Carmody, Tarwater finds the greatest force in favor of the call to religious fanaticism to be the strange, brooding silence that seems to surround him. "It was a strange waiting silence," the narrative consciousness writes. "It seemed to lie all around him like an invisible country whose border he was always on the edge of, always in danger of crossing." This silence is the larger realm of the spirit, the embodiment of the stark Yahwist vision of a fierce God overlooking all. Tarwater feels its presence everywhere, but most strikingly on clear nights when the stars "seemed to be holes in his skull through which some distant unmoving light was watching him. It was as if he were alone in the presence of an immense silent eye" (*VBIA*, 160, 85). The silent eye of God—and, one surmises, of the narrator, whose fundamentalism looms behind the world he or she creates—demands that Tarwater baptize Bishop and take up his religious calling.

Eventually both Rayber and Tarwater must have one final and absolute confrontation with the fundamentalist demands they carry within them. Rayber had tried to deny once and for all his fundamentalist self when he attempted to drown Bishop, an act of defiance not only against God (whose presence and likeness Rayber sees imaged in the retarded boy) but also against that all-consuming and irrational love that Bishop at times evokes in Rayber. But Rayber fails in his act, realizing during the attempt that Bishop somehow controls that love by keeping it focused. His life with the boy is thus one of taut balance, with Rayber, through his asceticism, attempting to keep his religious urges in check. His ultimate confrontation with these feelings comes when Tarwater drowns Bishop, for now he must confront the world and his surging irrational love without Bishop to control this love. To Rayber's surprise, however, no such feelings emerge; so intent has his fight against the fundamentalist imperative been, so withdrawn from life has he become, that he has won. ("He told himself that he was indifferent even to his own dissolution," the narrative consciousness reports him thinking. "It seemed to him that this indifference was the most human dignity could achieve. . . . To feel nothing was peace.") But in winning he is left with exactly what his life has become—nothing—and contrary to his earlier belief, feeling nothing is not peace: "He stood waiting for the raging pain, the intolerable hurt that was his due, to begin, so that he could ignore it, but he continued to feel nothing. He stood light-headed at the window and it was not until he realized there would be no pain that he collapsed" (*VBIA*, 200, 203). Such is Rayber's victory over his wise blood.

If Rayber defeats Old Tarwater and his fundamentalism—and in so doing is reduced to nothing, a man who has lost his soul—Tarwater believes that he achieves such a victory when he drowns Bishop. Although the words of baptism slip from his mouth as he drowns the boy, Tarwater sees them as just that—a slip, their significance nullified by the violent murder. He views the drowning as the ultimate repudiation of Old Tarwater and the beginning of his life of complete personal freedom. The narrative consciousness reports Tarwater's thoughts: "It was as no boy that he returned. He returned tried in the fire of his refusal, with all the old man's fancies burnt out of him, with all the old man's madness smothered for good, so that there was never any chance that it would break out in him. He had saved himself forever from the fate he had envisioned when, standing in the schoolteacher's hall and looking into the eyes of the dim-witted child, he had seen himself trudging off into the distance in the bleeding stinking mad shadow of Jesus, lost forever to his own inclinations" (*VBIA*, 220–21). But despite his claims otherwise, Tarwater has not won his battle; he is still wracked by his fierce hunger, still haunted by the ghostly figure of himself as mad prophet, still surrounded by invisible country. His fate yet awaits him.

Tarwater's final revelation, ushering in his ultimate identity and fate, comes after his rape by the homosexual (an obvious embodiment of the voice of Tarwater's friend, as is Meeks, the copper flue salesman who earlier also gave Tarwater a ride). The rape propels Tarwater out of the realm of everyday concerns and into the faraway country of Christ and the spirit; rather than resisting his prophetic destiny, he now rushes to it, returning to Powderhead to receive his revelation:

He felt his hunger no longer as a pain but as a tide. He felt it rising in himself through time and darkness, rising through the centuries, and he knew that it rose in a line of men whose lives were chosen to sustain it, who would wander in the world, strangers from that violent country where the silence is never broken except to shout the truth. He felt it building from the blood of Abel to his own, rising and engulfing him. It seemed in one instant to lift and turn him. He whirled toward the treeline. There, rising and spreading in the night, a red-gold tree of fire ascended as if it would consume the darkness in one tremendous burst of flame. The boy's breath went out to meet it. He knew that this was the fire that had encircled Daniel, that had raised Elijah from the earth, that had spoken to Moses and would in the instant speak to him. He threw himself to the ground and with his face against the dirt of the grave, he heard the command. GO WARN THE CHILDREN OF GOD OF THE TERRIBLE SPEED OF MERCY. The words were as silent as seeds opening one at a time in his blood. (*VBIA*, 242)

The novel ends with Tarwater's heeding the command, leaving Powderhead to return to the city as a prophet on his divine mission.

This final chapter, in which Tarwater returns to Powderhead, is some of the most exalted writing in O'Connor's fiction. Tarwater's acceptance of the fundamentalist imperative is celebrated in a language that suggests a significance extending far beyond the everyday. Early in the chapter the narrator writes that as Tarwater looks down a long hill at Powderhead, he "might have been Moses glimpsing the promised land" (*VBIA*, 236), and the language's tone and suggestiveness build from there. In many ways this celebratory final chapter is a fitting conclusion for the novel, as the thrust of the work has been moving relentlessly toward an affirmation of the fundamentalist path and the destruction of all others. By the end of the novel the other significant perspectives on reality seen in the work—Rayber's intellectualism and Tarwater's friend's ultimate freedom—have been thoroughly undercut. Rayber's intellectualism is revealed to be empty and meaningless, its abstract strictures and orderings of reality prohibiting any meaningful contact with self and others. The stranger's ideal of freedom leads in the end to a way of life embodied in the homosexual rapist—a thorough disregard for the welfare of others in a destructive pursuit of gratification. One thinks in this regard of The Misfit's words in "A Good Man Is Hard to Find"—"No pleasure but meanness" (*CS*, 132). The alternative (the only alternative in the eyes of the narrator) is the way of Old Tarwater, Lucette Carmody, and the narrator—a life that embraces the essential fundamentalist commitment. This is what Tarwater discovers after his rape, and thereafter he ceases all resistance to his religious calling. "He knew that he could not turn back now," the narrative consciousness writes. "He knew that his destiny forced him on to a final revelation" (*VBIA*, 233).

With this ending, and in the destruction of the alternative visions, the narrator seeks to create a novel that thoroughly justifies his or her starkly religious vision. If, returning to John Hawkes's observations on O'Connor's demonism, the narrator's voice is demonic in the sense of trying to destroy the pretensions of human rationality, it is not demonic in the sense of being a ravisher of souls. That demonism, the narrator makes clear, comes in the voice of Tarwater's friend and its several embodiments. By portraying this truly demonic voice— "That voice . . . is the Tempter, the Devil" (*HB*, 375), O'Connor wrote (February 14, 1960) to Elizabeth Fenwick Way—the narrator reveals what true demonism really is and in so doing suggests the great distance its vision stands from the narrator's. By underscoring the differences between the visions of Tarwater's friend and the narrator, the narrator thus discounts whatever similarities one might otherwise see in their shared violent means. The narrator thus draws the focus to the ends to which such violence is put.

The violence of the fundamentalist vision—its distortion, its willfulness, its single-mindedness that closes off a good deal of reality, its lack of charity—is thus affirmed in its opposition to the demonic voice, the taker of souls. Moreover, the violence of fundamentalism is shown to be necessary in the struggle for spiritual salvation. Given the fierceness of modern rationalism and the tenacity of individual freedom (seen, respectively, in the resistance to God's word by Rayber and Tarwater), violence, the novel says, is the only way to propel people to look beyond their narrow visions. As the very title of the novel (drawn from Matthew 11:12, "From the days of John the Baptist until now, the kingdom of heaven suffereth violence, and the violent bear it away") indicates, it is the violent—the violent fundamentalists, whose fierce commitment to Christ carries them beyond a life centered in the here and now—who bear away the kingdom of heaven.

The power of the narrative voice and its message is overwhelming in *The Violent Bear It Away*, and there is very little resistance to it. The ideal of Christian charity, significant to O'Connor's Catholic vision and present in a number of her works as a counterforce to fundamentalist rage, receives very little emphasis. The character who seems to suggest a more charitable and less extreme form of Christian vigor—Buford Munson—is a minor character whose presence does little to alter the fundamentalist thrust of the novel. Buford, who chides Tarwater for his failure to bury his great-uncle and who completes the task when Tarwater leaves, can merely back away, awestruck, from the consuming power of Tarwater's vision at the end of the novel. "The Negro trembled and felt suddenly a pressure on him too great to bear," the narrative consciousness writes. "He sensed it as a burning in the atmosphere. His nostrils twitched. He muttered something and turned his mule around and moved off, across the back field and down to the woods" (*VBIA*, 241). In the face of Tarwater's visionary presence even Buford is helpless; Tarwater's fundamentalism, not Buford's charity, reigns supreme and closes the novel.

If the narrative itself contains the seeds of destruction of the narrator's perspective, they come in the presence of Tarwater, particularly in the terrible cost to his selfhood inflicted by the assumption of his prophetic role. In a letter (August 4, 1962) to Roslyn Barnes, O'Connor wrote that "this is surely what it means to bear away the kingdom of heaven with violence: the violence is directed inward" (*HB*, 486), and such inwardly directed violence is what Tarwater inflicts upon himself. As Frederick Asals and Josephine Hendin have pointed out, Tarwater's religious destiny entails a pyschic mutilation—in Asals's words, "the fiery extirpation of the rational self"—that alienates him not only from the rest of the world but from the confines of his self.[5] By the end of the novel Tarwater is less a reasoning being than a boy consumed by the spirit (which has consumed his self) and driven to his destiny by the all-powerful force of an omnipotent God. For the narrator and that part of O'Connor given to fundamentalism, such a fate is Tarwater's glory; for those of less extreme persuasion, the victory is in all likelihood less clear.

Tarwater's loss of rational self has potentially disturbing implications for the narrator, whose fundamentalist vision is driven by the same forces that compel Tarwater. Like Tarwater at the end—and indeed like Old Tarwater and Lucette Carmody—the narrator is entirely closed off from rational thinking. Rather than engaging modern rationalism, testing and pressuring it to ascertain its values and limits, the narrator sets out in the novel to destroy it utterly. Rayber is shown to be empty and evil, and the Devil, seen in Tarwater's friend, speaks by and large in words of common sense and reasonableness (given that one views the world in secular terms). This rejection of reasoning and rationality on one level signals the victory of the fundamentalist vision, but on another it signals the monologic rejection of

5. *Ibid.*, 192; Josephine Hendin, *The World of Flannery O'Connor* (Bloomington, 1970), 59–60.

the true dialogic interplay between voices outside the self that is necessary for this victory. This fierce fundamentalist monologism is mirrored in Rayber's equally fierce rejection of the fundamentalist vision, and one of Rayber's most damning faults—that he manipulates people and engineers relationships for reasons other than charity—is precisely what the narrator does with the characters in the novel. If the narrator is charitable, it is only in the sense that in these dark days charity means cutting with the sword of Christ.

In some of O'Connor's other works where the religious issues are not so overt and riveting, the revelation of the monologic drive of the narrator (mirrored in the characters he or she attacks) and the narrator's extirpation of the rational self would thoroughly undermine his or her authority. This is what we saw, for instance, in "Everything That Rises Must Converge," discussed in the previous chapter. But in *The Violent Bear It Away*, where the narrator clearly draws the lines between Christ and the Devil, elevating the work to the level of the anagogic by openly suggesting that ultimate matters are at stake in Tarwater's struggles, such criticism of the narrator is deflected, itself undercut by the very force of the narrative voice.

Ultimately, then, the compelling force of the narrative voice carries the day; it is indeed the violent who bear it—if not the kingdom of heaven, then at least this novel—away. O'Connor herself as author, I would conjecture, was in this novel carried away too, her more charitable Catholic vision overwhelmed by her fundamentalist fanaticism. "The modern reader will identify himself with the schoolteacher," she wrote (September 13, 1959) to John Hawkes, expressing her own sympathies, "but it is the old man [Old Tarwater] who speaks for me" (*HB*, 350).

5

The Challenge of the Characters

In the previous two chapters we have focused our attention on O'Connor's narrator, and most particularly on the intense and complex dynamics that develop both between the narrator and the story told and between the narrator and the author, whose presence stands alongside, and in active interaction with, the work and its teller. We have seen how the narrator's stark fundamentalism, a decidedly monologic vision, is frequently pressured tellingly by the narrative told; characters the narrator sets out to expose and punish actually achieve the same end for the narrator, since their monologism on one level mirrors the storyteller's own. The dismantling of the narrator's monologism also profoundly affects the author, for it not only reveals the shortcomings of the fundamentalist vision with which a part of O'Connor was closely identified but also challenges her to free herself further from any temptation toward monologism, most obviously that demanded by the Catholic Church.

As we saw in the first chapter, O'Connor believed that to view reality only with the eyes of the Church was to ignore a large part of existence—that part that on the surface, at least, appeared to have little to do with the life of the Church. She argued that the best Catholic writers were those who saw with both their own eyes and the Church's, and did their best to work with the resulting tensions. "If the Catholic writer hopes to reveal mysteries, he will have to do it by describing truthfully what he sees from where he is," O'Connor wrote. "A purely affirmative vision cannot be demanded of him without limiting his freedom to observe what man has done with the things of God" (*CFO*, 48).

O'Connor was pressured not only by the narrator but also, as the narrator was, by the narrative, and particularly by the characters and their interactions. (O'Connor returned a pressure of her own as well.) Bakhtin frequently discusses this dynamic between author and characters, and he argues that in the best fiction characters exert profound pressure on the author. Through their value systems and points of view—Bakhtin would say their ideologies—characters introduce into the story or novel different perspectives and ways of seeing that, if not immediately rejected outright by the author in an act of monologic control, pressure the author's own perspective by dialogically interacting with it. In this situation the author is not wholly detached from the work but is actively participating in it. Brought into contact and intersection with other consciousnesses, the author engages them in what Bakhtin calls an activity "of a special *dialogic* sort"—"a questioning, provoking, answering, agreeing, objecting activity" that in its working out transforms the author's perspective. This dialogic growth involves not the renouncing of the author's views but the reworking of them; the author, writes Bakhtin, "must to an extraordinary extent broaden, deepen and rearrange [his or her] consciousness (to be sure, in a specific direction) in order to accommodate the autonomous consciousnesses of others."[1]

Bakhtin's observations speak tellingly to O'Connor's situation as an author who stands on the threshold of a number of various and charged consciousnesses. If her characters are not always entirely autonomous (O'Connor, through the narrator, has a tendency to manipulate her characters for religious ends; this tendency, mentioned in passing in previous chapters, will be explored fully in the next chapter on O'Connor and her audience), they nonetheless embody strong aspects of herself, as does the narrator's fundamentalism. By objectifying in Bakhtinian terms these internally persuasive voices, making them (in most cases) full-fledged consciousnesses in their own right, O'Connor frees herself from their control and gains perspective on their dimensions. In this way she sees aspects of herself from a perspective outside herself; she places these internal voices in situations that test and reveal their validity and authority. Likewise, these voices, liberated from O'Connor's consciousness, pressure

1. Bakhtin, *Problems of Dostoevsky's Poetics*, 285, 68.

O'Connor's authorial perspective in new and challenging ways. Making this dynamic even more complex—and lively—is the fact that in projecting aspects of herself into her characters, she sees herself through both her own eyes and those of the fundamentalist narrator; that is, from her essentially Catholic authorial perspective, she observes aspects of herself being shaped and judged by her own severe fundamentalist self. As she herself puts it in a letter (May 19, 1957) to Cecil Dawkins, she views her characters "from a standard of judgment from which they fall short," and this standard, she says later in the letter, "is what Tillich calls 'the ultimate concern'" (HB, 221).

In this dialogic interplay, then, O'Connor's characters are on one level refracted doubles of herself—refracted in that they embody specific dimensions of herself and that they are placed in contexts outside of O'Connor's consciousness that pressure and define their significance. Such refraction is at the heart of O'Connor's comments in a letter (November 14, 1959) to A. on Tarwater in *The Violent Bear It Away*: She says that Tarwater is neither a caricature nor a monster and that "I feel that in his place I would have done everything he did. Tarwater is made up of my saying: what would I do here?" (HB, 358). O'Connor's observation here is powerfully suggestive. With Tarwater, O'Connor bodies forth, one surmises, her own religious rebelliousness and, further, dramatically works out in his escapades the significance and authority of these feelings. Tarwater, it is clear, is not to be read as O'Connor, but as a version of her, a refracted version in a refracted context. What O'Connor herself learns from Tarwater is suggested in her comment in "The Catholic Novelist in the Protestant South" on the southern Catholic writer's affinities with religious fanatics: "These people in the invisible Church make discoveries that have meaning for us who are better protected from the vicissitudes of our own natures, and who are often too lazy and satisfied to make any discoveries at all" (MM, 207–208).

O'Connor frequently (but not entirely consistently) argued that artistic creation involved, besides technical skill, a good deal of self-exploration, and the dialogic challenge posed by her characters (including the narrator) was perhaps the most striking means for this growth and self-discovery. In "Some Aspects of the Grotesque in Southern Fiction," O'Connor writes that for a writer to understand the depth and dynamics of his or her fiction, "he will have to descend far enough into himself to reach those underground springs that give life to his work." This descent, she adds, "will, at the same time, be a descent into his region"—a descent, in other words, that reveals that the writer's inner self or selves are integrally bound up in the life of his or her home country. And for the writer, the life of the region— the life that the writer explores in fiction—embodies the artist's inner life in ways that alter vision and perspective. Continuing her discussion, O'Connor writes that the artist's descent into self/region carries the writer "through the darkness of the familiar world into a world where, like the blind man cured in the gospels, he sees men as if they were trees, but walking" (*MM*, 50). These mysterious figures that the writer sees, it might be understood, are the different selves of the writer, now given a life of their own in the fictional characters of the work.

To argue that O'Connor gave voice to her inner selves in the lives of her characters (in "The Catholic Novelist in the Protestant South" she quotes Conrad's saying that the artist "descends within himself, and in that region of stress and strife, if he be deserving and fortunate, he finds his terms of appeal") is not to suggest that she consciously wrote a story with this goal specifically in mind. Creating art, of course, is never that simple or formulaic—that is, if it is any good. Nor is art, as O'Connor wrote in "The Nature and Aim of Fiction," entirely "sunk in the self"; rather it is a give-and-take between the inner and outer worlds whereby a perspective built on the tension between the two ultimately ends up illuminating both. At times O'Connor downplayed the significance of art's role in the artist's self-discovery, saying that writers should simply start with a character—"a real personality, a real character," she says in "Writing Short Stories" (*MM*, 196, 82, 106)—and see what happens. But as O'Connor surely knew, no choice of character is entirely innocent, and it is clear from the pattern of characters that continually appear in her fiction— independent women, proud intellectuals, zealous prophet-freaks, struggling artists, to name some—that she wrote about certain types of characters not only because she could make them live but also because, in their hidden if not surface selves, they expressed some aspect of her own teeming personality.

For O'Connor, then, fiction had the potential for opening up the confines of the writer's conscious self and paving the way for an understanding of the deeper selves that battled for authority. In a letter (December 11, 1956) to A., O'Connor wrote that it was better for writers to discover than to impose meaning; she added that "nothing you write will lack meaning because the meaning is in you" (HB, 188). The meaning, she suggested in "The Nature and Aim of Fiction," embodies the artist's deepest selves, "its source in a realm much larger than that which [the writer's] conscious mind can encompass" and its expression in a work of literature always "a greater surprise to him than it can ever be to his reader" (MM, 83). Such revelations, she suggested further in an interview with C. Ross Mullins, Jr., not only reveal but shape the artist's self. "I suppose it's about fifty-fifty as to whether you create it or it creates you," she told Mullins, referring to the author and his or her work. "If it's a good story it's as much a revelation to you as it is to the reader" (CFO, 106–107).

By shattering the stronghold of the conscious mind, fiction drastically undermines whatever pretensions writers might have concerning their wholeness and completeness and as such is frequently a humbling, if not terrifying, experience. Only partly in jest did O'Connor write (March 24, 1956) to A. that her friend was able to see things in O'Connor's stories that she herself could not because "if I did see I would be too frightened to write [the stories]" (HB, 149). O'Connor in all likelihood knew the depths to which her art was taking her and did not, her claim notwithstanding, shy away from whatever disturbing knowledge she found there. To refuse to acknowledge what her art was telling her would be to shirk her responsibility as an artist and would weaken her art. "The more we learn about ourselves, the deeper into the unknown we push the frontiers of fiction," O'Connor wrote in "Novelist and Believer," suggesting the inextricable tie that binds self-knowledge and art; and to push back the frontiers, of both self-awareness and fiction, demanded effort and humility. "Art never responds to the wish to make it democratic; it is not for everybody; it is only for those who are willing to undergo the effort to understand it," O'Connor wrote in "Catholic Novelists and Their Readers," in words that speak to both writer and reader. "We hear a great deal about humility being required to lower oneself, but it requires an equal humility and a real love of truth to raise oneself and by hard labor to acquire higher standards" (MM, 165, 189).

Raising oneself means knowing oneself, and knowing oneself

means acknowledging one's many internal voices and recognizing that any attempt to assume a superior and monologic stance toward others closes oneself off from reality and belies the common identity of poverty and limitation that one shares with all humanity. The writer of fiction, says O'Connor, including herself, finds great satisfaction in writing about the poor—she cites in "The Teaching of Literature" Rudyard Kipling's observation that the writer should not chase the poor from his or her doorstep—not only because they have less to shield them from the raw forces of life but also, and more important, because their material poverty symbolizes the essential poverty of humanity. "When anyone writes about the poor in order merely to reveal their material lack, then he is doing what the sociologist does, not what the artist does," writes O'Connor in "The Teaching of Literature." "The poverty he writes about is so essential that it needn't have anything at all to do with money." But even beyond subject matter—seeing one's own poverty in that of others— O'Connor argues that the very act of fiction ultimately leads writers to a recognition of their fundamental poverty. In this same essay she explains: "The novelist writes about what he sees on the surface, but his angle of vision is such that he begins to see before he gets to the surface and he continues to see after he has gone past it. He begins to see in the depths of himself, and it seems to me that his position there rests on what must certainly be the bedrock of all human experience—the experience of limitation or, if you will of poverty" (MM, 132, 131–32).

This enlightening and humbling experience engendered by fiction for O'Connor could be an effective counterforce for the temptation of writers to see themselves as finalized and complete, as well as detached from, and superior to, those they write about. Such temptation, O'Connor was well aware, was particularly strong for Catholics (even if they saw themselves as fallen creatures, they were certain they—as opposed to everyone else—possessed the orthodoxy to attain salvation). As was discussed in some depth in the first chapter, Catholic writers often approached their art with the parochialism and insularity in which many Catholics lived their lives. As possessors of what they believed was the true faith, many Catholic writers ignored the complexities permeating their own selves and concrete reality, and instead manipulated the material of life and fiction in order to present the most agreeable vision possible. As O'Connor said in an interview at Vanderbilt University in 1959, the theological scaffolding of works of art created in this way frequently became so dominant that it effectively smothered the life of the characters. For those who responded to—rather than denied—the knowledge and challenge inherent in the creation of fiction, such tendencies could be overcome, and one's ties with the real world and with one's self, both of which were permeated with the mysteries of the divine, could be renewed.

Crucial to this positive response to fiction, as I have been suggesting, is the open and honest interaction of writers with their characters. Rather than closing themselves off from their challenges— challenges that force writers to see themselves as others would— writers must respond to these challenges and engage them dialogically. In this interchange writers probe and judge, and in turn are themselves probed and judged. Utterly opposed to such interaction, besides the simple refusal to engage in it, is what O'Connor labels the contemporary ideal of compassion. She points out in "Novelist and Believer" that compassion can be interpreted in two ways, one positive and one negative. The positive sense, an ideal generally shunned by modern writers, means "the sense of being in travail with and for creation in its subjection to vanity"; this attitude, she adds, "implies a recognition of sin; this is a suffering-with, but one which blunts no edges and makes no excuses." The negative sense, and the sense generally exalted in modern writing, means glossing over the hard facts of our fallen and sinful natures and excusing all failings in the name of sentiment. "It's considered an absolute necessity these days for writers to have compassion," O'Connor writes in "Some Aspects of the Grotesque in Southern Fiction." "Compassion is a word that sounds good in anybody's mouth and which no book jacket can do without. It is a quality which no one can put his finger on in any exact critical sense, so it is always safe for anybody to use. Usually I think what is meant by it is that the writer excuses all human weakness because human weakness is human" (MM, 165, 43). To feel compassion (in this latter sense) for one's characters—and, by extension, for oneself—is thus to short-circuit one's judgment of them and in turn their judgment of oneself; the frontiers of reality and the self remain obscured in a stultifying sentimentality.

O'Connor's fiction, together with her stance as author, embodies the positive sense of compassion. Hers is a fiction of participation, of "suffering-with," of challenge and being challenged. Her stance is similar to the one she finds in the work of Romano Guardini, who, though not a writer of fiction, nonetheless actively struggles in his writing with many of the same problems and concerns that O'Connor faces. In a review of Guardini's *The Rosary of Our Lady*, O'Connor notes that Guardini steers clear of pious cliché by always rethinking liturgical problems in terms of modern problems and preoccupations. She says that many others have attempted such examinations but have not fared as well as Guardini "because the attempt is made by one who sees these difficulties and preoccupations as being those of another." She continues, "With Monsignor Guardini, one feels that these difficulties are his own, that he does not stand on a height above the modern mind coping with its own agonizing problems but infused with grace" (*PG*, 17). Like Guardini, O'Connor is actively involved in her writing; the problems and conflicts she bodies forth are not those to which she is immune but those from which she suffers.

O'Connor's participation in her work puts her in a position not unlike that of her characters. Her characters, as Bakhtin found with Dostoevski's, live on what Bakhtin calls the "threshold"—they ultimately face "the breaking point of a life, the moment of crisis, the decision that changes a life (or the indecisiveness that fails to change a life, the fear to step over the threshold)."[2] Typically this turning point in a character's life comes in a blinding moment of violent confrontation with a force outside the character's self; with his or her old self shattered by the experience, the character must then make the choice, with eyes opened to an entirely new perspective, on how to proceed with life. From the works discussed in the previous chapters, one thinks in this regard of Asbury's realization that he is not dying and his encounter with the Holy Ghost in "The Enduring Chill," Julian's epiphany sparked by the death of his mother in "Everything That Rises Must Converge," Sheppard's final confrontation with Johnson and his discovery of his son's death in "The Lame Shall Enter First," Haze's meditations when the policeman pushes his car over the embankment in *Wise Blood*, and Tarwater's reaction to his drowning of

2. Mikhail Bakhtin: "Forms of Time and the Chronotope in the Novel," in *The Dialogic Imagination: Four Essays*, ed. Michael Holquist and trans. Caryl Emerson and Michael Holquist (Austin, 1981), 248.

Bishop and his own rape in *The Violent Bear It Away*. In all these situations the characters are forced to act beyond themselves in ways that reveal their true natures. O'Connor characterized these fateful and often violent encounters as moments when supernatural grace was offered to her characters, and she said that these episodes, together with the characters' responses to them, were what made her stories work as stories. In a speech introducing her reading of "A Good Man Is Hard to Find," O'Connor said that at the heart of all great fiction there must be an action or a gesture "that was both in character and beyond character; it would have to suggest both the world and eternity." She added that "it would be a gesture that transcended any neat allegory that might have been intended or any pat moral categories a reader could make. It would be a gesture which somehow made contact with mystery" (*MM*, 111).

In these startling moments when the mysteries of self and world are—at least momentarily—unveiled, a character's true identity emerges. O'Connor believed that our social selves, the selves we show forth in our typical everyday encounters, have little, if any, relevance to what we carry deep inside. "An identity is not be found on the surface; it is not accessible to the poll-taker; it is not something that *can* become a cliché," she wrote in "The Regional Writer." "It is not made from the mean average or the typical, but from the hidden and often the most extreme." One's identity, she added, is made up of "qualities that endure," and as she wrote elsewhere (in one of the selections collected as "On Her Own Work" in *Mystery and Manners: Occasional Prose*), these qualities surface most tellingly in violent situations. "It is the extreme situation that best reveals what we are essentially," she wrote, adding that "the man in the violent situation reveals those qualities least dispensable in his personality, those qualities which are all he will have to take into eternity with him" (*MM*, 58, 113, 114).

These enduring qualities of her characters are of course what are revealed in O'Connor's stories. In her fiction there is generally very little character development; most characters have fully developed perspectives, and these positions usually are put to the test in unusual and extreme situations. If there is change, it occurs not over time but in a blinding flash of recognition, usually at the end of the story. This sometimes-severe testing of her characters' outlooks is similar to that which O'Connor herself undergoes as author. Like the characters and narrators of her stories, O'Connor too stands on the threshold. As a participatory author, calling forth her many voices, she explores and pressures her essential values and beliefs with her characters.[3] The trials and sufferings of her characters, who are themselves embodiments of her own self or selves, in a sense become her own (although she experiences these versions of herself as other), and they severely impinge upon O'Connor's conception of herself, testing and retesting her positions in story after story.

Rather than remaining complacent and unbending in her outlooks, O'Connor instead does violence to her views by objectifying them and then severely challenging them. As violence returns her characters to themselves, revealing their true natures, so too the violence involved in O'Connor's participatory art returns her to herself, jarring her into recognizing the complexity of voices both within and without. This is in part what she means when she writes in "The Church and the Fiction Writer" that fiction is the antidote to the "tendency to compartmentalize the spiritual and make it resident in a certain type of life only" (*MM*, 151). Fiction opens the writer up to the world and the self, often with a violence; and the extremely violent events that occur in O'Connor's fiction merely mirror the encounters that O'Connor herself faces in her fiction.

In looking at O'Connor's characters, I want to limit my focus to several types: intellectuals, artists, and prophet-freaks (particularly those who resist their religious callings). I choose these three because they all embody aspects of O'Connor that, at their extreme, come into potential conflict with her overriding Catholic ideology, and indeed always exert a good deal of pressure on it.[4] The lives of intellectuals, writers, and prophet-freaks all represent temptations to the Catholic religious life, and in fleshing out these characters, O'Connor works through these temptations by showing their perspectives unchecked by her reigning Catholic orthodoxy. Her response to these tempta-

---

3. Claire Katz sees O'Connor's narrator as a scourge—as a superego that punishes aspects of O'Connor embodied in her characters. See Claire Katz, "Flannery O'Connor's Rage of Vision," *American Literature*, XLVI (1974), 54–67.

4. I omit a discussion of women and their identities, but refer those interested to Louise Westling, *Sacred Groves and Ravaged Gardens: The Fiction of Eudora Welty, Carson McCullers, and Flannery O'Connor* (Athens, Ga., 1985).

tions is complex. On one level her use of a fierce fundamentalist to chastise these rebellious characters embodies her harsh response to religious doubts and questionings, and it calls to mind her observation that she judges her characters by "the ultimate concern" (*HB*, 221). Yet as we have seen, frequently the narrator's fierce judgments themselves come undone in her fiction so that the dynamic that emerges among the various voices in her work (among author, narrator, and character) is one of interplay and pressure on all sides. Through this complex interplay O'Connor ultimately redefines her religious commitment, not leaving it unquestioned but bringing it to bear on all the problems and complexities that she knows and feels.

O'Connor's anti-intellectual bias is well known. As we have seen in several of her works, intellectuals come under fierce scrutiny and attack in her fiction. This stems in large part from her fundamentalist sympathies, which are embodied most strikingly in her narrators. Apparently O'Connor never tired of downplaying her own intellectual talents and capabilities, and she frequently donned in her letters the mask of a backwoods rube to express both her scorn for modern intellectuals and her insecurity before them. (Particularly in her use of a backwoods mask, O'Connor aligned herself in the tradition of Middle Georgia humor.) Not long before she left for a television interview in New York, she wrote (May 18, 1955) to Robie Mc-Cauley: "Everybody who has read *Wise Blood* thinks I'm a hillbilly nihilist, whereas I would like to create the impression over the television that I'm a hillbilly Thomist, but I will probably not be able to think of anything to say to Mr. Harvey Breit [the interviewer] but 'Huh' and 'Ah dunno.' When I come back I'll probably have to spend three months day and night in the chicken pen to counteract these evil influences." Although her words here are written partly in jest, there is a good deal of serious concern behind them, and they underscore her disquiet with intellectuals and her fear of their influence upon her. Frequently she was more straightforward in her comments, as she was to Granville Hicks, who had written asking her to submit an essay for the symposium he was then editing, *The Living Novel*. She sent him a copy of one of the talks she had given but said that she was sure he would see right off it was not the type of essay he wanted. "If the talk had been for a serious audience," she wrote (February 21, 1957), downplaying her paper, "I would not have been making it." To drive her point home, she added, "I'm not an intellectual and have a horror of making an idiot of myself with abstract statements and theories" (*HB*, 81, 202).

But of course O'Connor was an intellectual. As the scope and size of her personal library, together with her many references to her readings in her letters, attest, she was extremely well read, particularly (and not surprisingly) in literature and theology.[5] In her numerous book reviews she discusses difficult theological and philosophical issues with ease and grace; it is clear that she is in her element and that she has a thorough grounding in both fields. Given all this, it might seem that O'Connor's expressed anti-intellectualism should be largely discounted and interpreted as another instance of her comic imagination (playing off the learned against the vernacular) and/or as a manifestation of her insecurity and shyness as a southern Catholic woman facing the northern intelligentsia. Although there is a good deal of truth in both of these interpretations, O'Connor's attacks on intellectuals and intellectual endeavor go much deeper and are more central to her imaginative life.

What O'Connor feared and lashed out at was not intellectual activity itself—she was herself, as I have said, a thoroughgoing intellectual—but the dangers that a life of the mind was given to, particularly the temptation to locate all power and authority within the individual consciousness. To center the value and meaning of all creation, including the divine, in the mind was for O'Connor a devastating manifestation of intellectual pride, and one that had to be fiercely resisted. In a letter (January 30, 1956) to A., O'Connor wrote of the tyranny of the intellect, a tyranny that occurred when the mind had no authority other than itself, and she suggested that locating one's intellectual endeavors within a larger Christian framework controlled the mind's dangerous play for power. She wrote that as a person becomes deeply involved in the life of the Church, his or her "intellect will take its place in a larger context and will cease to be tyrannical, if it has been—and when there is nothing over the intellect it is usually tyrannical. Anyway, the mind serves best when it's

5. See Kathleen Feeley, *Flannery O'Connor: Voice of the Peacock* (New Brunswick, N.J., 1972); Lorine M. Getz, *Flannery O'Connor: Her Life, Library and Book Reviews* (New York, 1980); and Arthur F. Kinney, *Flannery O'Connor's Library: Resources of Being* (Athens, Ga., 1985).

anchored in the word of God. There is no danger then of becoming an intellectual without integrity." As we saw in the first chapter, O'Connor embraced what she called a Christian skepticism, an attitude that encouraged people to learn all that they could but at the same time to keep it all in perspective—a Christian perspective. When she wrote (May 30, 1962) to Alfred Corn, a college student whose faith was wavering, she advised him to cultivate such a skepticism, telling him that "it will keep you free—not free to do anything you please, but free to be formed by something larger than your own intellect or the intellects of those around you" (HB, 134, 478).

O'Connor's Christian skepticism in some ways characterizes her own approach to fiction: As a means for self-knowledge, she plumbs the depths of herself through her characters, all the while striving to keep what she discovers within a Christian perspective. As can be seen in her fiction, she polices the limits of the challenges to her faith with the rigorous fundamentalism of the narrative consciousness. Through the intellectuals in her fiction, O'Connor gives voice to that part of herself tending toward intellectual endeavor, exploring and exposing it in different situations and environments. Maryat Lee, in an essay remembering her relationship with O'Connor, suggests that O'Connor did indeed draw her intellectual characters from within. Lee says that O'Connor was able immediately to size her up at their first meeting because she viewed her "in some way as an incarnation of the rebellious intellectual young person who recurs in her writing, a character which ordinarily she drew from herself."[6] That O'Connor feared in herself the power of the intellect to overpower faith and reason (reason in the larger sense of one's overall judgment, not merely rationality) is suggested not only by her own harsh comments on herself but in the ferocious judgments in her fiction leveled against her intellectual characters by the narrative consciousness.

We have already seen the fate of several of O'Connor's intellectuals, most particularly Sheppard in "The Lame Shall Enter First" and Rayber in The Violent Bear It Away. Both of these characters suffer from an intellectual pride that elevates their own consciousness and perspective as ideals superior to those of all others. In their felt superiority they embrace their own self-sufficiency (an ideal preached so

6. Maryat Lee, "Flannery, 1957," Flannery O'Connor Bulletin, V (1976), 43.

fervently by Rayber) and see themselves as judges and saviors of those about them, all of whom they consider to be less wise and perceptive. These intellectuals lack, in all of this, an essential openness to, and charity for, other people, and both are severely taken to task by the narrative consciousness and, I think it is fair to say, by O'Connor as author. With these characters and other intellectuals like them, O'Connor embodies the voice of her own intellectual pride. Thus she frees herself, in a process of recognition and transcendence, from her own intellectual pretensions not only by voicing them but also by seeing them harshly punished by the fundamentalist narrator. Although drastically undercut, these intellectual characters and their perspectives nonetheless exert, as we have seen, profound if implicit pressure on the judgmental narrator, calling into question the narrator's own rigid and monologic vision. Through such dialogic pressuring, which cuts both ways, O'Connor's understanding of her self and its many voices is deepened and enriched.

Besides Sheppard and Rayber, one of O'Connor's most striking intellectual characters is Joy/Hulga Hopewell in "Good Country People." O'Connor herself noted several times in her letters that she shared some striking resemblances to Hulga, and of most significance to us here is Hulga's fierce intellectualism. A crippled woman who lives on a farm with her mother, Hulga is a sour and withdrawn intellectual who embraces nihilism; she sees a blank nothingness behind all existence. During the seduction scene with Manley Pointer, she confidently asserts her nihilist faith. "I don't have illusions," she tells him. "I'm one of those people who see *through* to nothing." Recognizing and accepting this nothingness, rather than living a life based on an illusory faith in the meaningfulness of existence, Hulga believes, is the only means for a person to achieve integrity. "We are all damned," she tells Manley, "but some of us have taken off our blindfolds and see that there's nothing to see. It's a kind of salvation" (*CS*, 287, 288).

That Hulga has achieved this salvation by accepting the nothingness of existence is what, in her eyes, sets her apart from everyone else. A passage she has underlined in one of her books, seen by Mrs. Hopewell, sheds light on her thinking. The passage asserts that science is wholly concerned with the what-is and shuns all knowledge of nothingness. "Nothing—how can it be for science anything but a horror and a phantasm?" the passage reads. "If science is right, then one thing stands firm: science wishes to know nothing of Nothing." Hulga, in contrast, wants to penetrate the what-is to know the nothingness behind it. Her frequently fierce attacks on her mother also focus on the avoidance of the real—of the nothingness—in her mother's case by glossing over reality with a shallow optimism that finally rests on clichéd expressions. The narrative consciousness writes of Mrs. Hopewell's proclivities: "Nothing is perfect. This was one of Mrs. Hopewell's favorite sayings. Another was: that is life! And still another, the most important, was: well, other people have their opinions too." Nothing seems to outrage Hulga more about her mother than her clichés; when she hears them, Hulga "would stare just a little to the side of her, her eyes icy blue, with the look of someone who has achieved blindness by an act of will and means to keep it" (CS, 277, 272–73).

Armed with what she sees as her penetrating vision and thoroughly rational mind, Hulga perceives herself as the potential savior of those about her. Like O'Connor's other intellectuals, she is given to teaching others lessons about life, lessons that call into question the very identities of those so taught. At one point during a meal, after her mother has mouthed one of her clichés ("A smile never hurt anyone"), Hulga stands up unexpectedly, "her face purple and her mouth half full," to shout at her mother: "Woman! do you ever look inside? Do you ever look inside to see what you are *not*? God!" Before her tryst with Manley Pointer, she imagines herself seducing him and then, in dealing with his remorse, leading him to a new awareness of life and his identity. "True genius can get an idea across even to an inferior mind," the narrative consciousness reports her thinking. "She imagined that she took his remorse in hand and changed it into a deeper understanding of life. She took all his shame away and turned it into something useful" (CS, 276, 284). Hulga sees Manley as similar to her mother: an innocent person blinded by a faith—in Manley's case a Christian vision that refuses to penetrate the real.

Hulga's startling unmasking comes, of course, in the seduction scene with Manley. He, it turns out, is no Bible-toting Christian after all—he just totes Bibles around to sell them and to get whatever else he can from those he meets. Hulga is no match for this experienced con artist, and her planned seduction and ensuing reeducation of him go completely awry. Rather than she, he is in total control of the situation, and in the end Manley walks away with Hulga's artificial leg, which is to Hulga the embodiment of her secret self, her "difference." As he leaves, Manley taunts her about her supposed wisdom: "You ain't so smart. I been believing in nothing ever since I was born" (CS, 291). The story ends with Hulga stranded in the loft of the barn, chastened and helpless.

The narrator's stunning rebuke of Hulga—it is she rather than Manley or her mother who has been taught a shocking lesson—thoroughly chastens her and reveals the emptiness of her professed (and professorial) knowledge. Here we find another example of what John Hawkes calls O'Connor's demonism—the fierce narrative voice that utterly destroys humanity's pretensions, particularly those reasoned and reasonable. The narrator's fundamentalism is closely allied in intent to Manley's devilishness (Manley's posing as a fundamentalist of sorts), with both relishing Hulga's downfall. Once again we find the narrator's fundamentalist perspective linked in disturbing ways to forces of evil; such links underscore the fine line separating fundamentalist rage from the demonic rage that arises when a person given to the fundamentalist perspective chooses not Christ but the Devil. As we have noted, O'Connor frequently employs this fierce voice in works dealing with intellectuals.

The overall dynamic of the story calls to mind that found in the Southwest humorists and in much American humor—the conflict between the vernacular and the genteel, with the vernacular exposing the limits and pretensions of the genteel and learned. The story is structured around this conflict, and the organizing center is the testing of Hulga's intellectualism. The narrator presents Hulga's position and perspective fully developed; and then with the action of the story, the narrator tests Hulga's stances and their limits in various situations, particularly in the crisis posed by Manley Pointer, the vernacular antagonist. As O'Connor was so well aware, extreme situations reveal a person's essential nature, and these situations are what characters in her work must endure.

Such testing also precisely defines the dynamic at work between O'Connor and Hulga. With Hulga, O'Connor isolates her own intellectual voice, freeing it from her consciousness and its place within the scheme of her Christian skepticism. In other words, O'Connor bodies forth her intellectualism so that it exists as an independent voice free from constraints and the higher calling to which O'Connor strives to put it. In this way O'Connor gains perspective on her intellectual voice as she sees how it responds in, and reacts to, different situations when unconstrained; she likewise gains a better understanding of what life would be like as an intellectual without the Church. Attaining such understanding was a crucial aspect for her in artistic endeavor, as she wrote (September 13, 1959) to John Hawkes: "There are some of us who have to pay for our faith every step of the way and who have to work out dramatically what it would be like without it and if being without it would be ultimately possible or not." Hulga's rigid and reductive intellectualism, together with that of O'Connor's other modern intellectuals, calls to mind the writer's own observation on modern thinking in a letter (August 28, 1955) to A.: "If I hadn't had the Church to fight it with or to tell me the necessity of fighting it, I would be the stinkingest logical positivist you ever saw right now" (HB, 349–50, 97).

O'Connor's comment to A. contains a significant word—fight— that signals O'Connor's prevailing attitude toward dealing with her intellectual self and its embodiments in her fiction. Although O'Connor establishes in her fiction a situation ripe for dialogic interchange—her intellectual self interacting with her authorial and prevailingly Catholic self—ultimately she envisions this interchange as less a dialogue than a battle. So strong, one gathers, is the temptation of intellectual pride in O'Connor that though she may free the intellectual voice from herself, she must at the same time seek to punish it. Louise Westling finds a similar pattern in O'Connor's works dealing with women who rebel from their designated places in the southern and Catholic scheme of things ("Good Country People" is one such story). Westling observes that O'Connor allows doubles of herself to act their feminist rebellions only to be later punished by O'Connor in an effort to reassert her dominant values.[7]

But this effort to punish her freed voices is more complex than both Westling and I have characterized it. Complicating matters is the fact that O'Connor uses as her agent of destruction, as we have seen, a fundamentalist narrator, and particularly in her works centering on intellectuals, this voice is almost always at its most extreme, becom-

7. Westling, Sacred Groves and Ravaged Gardens, chaps. 6–7.

ing, as O'Connor herself admitted in the case of "The Lame Shall Enter First," demonic in its ferocity. The use of this extremely harsh narrator reveals several things. First, it indicates the severe pressure that O'Connor's intellectualism levels on her authorial self; O'Connor must counter with her fiercest anti-intellectual voice. Even more significant, the presence of this harsh narrator underscores the complexity of this interchange, for the fundamentalist voice that seeks to destroy and dominate is open to many of the same criticisms—in stance if not belief—that it levels at the intellectual characters in the fiction. Indeed, as we have seen, this voice is frequently undercut in the stories, and this fact in turn forces a reassessment of the fundamentalist voice's attacks on modern thinking. Ultimately the narrator's efforts to punish the voice of intellectual thought reveal as much about the limitations of the narrator as they do about its targets, as well as underscore for O'Connor the dangers inherent in allowing voices to express a monologic control of others. If in "Good Country People" and other stories about intellectuals O'Connor works out dramatically what her intellectual voice might be without the Church, at the same time she works out with the narrator what her religious urges might be if likewise uninhibited. Such a dynamic chastens not merely the narrator's and the intellectual's voice but also the author's, for the final thrust of the story is ultimately delivered to O'Connor, chastising her for her monologic efforts to silence utterly her modern voice, a voice that she knew was an integral part of her consciousness.

Another set of characters who speak crucially to O'Connor are her artist figures. As she does with her intellectuals, with her aspiring artists (almost all of them are total failures) O'Connor isolates that part of herself given to artistic aspiration. In the process she frees this voice so it may go its own way without restraint or religious baggage. For this reason O'Connor's artist figures almost always are entirely committed to their art and rigidly uncompromising in their conceptions of their artistic ideals. In all of this O'Connor dramatically visualizes the workings of her artistic self freed from any faith except faith in itself.

O'Connor's artist figures are closely related to her intellectuals. Two characters we have already looked at primarily as intellectuals— Asbury in "The Enduring Chill" and Julian in "Everything That Rises Must Converge"—are aspiring artists whose approach to reality mirrors that of O'Connor's "pure" intellectuals, such as Rayber in *The Violent Bear It Away*. Both artists and intellectuals close themselves off within the isolated self and locate meaning and transcendence therein. Where they differ is in their self-worship: For O'Connor's artists the locus of transcendence is the unbridled imagination, free of all constraints and confining ties to anything outside itself, whereas for her intellectuals this locus is the rationality of the reasonable mind. Both the artists and the intellectuals are prone to suffering a stubborn and destructive pride, and we usually find them bloated in their conceptions of their own self-worth and clarity of vision.

Asbury and Julian both so suffer. Both men aspire to be writers but, in large part because of their monologic worship of self—which closes them off from meaningful contact with others and in turn denies them a realistic means of appraising the self and the world—are doomed to failure. Asbury is the more committed artist: He has moved to New York to make a go of the artistic life, seeing himself as the faithful servant of his deity, Art. His only explanation of his failure is that during his upbringing his mother destroyed all but his will to create; his imagination and talent, he thinks now, were domesticated and blighted by her smothering ways. It never crosses his mind that he in any way could be responsible for the miserable results of his artistic endeavors, since he believes he would have otherwise succeeded—he has done everything he should to mold himself into a lonely, suffering, and misunderstood (but ultimately great) artist.

Julian likewise aspires to be a writer, though he has yet to make a start at it. (He is a typewriter salesman, and in one of the story's funniest lines, a woman on the bus comments to Asbury's mother: "Well that's nice. Selling typewriters is close to writing. He can go right from one to the other.") There is no intimation that if Julian ever gets around to it he will succeed any better at writing than did Asbury, because he too suffers from seeing himself as the knower and arbiter of all things. Julian is thoroughly isolated in what the narrator calls his "mental bubble" (*CS*, 411), and there is a good deal of truth (though not as he interprets it) to his own belief that he is too intelligent to be a success. His overreliance on his own mental capacities, which he sees as infallible, will forever isolate him from the depths of himself and others.

Asbury and Julian both embody what O'Connor saw as a particularly destructive modern myth—that of the alienated writer. In "The Regional Writer" she says that "there is one myth about writers that I have always felt was particularly pernicious and untruthful—the myth of the 'lonely writer,' the myth that writing is a lonely occupation, involving much suffering because, supposedly, the writer exists in a state of sensitivity which cuts him off, or raises him above, or casts him below the community around him." O'Connor believed that writers who touted their alienation only further isolated themselves from the restorative community, and that such isolation usually in turn led to a form of what she called "self-inflation" that ultimately destroyed whatever gifts these writers had. This destruction frequently occurred when writers, unduly confident in the correctness and finality of their visions, put their art merely to utilitarian ends—to reform or to teach a lesson. This approach to art, according to O'Connor, suggests that the artist's self and vision are inviolable and that artistic creation entails no self-discovery or growth, or even any questioning, for that matter. Fiction written in such a way is flat and false; as O'Connor stresses in "The Catholic Novelist in the Protestant South," fiction of any depth and significance is for the writer not a utilitarian exercise but instead "a kind of personal encounter, an encounter with the circumstances of the particular writer's imagination, with circumstances which are brought to order only in the actual writing" (*MM*, 52–53, 82, 198).

Judging from the way they treat others, Asbury and Julian both approach art as utilitarian, as a means to teach lessons. Although we do not see their creative writing, it seems likely that their art would express the same basic approach to self and otherness as their interactions with people do; and this approach, as we have seen, is one of monologic dominance. Both characters are determined to chasten their mothers, to expose their faults and to open their eyes to what they, their sons, see as the true reality. Such is the intent of Asbury's long letter to his mother; as the narrative consciousness reports, Asbury hopes it will "leave her with an enduring chill and perhaps in time lead her to see herself as she was" (*CS*, 365). Asbury's letter is indicative of his own self-inflation in life and in art, a self-inflation from which Julian also suffers.

To succeed as people—and then perhaps as writers—both Asbury and Julian must break out of their monologic shells that define life as, and confine it into, the valorized self. They must enter, as both appear to be on the verge of doing at the end of their stories, the larger realm of the spirit—a realm that recognizes one's place among others and before God, described at the end of "Everything That Rises Must Converge" as "the world of guilt and sorrow" (*CS*, 429). As writers they must see that writing is more than merely teaching a lesson; it is rather, as O'Connor knew, a confrontation with the voices of one's deepest self or selves, voices that express the life both of one's consciousness and of one's region. At its richest this confrontation is dialogic, with the voices within interacting with the writer's prevailing self in a way that pressures and challenges its dominance, ultimately decentering the conscious self and forcing reflection, change, and growth. Writers, in other words, should not impose themselves upon others, but in a sense, through their art, open themselves to imposition from both within and without.

In her stories about artists, O'Connor enters into contact with that part of her that is given to pure artistic pursuit, and as in her stories about intellectuals, she uses a stern fundamentalist narrator to expose that voice's shortcomings. The thrust of the story extends far beyond that of the exposé, however. As we have seen in O'Connor's other fiction, the dynamics among author, narrator, and narrative are anything but simple and clear-cut, and they indeed work in dialogic ways, engendering tensions and pressures that challenge the authority of both author and narrator. Such complex dynamics are at work in another of O'Connor's stories about a failed artist, "The Partridge Festival."

"The Partridge Festival" centers on the artistic aspirations of a would-be writer, a young man named Calhoun, and to a lesser extent on those of another aspiring writer, a young woman named Mary Elizabeth. The narrative consciousness is characteristically severe and demanding, bringing great pressure upon both characters and ultimately exposing their ignorance and pretentiousness. Both Calhoun and Mary Elizabeth suffer from the self-inflation that plagued Julian and Asbury: They both see themselves as infinitely superior to the people about them (even each other), and both are bent on exposing what they see as the community's blindness and injustice.

The touchstone of their critique of society is the figure of Singleton, a man who, after being the butt of a community prank, burst in upon a town council meeting and shot and killed five council members and a bystander. Singleton is now confined to a mental institution, and both Calhoun and Mary Elizabeth lionize him because they see him, rather than those he killed, as the victim—the victim of a straitlaced, conservative society whose strictures destroy all who stand outside them, as Singleton did, all people who assert an individuality outside the norm. "He was an individualist," Calhoun tells the barber as he gets a haircut. "A man who would not allow himself to be pressed into the mold of his inferiors. A non-conformist. He was a man of depth living among caricatures and they finally drove him mad, unleashed all his violence on themselves." Calhoun adds that Singleton was committed to an institution instead of being brought to trial because "a trial would have brought out his essential innocence and the real guilt of the community" (*CS*, 431).

Calhoun sees in Singleton a version of himself—the victim of a stultifying society—and Singleton's shooting spree as an extreme version of his own antagonism toward, and efforts to expose, that society. Early in the story Calhoun closely examines Singleton's picture in the newspaper—he recognizes in Singleton's look "the composure of the man who knows he will and who is willing to suffer for the right to be himself" as he searches for the resemblances between himself and the killer. Except for their broad faces, however, he can find none; not disheartened, Calhoun decides, as the narrative consciousness reports, that the physical resemblances are finally insignificant, for "the real likeness between them was interior" (*CS*, 423). Calhoun desires to vindicate Singleton not only to expose the faults of the society from which he sees himself and Singleton as suffering but also to emulate Singleton's actions by lashing back at society and freeing himself once and for all from it.

Calhoun's ultimate goal is to become what he sees as the archetypal writer: the artist who stands on the fringe of society and pierces its pretensions. Although he is a quite successful salesman when he wants to be—he spends his summers selling so he can live free for the rest of the year—he sees his true self as the "rebel-artist-mystic." He hopes that his novel on Singleton will bring that self to fruition, something that he has not before now been able to achieve because he has been unable to liberate himself from what he calls his commercial instincts. As much as he portrays himself to his friends as a bohemian who scorns business and work, he knows deep down that he enjoys himself most when he is working a customer for a sale. "In the face of a customer," the narrative consciousness writes, "he was carried outside himself; his face began to beam and sweat and all complexity left him; he was in the grip of a drive as strong as the drive of some men for liquor or a woman; and he was horribly good at it" (CS, 424, 425).

It is from this part of him that Calhoun hopes to free himself, and he sees his visit to Singleton at the asylum and his projected novel on him as perhaps the best way to do it. Although he knows that his visit to Singleton will be a painful experience, he also sees it as opening him to salvation; if he just suffers enough, Calhoun believes, he can become an artist. "The sight of Singleton in his misery might cause him suffering sufficient to raise him once and for all from his commercial instincts," the narrative consciousness reports him thinking. "Selling was the only thing he had proved himself good at; yet it was impossible for him to believe that every man was not created equally as an artist if he could but suffer and achieve it" (CS, 437).

Mary Elizabeth's motives in writing about Singleton are not as clearly defined, though she reads the killer's acts in much the same way as Calhoun. As she points out to Calhoun, she is not much concerned with Singleton as an individual; she characterizes herself as a thinker, and so for her, Singleton and his acts are significant only on the level of abstract thought. "A Christ figure," she answers when Calhoun asks about her opinion of Singleton, adding quickly, "I mean as myth. . . . I'm not a Christian" (CS, 435). She agrees to go with Calhoun to visit Singleton as much because of Calhoun's goadings as anything else. She is clearly uneasy about the visit, for she knows that it is much simpler to confront reality, particularly its disturbing aspects, from afar—and particularly from the distance of the abstracted observer, uninvolved and safe in the world of one's own thoughts and feelings.

The visit with Singleton is a complete disaster for Calhoun and Mary Elizabeth. Singleton, it turns out, is a thoroughgoing madman, and his disturbing presence completely shatters Calhoun's and Mary Elizabeth's pretensions about themselves and their art. Where both had envisioned using Singleton's story to expose society's faults, both now suffer a complete reversal; as the narrative consciousness makes clear, Singleton's mad ravings expose not society's but Calhoun's and

Mary Elizabeth's blindness and self-deceptions. Both had approached their art in a way doomed to failure—to escape from, rather than to plunge into, reality. Calhoun wanted to manipulate his art to deny his true self—the master salesman, true heir of his grandfather's mercantile acumen—and to drive home a message about society's failings, whereas Mary Elizabeth intended to keep her art as abstract as possible in order to prop up her deluded vision of things and to keep herself buffered from everyday reality. Both saw meaning as located in their isolated selves, and artistic endeavor as a means to impose their beliefs and perceptions—false as they were—upon reality and their audience.

Singleton's madness reveals Calhoun's and Mary Elizabeth's, and the narrative consciousness makes it perfectly clear that the two deluded artists are indeed, just as Calhoun had earlier imagined himself to be, spiritual kin to Singleton. When Calhoun and Mary Elizabeth go to the asylum, they pose as Singleton's relatives (Calhoun Singleton and Mary Elizabeth Singleton) in order to get in. Both see the step as representing the cementing of their identity with Singleton and with each other. After their disastrous visit, the significance of their common identities becomes unmistakable: Calhoun and Mary Elizabeth, though not literally crazy like Singleton, nonetheless are, in their own ways, as out of touch with reality as he is. Both have isolated themselves from their own inner being and the reality about them; and both, in their efforts to strike out at society and to establish their own authority, are shown to be as ridiculous and misguided as Singleton was when he took on the city council with his loaded pistol. This is what the two learn when, sitting alone in their stopped car after fleeing the asylum, they look at each other and see in each other's faces "the likeness of their kinsman" (*CS*, 443)—Singleton. Such knowledge shatters the pretensions of both Calhoun and Mary Elizabeth and opens their eyes to their true selves. The story ends as Calhoun sees himself reflected in Mary Elizabeth's glasses—not as a suffering artist but as his grandfather, the master merchant, embodying the true inner self of Calhoun and the self he has gone to such great lengths, unsuccessfully, to deny.

There are a number of factors at work here concerning O'Connor and artistic endeavor as embodied in the story. To begin with, O'Connor uses a characteristically severe narrator to expose the limitations of those given entirely to artistic creation. The story suggests in Calhoun and Mary Elizabeth that the artistic impulse, if not firmly rooted in concrete experience and an openness to self, holds out a destructive temptation: to isolate oneself in one's own image of the gifted artist, and to cultivate that image further by assuming a superior stance to others (including the "others" within) that leads to a self-conception even more limited and distorted. To be such an artist leads to destruction not only of the self (through the stagnation of the isolated consciousness) but also of art, for creators such as Calhoun and Mary Elizabeth see their work merely as utilitarian, as a means to impose what they see as their unquestioned brilliance upon their audience and, along the way, to expose their audience's ignorance. Rather than participating in their art—growing through its discoveries and its dialogic challenges—writers of this sort remain thoroughly detached from it, believing that art administers entirely to the audience. The artist, from this standpoint, stands inviolate, supreme, and all knowing—a position that to O'Connor was a dangerous self-inflation.

As an artist, and one very much interested in getting her message across, O'Connor was susceptible to such temptation, if perhaps not in such a virulent form. As I suggested earlier, in "The Partridge Festival" and other stories about artists, O'Connor isolates and embodies her own inner voice of artistic temptation in her characters who aspire to be writers. If in so doing she frees that part of herself embodied by the voice of the artist, she also severely criticizes that voice, for she presents it in her fiction as conceived, perceived, and judged by a severe fundamentalist narrator. Such refraction gives O'Connor a perspective not only on her artistic voice but also on her fundamentalist voice, as the two play off each other. In this interaction the artistic voice is chastened, called to task for the ultimate freedom and the unquestioned worship of the self that it embraces.

But the chastening in this story goes much further, extending to both the narrator and the author. This surprising turnaround results from the intense pressure that Calhoun and Mary Elizabeth put on the narrator and on O'Connor, a pressure stemming from the similar approaches to art. This pressure is particularly intense on the narrator, for the story he or she tells—"The Partridge Festival"—is crafted much like the work envisioned by Calhoun and Mary Elizabeth, which the narrator roundly condemns, a work to expose and destroy, told from a perspective unassailable in authority and vision. The unmasking of Calhoun's and Mary Elizabeth's pretentious aspirations, ironically enough, thus at the same time unmasks those same pretensions in the narrator, and their downfalls suggest a similar fate for him or her.

Such pressure also extends to O'Connor as author, for the actions of Calhoun and Mary Elizabeth speak tellingly to her. Their approach to art—to stifle all other voices within and without—is a temptation that particularly plagues Catholic writers, as O'Connor pointed out time and again in her essays and letters; and there is every reason to believe O'Connor was so tempted. If Calhoun and Mary Elizabeth serve as a warning to O'Connor about what might happen were she to let her artistic sensibility rule entirely, they also suggest the danger in allowing *any* single voice to maintain total control and power. That O'Connor uses a fierce fundamentalist narrator to lash out at embodiments of her self—even if on one level she does so to free up her fundamentalist self and gain a perspective on it—suggests that she was frequently susceptible to this monologic temptation to suppress and punish, a temptation directly opposed to her ideal of engaging perspectives and voices outside one's conception of a univocal and finalized consciousness. Such ferocity, as we have seen, occurs in a number of her works, particularly those centering on intellectuals and artists, where the narrator's ire is particularly fierce and unrelenting.

Even in their suppression, however, characters like Calhoun and Mary Elizabeth remain powerful forces, since their fates are so integrally tied up with those who, on the level of narrative, seek to suppress them. The attacks on Calhoun and Mary Elizabeth are ultimately turned back on those assailing them (the narrator and the author) so that the assailants too, as Calhoun does at the end of the story, see images of themselves (images embodying voices from within that are usually denied) that must be acknowledged and integrated into a multi-voiced conception of self. Only then can a person achieve a self-knowledge that opens into vision.

O'Connor's deep kinship with backwoods religious fanatics and their fundamentalist faith is a matter we have already explored in some depth. As we have seen, this closeness is expressed most significantly in O'Connor's use of a charged fundamentalist narrator and in her occasional fanatical characters, such as Old Tarwater and Lucette Carmody in *The Violent Bear It Away*. These intensely religious figures embody what I believe is O'Connor's essential religious temperament (O'Connor has said as much), one given to intense fervor and extreme demands and commitment. On one level these figures represent versions of O'Connor without her Catholic faith; and though extremely attracted to these figures' fierce religiosity, O'Connor also knew that their extremes were limiting and potentially destructive. Part of her artistic power derives from her not denying this fundamentalist aspect of herself but integrating it, in all of its complexity and in all of the conflicting feelings it generated, into her artistic vision.

Closely related to O'Connor's fascination with southern fundamentalists are her feelings for another brand of fanatics—those who are aware of the fundamentalist imperative of making a commitment, total in scope and intensity, for Christ or the Devil and who have made the satanic choice. These characters have resisted what O'Connor liked to call their wise blood, the searing and elemental awareness of Christ's presence in human history. Their choice to live without Christ is in no way one of compromise or complacency, the type made by many people who live essentially nonreligious lives even when they go to worship one day a week; rather the choice is fired with an intensity and fervor matching that of their opposites, the fundamentalist Christians.

These religious rebels—and they are indeed religious in their wrestlings with profound spiritual matters—are important to O'Connor for several reasons. Their religious struggles pressure O'Connor's own faith and challenge her beliefs in the intensity of their questionings and their resistance to Christ. "These unbelieving searchers have their effect even upon those of us who do believe," O'Connor writes in "Novelist and Believer" in an observation not specifically about her fictional characters but certainly relevant to them. "We begin to examine our own religious notions, to sound them for genuineness, to purify them in the heat of our unbelieving neighbor's anguish" (*MM*, 160). Even more searchingly, these characters, as indicated by her earlier-cited words on Tarwater from *The Violent Bear It Away* ("Tarwater is made up out of my saying: what would I do here?" [*HB*,

358]), embody O'Connor's own religious doubts, pressuring and testing them in situations and encounters outside her own consciousness.

Although a devout and committed Catholic—as rigorous in her faith as the fundamentalists she wrote of were in theirs—O'Connor nonetheless, as she freely admitted in her letters, was torn by religious doubt, in part because of her refusal to close herself off within her faith. O'Connor frequently railed about those she called vapid Catholics, believers who never allowed their faith and its tenets to be challenged or examined in any critical way. To Father John McCown, she complained (December 23, 1958) that priests should be doing more "preaching about the harm we do from the things we do not face and from all the questions that we give Instant Answers to." Such probings and challenges, even if they gave rise to questions of unbelief, were for O'Connor a bedrock of faith. As she wrote (May 30, 1962) to Alfred Corn, Peter's prayer, "Lord, I believe. Help my unbelief," is "the foundation prayer of faith" (*HB*, 309, 476).

O'Connor's religious dissenters dramatically worked out her own challenges to, and questionings of, faith. In *Wise Blood* and *The Violent Bear It Away* we saw two such religious dissenters, Hazel Motes and Tarwater, both of whom struggle violently to disavow their religious callings. After their intense and extreme rebellions, which ultimately lead them to profound encounters with Christ's presence in the world and the self, Haze and Tarwater wholeheartedly embrace the knowledge that their wise blood has been driving them all along: that the center of life is the Incarnation and that to be true to Christ one must make a total commitment to him. This image of a person's wise blood is fitting for O'Connor's own religious faith at its most fundamental—an intense desire to accept Christ, to follow him and his authority despite whatever doubts. The conflict arising from the severe demands of this elemental drive and the resistance to them is a central tension in O'Connor's artistic imagination, and one that is dramatically worked out time and again in her fiction.

If O'Connor liberates her own religious doubts and rebellious urges in her fiction, and particularly in her prophet-freak dissenters, she also uses the harsh fundamentalist narrator to police these desires and the characters who embody them. Haze and Tarwater, as we have seen, are violently chastened in their returns to faith; the narrators of both of these novels strive to assert their fundamentalist perspective using a rigid authority that matches that of their faith. Complicating—and enriching—this interplay is the fact that the narrator's authority is itself pressured and called into question by the narrative and the author. Such dynamics point to the open-endedness of O'Connor's fiction and of the religious struggles found therein, even when on one level the fiction appears to assert a firm resolution of both. The many voices of O'Connor's fiction—and self—go on speaking despite any efforts to silence them.

Surely the most noteworthy religious rebel in O'Connor's stories is The Misfit in "A Good Man Is Hard to Find." Like O'Connor's other prophet-freaks, The Misfit is forthrightly aware of the fundamentalist imperative. Of Jesus, The Misfit says: "He thrown everything off balance. If He did what He said, then it's nothing for you to do but throw away everything and follow Him, and if He didn't, then it's nothing for you to do but enjoy the few minutes you got left the best way you can—by killing somebody or burning down his house or doing some other meanness to him. No pleasure but meanness." As strong as his awareness of Christ is (note the capitalized pronouns referring to Christ), The Misfit has let his faith fall prey to the reasonings and literalism of the rational mind. In simple terms, his will to believe is distorted by his modern sensibility that demands that everything, including the irrational, be explained rationally. (This concern for reasonableness is also underscored by his anger at what he sees as his unjustified punishment by the penal system. "I call myself The Misfit," he says, "because I can't make what all I done wrong fit what all I gone through in punishment.") Because he did not witness Christ performing his miracles, The Misfit cannot be absolutely sure if Christ is true or not; and without this certainty—the certainty of a divine force operating outside the bounds of reason that, as The Misfit says, "thrown everything off balance"—he cannot make a commitment to Jesus. "I wisht I had of been there," he says to the grandmother. "It ain't right I wasn't there because if I had of been there I would of known. Listen lady . . . if I had of been there I would of known and I wouldn't be like I am now" (CS, 132, 131, 132). The Misfit cannot accept a paradox O'Connor found so central to faith: that, as she put it in a letter (January 11, 1960) to Cecil Dawkins, "you must believe in order to understand, not understand in order to believe" (*HB,* 370).

In turning away from Christ, The Misfit embraces the alternative—a life of "meanness"—with the type of total commitment he sees Christ demanding of his followers. His is a life of principled violence and crime (not unlike Johnson's life in "The Lame Shall Enter First") and is quite different from that of his henchmen, who act with a mindless abandon. This determined willfulness signifies—for us and for O'Connor—the extremes to which a religious renunciation can extend, particularly from a person rooted in a fierce fundamentalism like The Misfit, and indeed like O'Connor. On one level, then, The Misfit's rebellion can be seen as embodying O'Connor's own religious doubts, a voice now freed from her control and flourishing in all its intensity. O'Connor gains perspective on this voice by observing it outside herself, but at the same time she is also severely challenged by it. Although the grandmother, in her simpleminded life of platitudes and clichés, is nothing like O'Connor, the pressure The Misfit puts on her is not unlike that which O'Connor feels from him. As Christ is for him, The Misfit is for the grandmother a force that throws everything off balance; in the face of the violence he initiates and of his piercing awareness of Christ, the grandmother's life and her cherished views are severely tested. During their dialogue, The Misfit and the grandmother engage in a verbal duel that ultimately undoes the old woman and destroys her life of easy sentimentality. With this destruction, however, and still under The Misfit's intense pressure, the grandmother is propelled into a fuller awareness of the world and its spiritual dimensions. No longer just a silly old lady, she reaches out in a Christ-like gesture to touch The Misfit, declaring that he is one of her children. The Misfit recoils in horror, aware that the grandmother has opened herself to the Christian mysteries and therefore is threatening, if not totally undoing, his life founded on the impossibility of knowing Christ. He immediately shoots her three times in the chest.

If not quite as violently, The Misfit and O'Connor also engage in a duel of sorts, and the character exerts intense pressure on the author. In his dedicated turning away from Christ and in his ferocious quest for meanness, The Misfit tests O'Connor's religious faith by forcing her to work through the challenges that his rebellion poses. O'Connor faces her religious doubts and questionings in her interplay with The Misfit (and, more generally, with her fiction). The Misfit's religious doubts, which are extensions of O'Connor's own, are those that she must not only acknowledge but also respond to, and in the interchange learn and grow. Such dialogic encounters, as she well knew, helped make her faith deep and rich, and kept her from sliding into the easygoing and unquestioned piety that she so deplored. As the grandmother opens herself to a clearer and fuller spiritual knowledge through The Misfit's challenges, so too does O'Connor, herself thrown off balance and goaded to develop a larger sense of things.

Besides pressuring O'Connor's faith, The Misfit also sheds light on the fundamentalist sensibility, a sensibility that, as I have been arguing throughout, was an important voice in O'Connor's consciousness. Like Hazel Motes, The Misfit on one level reveals the closeness between those fundamentalists who resist God's presence and those who embrace it. In intensity and severity, The Misfit's attacks on others mirror, in spirit if not in deed, those of O'Connor's fundamentalists, most particularly her fundamentalist narrators here and in other stories. (Ironically enough, The Misfit's "preaching" to the grandmother "converts" her to Christ; her reaching out to The Misfit, furthermore, is an act signifying the fundamentalist rejection of the world for Christ, and fittingly, she literally loses her life in making the step.) Once again, then, we find the severity of the fundamentalist vision called into question, undercut by the very narrative meant to confirm it.

Near the end of the story, with the grandmother and the rest of the family lying dead, one of the henchmen, Bobby Lee, says to The Misfit that the grandmother was a great talker. "She would of been a good woman," The Misfit answers, "if it had been somebody there to shoot her every minute of her life" (CS, 133). The Misfit's reply suggests the great power of challenge and pressure in opening up one's sensibility to a larger vision of things, and it is such pressure and challenge that O'Connor sought and received from her stories, and frequently from her characters. Through these encounters O'Connor deepened her self-knowledge and her faith, and with this growth enriched her artistic imagination and her fiction.

6

Flannery O'Connor and Her Readers

Up until now we have been exploring almost exclusively the interplay among author, narrator, and narrative in O'Connor's fiction and looking closely at the often charged tensions involved in the confrontations between opposed visions and interpretations of reality. The tensions that the conflict between monologic and dialogic perspectives engenders have been central in these confrontations. In this chapter we turn to another area of interplay, that between the author and reader—via the work of art—and pay particular attention to how O'Connor shapes her fiction in order to communicate with her audience. Here too we find complex dynamics at work, with an unsettled interplay between monologic and dialogic visions.

As her letters and essays clearly indicate, O'Connor was very much concerned with her reading audience. Her comments on her audience and how it affected her as an artist, however, were not entirely consistent, and it seems clear that O'Connor was of two minds on the subject.[1] One part of O'Connor downplayed the significance of the audience, saying that artists should be concerned with one thing—their art—and that they bear no responsibility to the audience. By this line of thinking writers concentrate on making their fiction—the characters and their worlds—come alive, and they make sure that the story works as a story and not as a medium for expressing an abstract statement. The meaning of a piece of fiction, O'Connor insisted, was the entire experience one has with it and was not a statement imposed

1. The most extensive discussion of O'Connor's interpretation of her audience is in Carol Shloss, *Flannery O'Connor's Dark Comedies: The Limits of Inference* (Baton Rouge, 1980).

on it that could then later be extracted and held up as its "message." Such thinking was central to the advice she wrote (December 11, 1956) to A. about writing fiction. O'Connor wrote that a writer should merely "start simply with a character or anything that you can make come alive." She continued, "When you have a character he will create his own situation and his situation will suggest some kind of resolution as you get into it. Wouldn't it be better to discover a meaning in what you write than to impose one?" (HB, 188).

Behind O'Connor's thinking is the thought of Saint Thomas Aquinas, whom O'Connor frequently cites. For Aquinas a work of art is, as O'Connor points out in "Catholic Novelists and Their Readers," "a good in itself," being "wholly concerned with the good of that which is made." As such, it "glorifies God because it reflects God," and writers have no cause to put their work to any other end; such endeavors only undermine the integrity of the vision and sully the purity of the art. Modern writers, O'Connor says in this same essay, by and large fail to heed Aquinas's lesson and instead wrench their art to make it fit utilitarian ends. For her, in contrast, "the artist has his hands full and does his duty if he attends to his art. He can safely leave the evangelizing to the evangelists" (MM, 171, 173, 171).

Catholic writers, in O'Connor's eyes, were particularly prone to distort their fiction for utilitarian purposes—to make it do something rather than be something. Particularly disturbing to her were those writers, in part goaded by the Catholic press, who wrote in pious language about the pieties of the Church. O'Connor's attitude toward this type of fiction was sharp: "As for the fiction," she wrote (February 19, 1956) to John Lynch, "the motto of the Catholic press should be: We guarantee to corrupt nothing but your taste" (HB, 138). In ignoring the realities of the here and now outside the Church, such fiction was for O'Connor little more than religious propaganda, the stuff one expects to find in the vestibules of churches but not in bookstores. These writers, she believed, were too concerned with presenting the Church in a favorable light and tending to their readership's spiritual needs; O'Connor's answer to them was that in writing fiction the Catholic writer "does not decide what would be good for the Christian body and proceed to deliver it" (MM, 183). Instead, as we have seen O'Connor stressing, writers must work within the limitations of their vocation to create the best story—not tract—possible.

"The writer is only free when he can tell the reader to go jump in the lake," O'Connor said in one of her interviews, stressing the artist's independence from the audience. She added that though the writer of course wants to communicate a personal vision, "whether [the reader] likes it or not is no concern of the writer" (*CFO*, 39).

If in this way O'Connor downplayed the significance of the audience, she also frequently said something quite different. She argued that the audience played a crucial role in artistic creation and that writers always had to be aware of, and to take account of, their audience. She spoke of this connection in "Catholic Novelists and Their Readers," saying that "it takes readers as well as writers to make literature," and she added in "The Catholic Novelist in the Protestant South" that "it is what writer, character, and reader share that makes it possible to write fiction at all." Elsewhere (in "Novelist and Believer") O'Connor wrote that fiction was ultimately an attempt at communication; successful writing, she added, was not merely a rendering of the artist's vision but a rendering of it in such a way that the reader could understand it. "The novelist doesn't write to express himself, he doesn't write simply to render a vision he believes true, rather he renders his vision so it can be transferred, as nearly whole as possible, to his reader," she wrote. "You can safely ignore the reader's taste, but you can't ignore his nature, you can't ignore his limited patience. Your problem is going to be difficult in direct proportion as your beliefs depart from his." She echoes this observation in "Some Aspects of the Grotesque in Southern Fiction," saying that the writer's vision "has to be transmitted and that the limitations and blind spots of his audience will very definitely affect the way he is able to show what he sees" (*MM*, 182, 204–205, 162, 47).

When speaking of her own audience, O'Connor almost always stressed the great distance she felt between herself and her readers and pointed to the ways this gulf pressured and limited her as a writer. She believed that she and other American Catholic writers lacked a significant and responsive audience, and that this situation stifled imaginative growth and artistic expression. O'Connor found several reasons for this development. Central to the Catholic writer's plight, O'Connor believed, was the fact that in America Catholic writers lacked a distinctive social and cultural heritage based on religious identity. In "The Catholic Novelist in the Protestant South" she asserts that "the writer whose themes are religious particularly needs a region where these themes find a response in the life of the people." She then adds: "The American Catholic is short on places that reflect his particular religious life and his particular problems. This country isn't exactly cut in his image." She goes on to say that even in areas where there are large numbers of Catholics, Catholic life there lacks "the significant features that result in a high degree of regional self-consciousness" and so offers the Catholic writer few "exploitable benefits." O'Connor's analysis of Catholic writers continues: "They have no great geographical extent, they have no particularly significant history, certainly no history of defeat; they have no real peasant class, and no cultural unity of the kind you find in the South." She adds that Catholics usually "blend almost imperceptively into the general materialistic background." This lack of a strong cultural tradition and a supportive audience greatly burdens Catholic writers, impoverishing their imaginative life and art. "If the Catholic faith were central to life in America, Catholic fiction would fare better, but the Church is not central to this society," O'Connor continues. "The things that bind us together as Catholics are known only to ourselves. A secular society understands us less and less. It becomes more and more difficult in America to make belief believable" (MM, 200, 201).

These final words point to the second reason American Catholics lack a supportive audience: The larger society they write from and to is overwhelmingly secular and materialistic, money based rather than religion based. O'Connor, as we saw in the first chapter, was well aware of the trends in modern social and intellectual thought that since the Enlightenment have been validating and valorizing the human consciousness and rationality while undermining and reducing the significance of the religious. In a letter (October 19, 1958) to T. R. Spivey, O'Connor wrote that by and large people in today's society have "no sense of the power of God that could produce the Incarnation and the Resurrection. They are all so busy explaining away the virgin birth and such things, reducing everything to human proportions that in time they lose even the sense of the human itself, what they were aiming to reduce everything to" (HB, 300). Because moderns lacked a faith in transcendent values and order, O'Connor, as she said in "Some Aspects of the Grotesque in Southern Fiction," saw the age as one "which doubts both fact and value, which is swept this way and that by momentary convictions" (*MM*, 49). O'Connor found such relativism particularly disturbing, and this in part explains her strong attraction to the fundamentalist imperative that defines all values according to the simple—but total—choice of being for either Christ or the Devil.

Given these trends and developments, O'Connor saw her own position, as well as that of almost all American Catholic writers, as being particularly precarious in terms of communicating with her readership. O'Connor frequently asserted in her letters that she could consistently count on only a handful of informed readers—an assertion largely borne out by the number of vicious and misinformed readings her work received, particularly early on—and that she had to make these readers go a long way in her life as an author. O'Connor knew hers was not the type of fiction that most Catholic readers yearned to read—not, in other words, fiction that was thoroughly positive and that went out of its way to celebrate the life of the Church. She characterized the general Catholic reader as unthinking, and she said that this reader "is so busy looking for something that fits his needs, and shows him in the best possible light, that he will find suspect anything that doesn't serve such purpose" (*MM*, 182). Elsewhere, in a letter (May 4, 1963) to Sister Mariella Gable, she wrote that those Catholic readers who demand that the writer make Christianity look desirable are asking the writer to describe Christianity's essence and not what the writer actually sees. "Ideal Christianity doesn't exist, because anything the human being touches, even Christian truth, he deforms slightly in his own image," she wrote, adding a bit later that the tendency of the Catholic readers she had been discussing "is always toward the abstract and therefore toward allegory, thinness, and ultimately what they are looking for is apologetic fiction. The best of them think: make it look desirable because it is desirable. And the rest of them think: make it look desirable so I won't look like a fool for holding it" (*HB*, 516). Such readers would find little to like in O'Connor's fiction and in all likelihood would see it as a good deal more than suspect—subversive, probably.

O'Connor of course felt an even greater distance from what she saw as the thoroughly secular and unbelieving general reader, the reader to whom she claimed she primarily wrote. In "The Catholic Novelists and Their Readers" she said that Catholic readers make a great mistake in supposing that Catholic writers write exclusively for them. "Occasionally this may happen," she wrote, "but generally it is not happening today" (MM, 185), and O'Connor made it clear elsewhere that it was not happening in her fiction. To A., O'Connor wrote (August 2, 1955) of the audience she perceived, saying that "one of the awful things about writing when you are a Christian is that for you the ultimate reality is the Incarnation, the present reality is the Incarnation, and nobody believes in the Incarnation; that is, nobody in your audience. My audience are the people who think God is dead. At least these are the people I am conscious of writing for" (HB, 92). Trying to bridge this gap between believing author and unbelieving audience was a terrible burden for O'Connor, and one that haunted her throughout her career. In a review of Caroline Gordon's The Malefactors, O'Connor wrote that "making grace believable to the contemporary reader is the almost insurmountable problem of the novelist who writes from the standpoint of Christian orthodoxy," an observation that speaks crucially to O'Connor's own situation in communicating with her audience (PG, 16).

O'Connor further perceived her audience as making demands that she was not prepared to meet—ever. She complained in "Some Aspects of the Grotesque in Southern Fiction" that her freedom as a writer was always under pressure, since everywhere "the novelist is asked to be the handmaid of his age." She wrote, "Whenever the public is heard from, it is heard demanding a literature which is balanced and which will somehow heal the ravages of our time." This literature, she said elsewhere in this essay, was based on what she called "a realism of fact"—a realism that associated "the only legitimate material for long fiction with the movement of social forces, with the typical, with the fidelity to the way things look and happen in normal life." Such realism, she added, limited both the scope of the imaginative vision of artists and their fiction. As O'Connor noted here and elsewhere, her own fiction was written with a realism of an altogether different sort—a realism that sought not to mirror the typical but to reveal the spiritual. To this end, she says in "Novelist and Believer," the writer "is bound by the reasonable possibilities, not the probabilities of his culture" (MM, 46, 39, 165).

If the overall critical environment established its own orthodoxy for fiction, O'Connor also saw general readers establishing their own expectations and demands for what they should experience in the act of reading. She characterized the general readers as being "tired," of wanting what she called at one point "Instant Uplift"—that is, wanting to have their spirits raised in an act of easy compassion and sentiment. This demand for uplift and the redemptive act, O'Connor notes in "Some Aspects of the Grotesque in Southern Fiction," is a characteristic human need, and one that both the storyteller and the listener find particularly compelling in narrative. What bothers O'Connor is not that the reader seeks this motion in fiction but that the reader "has forgotten the cost of it." She explains that the modern reader's "sense of evil is diluted or lacking altogether, and so he has forgotten the price of restoration. When he reads a novel, he wants either his senses tormented or his spirits raised. He wants to be transported, instantly, either to mock damnation or a mock innocence." To underscore the risks the writer takes in ignoring such readers, O'Connor writes in this same essay that there are those who "say that the serious writer doesn't have to bother about the tired reader, but he does, because they are all tired. One old lady who wants her heart uplifted wouldn't be so bad, but you multiply her two hundred and fifty thousand times and what you get is a book club" (*MM*, 165, 48–49).

O'Connor saw her problems with her audience as being further aggravated by her southern identity. Although we have already seen that O'Connor believed that being from the South provided her with a number of important advantages as a writer, she also felt that being labeled a southerner further separated her from her audience because it immediately placed her, in the eyes of the general reader, into a school of writing that was concerned primarily with degenerate and grotesque lives. In "The Fiction Writer and His Country" she wrote that the term "Southern school" usually "conjures up an image of Gothic monstrosities and the idea of preoccupation with everything deformed and grotesque," and she added that most southern writers are looked upon as "unhappy combinations of Poe and Erskine Caldwell" (*MM*, 28).

O'Connor found her own particular delineation as southern writer particularly unsettling. In "Some Aspects of the Grotesque in Southern Fiction" she writes: "When I first began to write my own particular bête noir was that mythical entity, 'The School of Southern

Degeneracy.' Every time I heard about The School of Southern Degeneracy, I felt like Br'er Rabbit stuck on the Tarbaby" (*MM*, 38). Being so perceived of course threw up an additional barrier for O'Connor in her efforts to reach her audience, particularly in communicating her Christian vision. In an interview with C. Ross Mullins, Jr., O'Connor spoke specifically of this problem, saying that most readers fail to note the religious dimensions of her work because these religious concerns are worked out in southern situations, and as O'Connor says, "this creates confusion, as most readers rely on various critical clichés to explain Southern literature that don't explain anything" (*CFO*, 103).

For a writer who at times claims that the writer bears no responsibility to the audience and should therefore by and large ignore it, O'Connor clearly rarely follows her own dicta; as we have seen, she is profoundly aware of her intended audience and deeply affected by her perceptions of it. O'Connor's apparent inconsistency is particularly intriguing, for I believe it embodies the same type of dialogic pressuring to which O'Connor submitted her faith in her fiction. As we have already seen, in her stories and novels O'Connor tests and pressures the limits and dimensions of her reigning Catholic faith by bringing this faith into dialogic contact with other perspectives, found in the narrators and the characters. Such interplay is also at work in her nonfiction in her discussions of art and the artist. Her established and regnant view of art is that drawn from Aquinas—primarily through the work of Jacques Maritain, particularly *Art and Scholasticism*— that art is a good in itself and that the reader's role in its creation is minimal. This rather theoretical understanding of art, a cornerstone of which is Christian faith, is put under intense pressure by O'Connor's immediate situation of being a Catholic writer in an unbelieving world. In other words, her efforts to interact with her readers and to form a bridge of communication with them severely test her regnant notions of art; in this testing, her Thomist views are forced to take new shape and to adapt to the extreme situation in which O'Connor finds herself. Rather than ignoring the readers, O'Connor feels that when she actually begins writing she has to open her art to them and mold it in such a way that she can engage in meaningful communication.

The pressure the reader exerted on O'Connor in this process was severe, and she described it in a lecture delivered at Georgia State College in graphic and unpleasant terms: "When I sit down to write, a monstrous reader looms up who sits down beside me and continually mutters, 'I don't get it, I don't see it, I don't want it.' Some writers can ignore this presence, but I have never learned how." O'Connor went on to say that she felt both an intense resistance to this reader and a compelling need to communicate with him or her: "I know that I must never let him affect my vision, must never let him gain control over my thinking, must never listen to his demands unless they accord with my conscience; yet I feel I must make him see what I have to show, even if my means of making him see are extreme."[2] Despite her claims here, O'Connor's vision certainly was deeply affected by her perceived presence of her audience; for even if this audience did not literally control her thinking, nonetheless it clearly penetrated her consciousness, making her reshape her vision so that it took account of her audience and its demands. As she admitted, in everything she wrote she always had in mind that disturbing—and distorting—presence of the general reader and how this reader would react to her words.

Discovering the means to communicate with her unbelieving audience was a crucial problem for O'Connor, and one not easily solved. Just as she made varying comments on the significance of the audience, here too she holds conflicting views that ultimately embody a dialogic interplay between a ruling view she endorsed largely only in theory and one that she actually used in practice. O'Connor's predominant view embraced a realism that emphasized a fidelity to the here and now. This was not, as O'Connor was quick to point out, a realism of social fact but was what she called a "Christian realism"—a realism that accurately portrayed reality to suggest ultimately the Christian mysteries that lay beyond.[3] O'Connor liked to compare her method to Joseph Conrad's, saying that like him she sought "to render the highest possible justice to the visible universe" (*MM*, 80); doing justice to the visible, she added, suggested the invisible. "For

---

2. Quoted in Kathleen Feeley, *Flannery O'Connor*, 45.

3. John Desmond sees O'Connor's art as incarnational—derived from her belief in Christ's Incarnation and characterized by an analogical vision that provided O'Connor with a way to perceive reality in all its divine mystery. See Desmond, *Risen Sons*.

me the visible universe is a reflection of the invisible universe," she wrote (January 13, 1956) to A. "Somewhere St. Augustine says that the things of the world poured forth from God in a double way: intellectually into the minds of angels and physically into the world of things." Portraying the world of things—"accurate[ly] naming the things of God," she wrote in this same letter—is the duty of the artist (*HB*, 128).

By this line of thinking, O'Connor's role as artist was not to pound home to the readers overt religious messages but instead to make them see the physical world with a clarity of vision that would open up its mysteries. Once again she returned to Conrad to define the artist's purpose and relationship with the general reader:

If the [artist's] conscience is clear, his answer to those who in the fullness of a wisdom which looks for immediate profit, demand specifically to be edified, consoled, amused; who demand to be promptly improved, or encouraged, or frightened, or shocked or charmed, must run thus: My task which I am trying to achieve is, by the power of the written word, to make you hear, to make you feel—it is, before all, to make you *see*. That—and no more, and it is everything. If I succeed, you shall find there, according to your deserts, encouragement, consolation, fear, charm, all you demand—and, perhaps, also that glimpse of truth for which you have forgotten to ask.

Using other terms, O'Connor commented in "The Teaching of Literature," this time drawing on the insights of Henry James, that the artist should reveal "mystery through manners." She explained what James means: "The mystery he was talking about is the mystery of our position on earth, and the manners are those conventions which, in the hands of the artist, reveal that mystery" (*MM*, 80, 124).

At the center of O'Connor's thinking was her conviction that the writer of fiction can express the mysteries of existence only as embodied in concrete and human experience. In "Catholic Novelists and Their Readers" she cites several observations by Baron Friedrich von Hügel on the concreteness of spiritual experience—"The Spiritual," he says, "generally is always preceded, or occasioned, accompanied or followed, by the Sensible. . . . The highest realities and deepest responses are experienced by us within, or in contact with, the lower and lowliest"—and then notes the relevance of von Hügel's insights to the artist. O'Connor explains that if the writer "is going to show the supernatural taking place, he has nowhere to do it except on the literal level of natural events, and that if he doesn't make these natural things believable in themselves, he can't make them believable in any of their spiritual extensions." Her emphasis here and elsewhere is that only by making their stories believable on a dramatic level can Christian writers suggest what she frequently called the "added dimension"—the Christian mysteries. She writes in "The Church and the Fiction Writer" that "the reality of the added dimension will be judged in a work of fiction by the truthfulness and wholeness of the natural events presented" (*MM*, 176, 150), and for this reason, as she argues in "Catholic Novelists and Their Readers," the Catholic writer's obligation to depict the natural world truthfully is even greater than that of the writer without faith.

In a departure of sorts, O'Connor suggests in several places that her Christian realism is very close in spirit and method to Nathaniel Hawthorne and the nineteenth-century romance tradition. To John Hawkes she wrote (November 28, 1961): "I think I would admit to writing what Hawthorne called 'romances,' but I don't think that has anything to do with the romantic mentality. Hawthorne interests me considerably. I feel more of a kinship with him than with any other American" (*HB*, 457). Like Hawthorne, O'Connor envisioned the writer as not being bound to the probable and the everyday, and as free to rearrange aspects of the natural world—only after accurately describing them—to suggest the mysteries that lay beyond. O'Connor was almost certainly aware of Hawthorne's prefaces, and she in all likelihood had in mind his well-known discussion of the differences between a novel and a romance, found in the preface to *The House of the Seven Gables*:

When a writer calls his work a Romance, it need hardly be observed that he wishes to claim a certain latitude, both as to its fashion and material, which he would not have felt himself entitled to assume, had he professed to be writing a Novel. The latter form of composition is presumed to aim at a very minute fidelity, not merely to the possible, but to the probable and ordinary course of man's experience. The former—while, as a work of art, it must rigidly subject itself to laws, and while it sins unpardonably, so far as it may swerve aside from the truth of the human heart—has fairly a right to present that truth under circumstances, to a great extent, of the writer's own choosing or creation. If he think fit, also, he may so manage his atmospherical medium as to bring out or mellow lights and deepen and enrich the shadows of the picture. He will be wise, no doubt, to make a very moderate use of the privileges here stated, and, especially, to mingle the Marvellous rather as a slight, delicate, and evanescent flavor, than as any portion of the actual substance of the dish offered to the Public. He can hardly be said, however, to commit a literary crime, even if he disregard this caution.[4]

Echoing Hawthorne's observations here in "Some Aspects of the Grotesque in Southern Fiction," O'Connor said that she wrote in "the modern romance tradition," a tradition that stood opposed to that of the realistic novel and whose works "leaned away from typical social patterns, toward mystery and the unexpected." In these works, O'Connor adds, "the writer has made alive some experience which we are not accustomed to observe every day or which the ordinary man may never experience in his ordinary life. We find that connections which we would expect in the customary kind of realism have been ignored, that there are strange skips and gaps which anyone trying to describe manners and customs would certainly not have left. Yet the characters have an inner coherence, if not always a coherence to their social framework" (MM, 39, 40).

In communicating with the reader, according to this type of Christian realism, O'Connor depends on both the fidelity and the suggestiveness of her fictional world. Unlike Hawthorne, she shuns allegory; she believes that allegory leads to thinness and abstraction and, in any case, is impossible to employ effectively given the relativism of the modern world.[5] But like Hawthorne, O'Connor declares that a writer cannot impose meaning on a story and that reaching the reader takes a subtle and patient hand. Hawthorne's observations, again drawn from his preface to *The House of the Seven Gables*, could easily be O'Connor's comments on her own work as a Christian realist:

When romances do really teach anything, or produce any effective operation, it is usually through a far more subtle process than the ostensible one. The Author has considered it hardly worth his while, therefore, relentlessly to impale the story with its moral, as with an iron rod—or, rather, as by sticking a pin through a butterfly—thus at once depriving it of life, and

4. Nathaniel Hawthorne, *The House of the Seven Gables* (1851; rpr. Columbus, Ohio, 1965), 1.

5. See O'Connor's comments in Rosemary M. Magee (ed.), *Conversations with Flannery O'Connor* (Jackson, Miss., 1987), 87; and in Flannery O'Connor, *Mystery and Manners: Occasional Prose*, ed. Sally Fitzgerald and Robert Fitzgerald (New York, 1969), 49.

causing it to stiffen in an ungainly and unnatural attitude. A high truth, indeed, fairly, finely, and skilfully wrought out, brightening at every step, and crowning the final developement of a work of fiction, may add an artistic glory, but is never any truer, and seldom any more evident, at the last page than at the first.[6]

In this mode of thinking and art O'Connor vows to stay grounded in the here and now, to manipulate but not to falsify reality, to make her stories work first as stories and then, if the reader responds to the suggested meaning, as gateways to vision. Much of her hope, as mentioned earlier, is based on her Thomist view that everything good in itself glorifies God's majesty.

A quite different approach to communicating with her audience, however—one based on distortion and exaggeration—also emerges in O'Connor's art and thinking. If as a Christian realist and modern romancer her primary method of revealing the Christian mysteries is suggestion, as a writer of this more extreme approach her fundamental method is shock and distortion. In her great concern over the distance separating her from what she perceived as her unbelieving and unsympathetic audience, O'Connor early on began developing a number of severe fictional strategies that she hoped would speak to her readers. One thing she hoped to gain from these strategies was the readers' attention; she wanted to jar them from the complacency with which she saw readers characteristically approaching fiction. "You see people who are supposed to be highly educated who don't know trashy fiction from any other kind," she said in an interview with Margaret Turner. "If you have the values of your time, you can usually write without having to shock anyone to attention; but if you want to show something that the majority don't believe in or wish to see, then you have to get and hold their attention usually by extreme means" (CFO, 43). Even more significant than getting her audience's attention, as O'Connor saw it, was the role of the violence of her fiction as the means of communicating her vision. She writes in "The Fiction Writer and His Country" that "when you can assume that your audience holds the same beliefs you do, you can relax a little and use more normal means of talking to it; when you assume that it does not, then you have to make your vision apparent by shock—to the hard of

6. Hawthorne, *The House of the Seven Gables*, 2–3.

hearing you shout, and for the almost-blind you draw large and startling pictures" (MM, 34).

One of O'Connor's most effective literary techniques, as the words "large and startling pictures" suggest, was the use of the grotesque, and particularly the depiction of odd and freakish characters.[7] She liked to quote Thomas Mann's observation that the grotesque was the true antibourgeois style, and in large part she used it just so—to assault the complacent and bourgeois mind. "The freak in modern fiction is usually disturbing to us because he keeps us from forgetting that we share in his fate," O'Connor writes in "The Teaching of Literature," adding elsewhere that in today's society, dominated as it is by a liberal doctrine of human perfectibility, people often refuse to make this disturbing connection and instead read the freak as something entirely "other," an object worthy of compassion (in the pejorative sense in which O'Connor usually used the term). In other words, modern readers view the freak from an elevated and distanced vantage point, remaining there separate and superior. O'Connor, in contrast, sought to undermine this superiority and to bring the reader down to the level of the freak and into contact with him or her—just as she as author was. Such repositioning was of course not easily achieved, and in "The Fiction Writer and His Country" O'Connor notes that its success involves the reorientation of the reader's vision: "The novelist with Christian values will find in modern life distortions which are repugnant to him, and his problem will be to make these appear as distortions to an audience which is used to seeing them as natural" (MM, 133, 33).

Geoffrey Galt Harpham, in his brief discussion of O'Connor in *On the Grotesque: Strategies of Contradiction in Art and Literature*, suggests how the grotesque is particularly well suited to such a task. Harpham points out that coming to terms with grotesque forms requires a great amount of interpretative energy. "Meaning is made

7. The fullest discussions of O'Connor's use of the grotesque come in Gilbert H. Muller's *Nightmares and Visions: Flannery O'Connor and the Catholic Grotesque* (Athens, Ga., 1972) and Gentry's *Flannery O'Connor's Religion of the Grotesque*. Muller argues that O'Connor uses the grotesque to assault her readers and shock them into grasping the spiritual foundations of reality. In contrast, Gentry, drawing from the work of Mikhail Bakhtin, sees O'Connor as working with a more positive interpretation of the grotesque. See my discussion of Gentry in chapter 2.

through connections, by linking something with something else out-side itself," writes Harpham; "it is made by establishing relations both within and outside the text, by ascribing intentionality to things that do not inherently possess it, by seeing elements in contexts other than the ones in which they occur, by seeing one thing as another."[8] The grotesque, Harpham adds, requires readers to engage this inter-pretative process at a particularly high intensity, thereby being jarred into reexamining their everyday understanding of the world and their ways of perceiving it.

O'Connor's efforts at communicating with her readers were not limited to her use of the grotesque. She points out in "Some Aspects of the Grotesque in Southern Fiction" that because of the extremes to which she pushes her art and the discrepancies that she strives to combine in it (those arising from seeing the supernatural in the natu-ral), her fiction will always have a wild look characterized by intense violence and wrenching comedy. These violent and comic extremes, in part there to shake her readers' confidence in their rational sen-sibilities and to open their eyes to the facts of Christ's suffering and humanity's redemption, are shaping forces of her fiction. O'Connor makes it clear in "Novelist and Believer," in a statement referring to *The Violent Bear It Away*, that her technique of deliberate distortion extends to all aspects of her work:

When I write a novel in which the central action is a baptism, I am very well aware that for a majority of my readers, baptism is a meaningless rite, and so in my novel I have to see that this baptism carries enough awe and mystery to jar the reader into some kind of emotional recognition of its significance. To this end I have to bend the whole novel—its language, its structure, its action. I have to make the reader feel, in his bones if nowhere else, that something is going on here that counts. Distortion in this case is an instru-ment; exaggeration has a purpose, and the whole structure of the story or novel has been made what it is because of belief. This is not the kind of distortion that destroys; it is the kind that reveals, or should reveal. (*MM*, 162)

O'Connor wanted the experience of reading her work itself to be a process of reorientation, a refocusing of the mind's light toward the mysteries of human creation—mysteries that cannot be accounted

8. Geoffrey Galt Harpham, *On the Grotesque: Strategies of Contradiction in Art and Literature* (Princeton, 1982), 187.

for merely by social and psychological determinations, or by any human formula, for that matter. Somewhat ironically, O'Connor's descriptions of the fiction she writes to bring the reader to this understanding, including her observations in the passage just above, make the writing appear formulaic; every element of her work, she says, is carefully constructed to guide the reader along the path to enlightenment. At the end of this path, she says, she hopes that the reader's eyes will, like Tarwater's at the end of *The Violent Bear It Away*, be burned clean; the reader will then be able to perceive God's presence in the world and human history, and will understand his or her place and role in God's plan.

The extremes of O'Connor's descriptions of her intentions and methods in her fiction, together of course with the fiction itself, indicate the difficulty that O'Connor envisioned in reorienting the reader's secular vision. Her task was made even more tricky by her realization that she could not be explicit in portraying the religious dimensions of her work—secular readers would have none of that— nor could she rely on traditional religious vocabulary to express her vision. "The old words of grace," observes Walker Percy (another southern Catholic novelist, and one who was influenced by O'Connor in more depth than is generally acknowledged), "are worn smooth as poker chips and a certain devaluation has occurred, like a poker chip after it is cashed in."[9] In a letter (February 21, 1957) to A., O'Connor criticized one of her friend's short stories for being too obviously and explicitly religious, particularly in its conclusion. "The ending is too obvious," she wrote. "You can suggest something obvious is going to happen but you cannot have it happen in a story. You can't clobber any reader while he is looking. You divert his attention, then you clobber him, and he never knows what hit him" (*HB*, 202). As these words indicate, O'Connor saw the religious writer as the antagonist of the reader; the writer must use guile and deceit to set the readers up for a stunning "clobbering" that will force them to see that their rationalist vision, generally understood to be sophisticated and complete, is wholly inadequate to comprehend the divine mysteries.

9. Walker Percy, "The Delta Factor," in *The Message in the Bottle: How Queer Man Is, How Queer Language Is, and What One Has to Do with the Other* (New York, 1975), 16.

O'Connor's own assaults usually occur most tellingly in the sudden reversals that mark the endings of most of her works, where, in a moment frequently marked by extreme violence, the pretensions of a character are suddenly shattered. The shattering of these willful characters on one level mirrors what O'Connor hopes will also be the story's effect on readers—the shocking destruction of their limited and pretentious visions.

This severe and radical approach to fiction and the reader stands directly opposed to O'Connor's less belligerent views, based on her Thomism, that art is a good in itself and that the Christian writer communicates with the reader by maintaining a fidelity to reality in order to suggest Reality. To understand the extremes to which she carried her views of fiction, particularly in light of what she professed elsewhere, one might recall the warnings she delivered to all writers who sought to put their art to utilitarian ends; such fiction, she said, lacked depth and was finally false, an imposition of the will rather than an avenue for self-discovery. The writer, she said in a passage cited previously, "can safely leave the evangelizing to the evangelists" (*MM*, 171). And yet, of course, in her admonition that the writer must assault the secular reader, must shock and disorient so as to open up the rational mind to the divine, O'Connor was endorsing a utilitarian art and was by no means leaving "the evangelizing to the evangelists." The dynamics involved in embracing these contradictory stances, I would offer, are similar to those at work in her conflicting attitudes toward the significance of the audience both in and to artistic creation: In both kinds of dynamics we see an essentially theoretical understanding of art and audience severely pressured by another perspective that arises during the actual struggle in writing. In this case O'Connor's Thomism was intensely challenged by a severe evangelism, one that depended less on fidelity to the real than to the real's distortion and exaggeration. As O'Connor herself admitted in an interview with Joel Wells, this severe approach to art was an automatic response when she wrote. "I don't consciously set out to be more drastic," she told Wells, "but this happens automatically. . . . I have to distort the look of the thing in order to represent as I see them both the mystery and the fact" (*CFO*, 88–89).

Particularly intriguing for our study is the fact that O'Connor's evangelical impulse precisely describes the approach to art embodied in the narrators of her fiction. Indeed when O'Connor argues for the religious writer to assault the secular reader—to evangelize—she speaks more as a fundamentalist than as a Catholic. As she noted in a letter (January 30, 1956) to A., Catholics generally spurn making any evangelical calls to nonbelievers. O'Connor said that before her friend was converted to the Church, she did not send her any books on Catholic thought because she did not want her to think she "was trying to stuff the Church down [her] throat." O'Connor continued, "This is a peculiar thing—I have the one-fold one-Shepherd instinct as strong as any, to see somebody I know outside the Church is a grief to me, it's to want him in with great urgency. At the same time, the Church can't be put forward by anybody but God and one is apt to do great damage by trying; consequently Catholics may seem remiss, almost lethargic, about coming forward with the Faith. (Maybe you ain't observed this reticence in me.)" (HB, 134).

Whatever reticence O'Connor may have felt about voicing her "one-fold one-Shepherd instinct" to her friends, she freed herself from this restraint in her fiction by embodying her evangelical impulse in her fundamentalist narrators and the stories they told. In doing so O'Connor reworks the tensions between the opposing views of art and audience into the tensions at work between author and narrator—a dialogic interplay between the author's learned and orthodox Catholicism and the narrator's fierce down-home fundamentalism. Such a conceptualization not only liberates O'Connor's evangelical voice but also unleashes its fury at her secular readers; at the same time this voice pressures O'Connor's regnant vision, putting her Catholicism into an alien context, and is itself pressured in turn by the authorial vision. Finally, and of most significance to us here, O'Connor establishes with her evangelical voice a complex relationship with her readers.

The narrator's fierce attack on the secular reader does not define but merely initiates O'Connor's interactions with her audience. In a letter (October 19, 1958) to T. R. Spivey, O'Connor writes that self-knowledge "has to be the first step in conversion" (HB, 299), an observation that speaks tellingly to O'Connor's own motives with her audience. Through the narrator's fierce attacks on the readers, O'Connor hopes to prepare them for a deeper knowledge of self by shattering their monologic intellectualism and thereby opening them up to a more profound dialogic understanding. If her readers respond to her work, achieving in the process this larger understanding of self and world, O'Connor then hopes they will come to a vision mirroring not the narrator's but her own—a vision, in other words, that sees the work of fiction, as well as everything else in the world, as a good-in-itself glorifying God, and a vision that leads the readers to embrace the world and its many voices (including those within) rather than closing themselves off within the monologic self. Such is the true end of a dialogic vision as seen by O'Connor: the celebration of God.

The strategies that the narrators use in shaping their fiction into an evangelical tool to shake up the reader are very similar to those of fundamentalist preachers. At the heart of an evangelical sermon is the preacher's goal of bringing the listeners to a point where they make active commitments to accept Christ into their lives—that is, the preacher wants them to be "born again" into Christ's fold, having decided to shuck off their old identities and to open themselves to Christ's presence. To move the audience to an emotion-charged state that will lead them to seek their salvation, the evangelical preacher typically first pounds home to the listeners the emptiness of their secular lives and the lowliness of their sinful natures in the eyes of the Lord. The preacher's aim is to disorient the listeners by challenging and pressuring their way of life; the preacher wants to make them see their lives from a perspective outside their own—from God Yahweh's towering and judgmental perspective. From this vantage and by the light of their enlarged understanding, the preacher wants his audience to see, their lives are not merely meaningless but diabolic. The preacher customarily uses a highly rhetorical style punctuated by illustrative stories and anecdotes to draw the listeners into the sermon and to electrify their sensibilities. This done, the preacher starkly asserts that there is no middle ground for belief: One either accepts Christ and lives by that commitment, or one does not and instead lives by the Devil. The sermon ends with the preacher's appeal to the audience to step forward, to let Christ enter their now shattered lives, and to begin life anew.

For obvious reasons, the fundamentalist narrator of O'Connor's fiction uses a style much less explicit than that found in an evangelical sermon—the narrator is, after all, telling a story, not delivering a sermon, even if on one level the intentions are similar to the preacher's. Nonetheless, the narrator's underlying strategies of shock and distortion mirror those of the fundamentalist preacher, and the narrator's rage of vision is every bit as fierce as is the religious counterpart's. Indeed, at the risk of overreading, I would suggest that the revival scene in *The Violent Bear It Away*, with Lucette Carmody on the stage and Rayber huddled at a window and listening, is a revealing embodiment of what O'Connor perceived as the relationship between her fundamentalist narrator and the modern audience.

In this scene Lucette, a child evangelist, delivers a fierce and increasingly strident sermon warning her listeners of Christ's Second Coming and the necessity to get right with him before it is too late. "If you don't know Him, now," she cries out, "you won't know Him then. Listen to me, world, listen to this warning. The Holy Word is in my mouth!" From his detached and distanced perspective, Rayber all but ignores Lucette's words; instead, her presence calls to mind what he remembers as his own religious sufferings as a child when his uncle, Old Tarwater, had kidnapped him from his worldly parents and baptized him. As he continues to watch Lucette, these feelings quickly expand into a strong pity for her and all exploited children. Typically, as an intellectual in O'Connor's fiction, Rayber refuses to see himself as a child of God and therefore as a limited being suffering from humanity's fallen nature. Rather, because of his intellectual pride and his capacity for that type of negative compassion that O'Connor saw excusing all weakness and error by a hazy sentimentality that destroyed the capacity for moral judgment, he sees himself, not Christ, as the child's savior. So certain of himself is he, and so determined to mold Lucette into his own image, that when the girl turns her eyes to him he believes she experiences a shock of recognition, a realization that her redeemer waits at the window. "He was certain that the child had looked directly into his heart and seen his pity," the narrative consciousness reports Rayber thinking. "He felt some mysterious connection was established between them." Rayber's vision of himself as the child's savior intensifies as Lucette continues her harangue for Christ. At one point he imagines himself "moving like an avenging angel through the world, gathering up all the children that the Lord, not Herod, had slain"; at another he sees himself "fleeing with [Lucette] to some enclosed garden where he would teach her the truth, where he would gather all the exploited children of the world and let the sunshine flood their minds" (*VBIA*, 133, 131, 132, 133).

Rayber's dreams of saving Lucette, of freeing her mind from the bondage of religious discipline so it may exist free, glorifying itself and nothing else, are soon shattered, however. When Lucette once again fixes her gaze upon Rayber and walks toward him, Rayber believes she ignores her congregation for him because she sees the truth in her new savior. He calls to her in his thoughts, "Come away with me! . . . and I'll teach you the truth, I'll save you, beautiful child." Rayber's excitement grows as she steps closer, since he is now certain that Lucette "alone in the world was meant to understand him" and that "in the space between them, their spirits had broken the bonds of age and ignorance and were mingling in some unheard knowledge of each other." Rayber is utterly transfixed. But then the unexpected happens: Lucette suddenly points her arm at Rayber and shrieks to the congregation: "I see a dead man Jesus hasn't raised. His head is in the window but his ear is deaf to the Holy Word!" (*VBIA*, 134).

Lucette's ferocious words shatter Rayber's spell, and stunned, he crashes to the ground and fumbles to turn off his hearing aid. Before he can find the switch (thus becoming truly deaf to God's word), however, he hears the girl's warning that "the Word of God is a burning Word to burn you clean" and her challenge to be consumed in this fire. "Be saved in the Lord's fire or perish in your own!" she calls out. With his hearing aid finally turned off, Rayber attempts to regain his composure; he meets up with Tarwater, whom Rayber had followed to the revival, and they head home. But something has happened to Rayber. Within him burns a fury that seems "to be stirring from buried depths that had lain quiet for years and to be working upward, closer and closer, toward the slender roots of his peace" (*VBIA*, 134–35, 137). How Rayber responds to this inner fury, as we have already seen, is worked out in the rest of the novel.

I point to this passage because the interaction between Lucette Carmody and Rayber seems to work out dramatically the type of "clobbering" that O'Connor said the Catholic writer must deliver to the reader. Through her gazes at, and her walking toward, Rayber, Lucette, aided too by Rayber's own pride and self-conceit, lulls him into a false sense of security and sets him up for the tremendous shock and indictment she has prepared for him. Rayber is caught totally off guard by Lucette's assault; her fundamentalist indictment strikes to his deepest being and challenges his understanding of self and world. Although, as we have noted, Rayber is not an immediate convert (nor a later one), the religious challenge has been so fiercely delivered that he can no longer deny its reality as a force with which he must deal. Escaping God and his judgments is not merely a matter of turning off a hearing aid or returning home; Rayber's entire identity, he now understands, is entirely wrapped up in his relationship with God.

Achieving such disorientation in the reader, forcing a reassessment of identity and values that must account for, if not embrace, the Christian mysteries, is what O'Connor sees the Catholic writer striving to accomplish in fiction and what her own fundamentalist narrators seek. Like Lucette, O'Connor's narrators work with guile and cunning, hoping to create works of fiction that set the reader up for a climactic reversal that speaks compellingly to the reader's own limited condition and points to the fundamentalist imperative as a way to understand humanity's plight. The narrator's basic strategy is to draw the reader into what appears to be one type of story only to have it suddenly become a type quite different. This strategy follows closely what Brainard Cheney, in his essay of appreciation, "Flannery O'Connor's Campaign for Her Country," sees as the characteristic pattern in her work. Cheney argues that the narrative structures of O'Connor's stories embody a new form of humor; he points out that her stories begin innocently enough, "with familiar surfaces in an action that seems secular, and in a secular tone of satire or humor." But, Cheney continues, "before you know it, the naturalistic situation has become metaphysical and the action appropriate to it comes with a surprise, an unaccountability that is humorous, however shocking. The *means* is *violent*, but the end is Christian."[10] This surprising turnaround, I would argue, challenges the way the reader has been interpreting not only the story but also self and world.

One does not have to look far to find an O'Connor story that follows Cheney's pattern; any number of stories come immediately

10. Brainard Cheney, "Flannery O'Connor's Campaign for Her Country," *Sewanee Review*, LXXII (1964), 556.

to mind, indeed almost all of those we have already discussed, including perhaps most significantly "A Good Man Is Hard to Find." In that story, for instance, the direction and tone shift several times, each time with a heightening of interpretative and metaphysical significance; each shift forces the readers to reassess their own position in regard to the story and the meanings they draw from it. By the end of the story the readers are brought face to face with what the narrator considers the ultimate theological questions facing humanity.

"A Good Man Is Hard to Find" opens, and for a while develops, as a relatively gentle satire on the American pastime of the family vacation. We watch the antics of what appears to be a fairly typical family—husband, wife, son, daughter, baby, and grandmother— from the perspective of a narrator who touches everything with satiric scrutiny and judgment. Much of what I identify as this first section (the story is not formally divided) is quite funny, as in the following description of life in the car: "John Wesley kicked the back of the front seat and June Star hung over her mother's shoulder and whined desperately into her ear that they never had any fun even on their vacation, that they could never do what THEY wanted to do. The baby began to scream and John Wesley kicked the back of the seat so hard that his father could feel the blows in his kidney." Most closely scrutinized is the grandmother, who slyly tries to get her way in everything and whose clouded vision seems the fitting embodiment of the clichéd sentimentality that marks the legends of Old South thinking. "Oh look at the cute little pickaninny!" she says as they drive by a shack in the country. "Wouldn't that make a picture, now?" (*CS*, 123, 119). She is as lost in the modern world as she is when she gives her son directions to a plantation house that she remembers to be in Georgia but that is actually in Tennessee.

The tone and direction of the story take a sudden and drastic turn after the family's car overturns and The Misfit and his two henchmen drive up.[11] What began as a satire of the family vacation now becomes a tale of terror as The Misfit first orders the father and son and then the mother, daughter, and baby off into the woods to be shot. During this time The Misfit talks primarily with the grandmother, telling her

11. Martha Stephens gives a full discussion of the two-part structure of "A Good Man Is Hard to Find." See Stephens, *The Question of Flannery O'Connor*, 18–36.

about his upbringing and his days at the penitentiary. Armed only with her empty clichés, the grandmother pleads her case, trying to stave off the inevitable. "You could be honest too if you'd only try," she tells The Misfit at one point. "Think how wonderful it would be to settle down to live a comfortable life and not have to think about somebody chasing you all the time" (CS, 129).

In this second section the reader is in a much more uncomfortable position. The satiric humor of the first section positioned the reader, along with the narrator, in a detached and distanced perspective that embodied clear superiority to the rather ludicrous vacationers. With the terror of the second section, however, the distance between the reader and the characters narrows. The satiric dimension all but disappears as the family is systematically murdered; once so foolish and worthy of the reader's laughter, the doomed family, particularly the husband and wife and their children, now appear to possess quiet dignity and courage. Even the grandmother, who still rambles on, seems in her face-off with The Misfit less ludicrous and more human.

The reader, then, is directed in this second section toward forming a bond of sympathy with the family, a move of crucial importance in the narrator's strategy for delivering a startling turnaround to the reader. By guiding the reader into this closer relationship with the family, the narrator seeks to cloud the reader's eyes with the sentimental compassion that O'Connor frequently railed against (that which excuses human weakness because weakness is human) and so divert the reader's attention from the stunning climax—the clobbering—that is about to occur. The story at this point seems to be working securely on an ethical plane and pushing toward a moral that says that one should not be overly critical of others—as the reader was with the family early on—because even in their weakness people carry the seeds of courage.

The ethical gives way to the theological in the story's charged third section, which begins after the mother, daughter, and baby have been taken into the woods and The Misfit and the grandmother now stand alone together. The religious dimension openly enters the story when The Misfit unexpectedly reveals that he is a man wracked by deep spiritual struggles. Up until this third section The Misfit has appeared to be a cold and calculating murderer with little interest in anything except what will further or hinder his escape. He has characterized himself in terms that make him seem a recognizably typical criminal: a rebellious boy gone bad, misunderstood by family and society, and now on the run and living the only way he can—by the gun. Only his politeness seems to set him apart, and that only adds to the terror of the situation. All this changes after the grandmother in her fears mutters "Jesus, Jesus" (CS, 131) in a way that sounds as if she is cursing. The Misfit then launches into an explanation that he is deeply aware of the fundamentalist imperative but has chosen the way of the Devil. He is, it turns out, no typical criminal at all (as his henchmen are) but a man forever confronting ultimate matters, even if he has chosen the diabolic. As we saw in our earlier discussion of the story, the intensity of The Misfit's commitment to rejecting Christ, together with her own shock at her family's death and her fear of her own, propel the grandmother beyond her sentimental existence and into a higher realm of charity and grace. She reaches out to The Misfit, who immediately recoils in horror and shoots her dead.

This unexpected turn of events in the third section is the clobbering the narrator has prepared for the reader. With the transformations of The Misfit and the grandmother, who both in their own ways have become religious seekers, the narrator undoes the ethical issues previously established and elevates the concerns of the story to the realm of the spirit. For the reader this is a particularly disturbing jolt, because it challenges the reader's interpretative authority by undercutting the significance and the wisdom of the compassion that he or she had fixed upon to understand the story. Indeed, just as the grandmother's compassion is shown to be worthless until it becomes selfless and all giving (in other words, a fundamental love of creation because it is God's), the reader's compassion by implication is just as insignificant before the larger theological vision that now clearly structures the story. The grandmother's fate further suggests what the narrator intends for the reader. Although not acting with the intentionality of the narrator, The Misfit pressures the grandmother with violence and religious vision (perverted as it is) into a higher understanding of Christ's presence in the world; likewise the narrator strives to achieve this end with the reader, using means in some ways as jolting and severe as The Misfit's. The Misfit's comments that the grandmother "would of been a good woman if it had been somebody there to shoot her every minute of her life" (CS, 133) rings true for the reader: The secular reader would be a good person—that is, one in touch with ultimate matters—if there were somebody to clobber him or her every minute.

If the narrator's intentions end here, with the reader's secularism shattered by the narrator's assault and now open to a fundamentalist appreciation of reality, O'Connor as author, I believe, hopes for more. Rather than seeing the narrator's evangelism as an end, she sees it as a means to prepare the reader for a larger vision based on a more receptive and dialogic appreciation of the world and self. This vision sees God's presence as permeating all creation—all things and people, all voices of others (including all the voices in the multi-voiced self)— and calls for a person to embrace, understand, and adapt to these voices, all within a Christian vision. If The Misfit's fundamentalist either-or imperative is the narrator's, the grandmother's act of charity, her reaching out to another to embrace an alien voice as her own, is the author's. ("Why you're one of my babies. You're one of my own children!" she says to The Misfit as she touches him [CS, 132].) But, as I have suggested, for the readers to achieve such a vision, O'Connor believed that they had to be first bashed about by the narrator. Rephrasing Cheney's previously cited observation, in O'Connor's relationship with her readers the means are monologic but the end is dialogic.

O'Connor found the short story particularly suited to the type of manipulation of the reader she wanted, its form well structured for the strategy of setting up the reader for a shocking turnaround at the story's climax. The extended form of the novel, however, was more problematic. As in her stories, in her novels O'Connor also relied on a shocking reversal at the end to disorient the reader, but in the longer works she had somewhere around two hundred pages, rather than twenty, to get to this startling moment. There was certainly more room for error in the novels, particularly in maintaining the proper tone to achieve the religious ends O'Connor sought. As in her short stories, O'Connor, again through a crafty fundamentalist narrator, early on establishes the novels along the lines of works in distinctly secular traditions, only then to have them later reverse themselves to affirm starkly religious visions. Wise Blood thus in many ways appears to be a modern absurdist novel until the end, when with Haze's blinding, it becomes a novel of faith, what O'Connor said was the story of a Protestant saint. A similar motion occurs in *The Violent Bear It Away*, the work to which I wish briefly to return to close this chapter.

Even though all of the action of *The Violent Bear It Away* takes place within a week or so, the narrator molds the novel in such a way that it comes very close to resembling the form of the bildungsroman, or apprenticeship novel. The bildungsroman paradigm, expressed very simply, follows an apprentice-hero on a search for identity and meaning. In this quest the hero encounters a succession of people offering advice and guidance, but none of these people ultimately is able to answer the hero's most urgent questions. Finally, after long struggling, the hero discovers the key both to personal identity and to the meaning of the world at large. Typically this revelation occurs in a vision received only after the hero has solved a riddle that has long been held before him or her and with which the hero has known all along that he or she must somehow come to terms.

Up until its conclusion, when the narrator turns everything around, *The Violent Bear It Away* closely follows this basic paradigm. Through a series of flashbacks, the narrator presents quite a full picture of Tarwater's upbringing from infancy to adolescence, and in Tarwater's journey from and then back to Powderhead the narrator telescopes the generally more protracted bildungsroman quest. On his journey Tarwater strives to solve his central problem—whether or not to baptize Bishop—and hears the advice of a number of people. Eventually Tarwater solves his enigmatic problem and receives his vision—though, as I have suggested and shall discuss shortly, the ending is something quite unexpected.

The Violent Bear It Away resembles in basic structure not only the classic bildungsroman but, even more tellingly, its American version, a form that heavily stresses individualism and fierce independence and that is perhaps best typified by *The Adventures of Huckleberry Finn*. Echoes of *Huckleberry Finn*, in fact, abound in O'Connor's novel. Old Tarwater, for instance, bears a suspicious resemblance to Pap Finn, that archetypal tyrant whose death sets Huck free; both are wild old hard-drinking men who flee to the woods to escape the snares of civilization, each taking with him a shrewd child who later grows restive under the patriarch's heavy thumb. Young Tarwater by the same token seems a direct descendant of Huck Finn; he is another of those familiar "good-bad" boys of American literature who reject parental authority and set out on their own quest for maturity and wisdom. Like Huck, Tarwater is quick and resourceful, and adept at shutting out civilizing influences. While living with Old Tarwater, for instance, he puts on a strikingly Huck-like masquerade of idiot innocence before the truant officer, and then later, on his journey from Powderhead, he resists the enticements of Mr. Meeks, the copper flue salesman who wants Tarwater to come work for him. Tarwater likewise fends off the attempts to reform him by Rayber, his main antagonist other than the ghost of his great-uncle. The narrator reports that from his first night in the city Tarwater "had seen once and for all that the schoolteacher was of no significance—nothing but a piece of bait, an insult to his intelligence" (*VBIA*, 160); and indeed the boy never yields the man an inch. In all of this, the narrator strives to place the novel in the *Huckleberry Finn* tradition, thereby establishing for the reader an interpretative framework for understanding its action. By this interpretative scheme, to attain freedom Tarwater must act out his rejection of his great-uncle; he must, in other words, go his own way and not baptize Bishop.

With Tarwater's drowning of Bishop, he appears to commit the violent initiation rite needed to propel him beyond the innocence of childhood and the bondage of Old Tarwater and into the unsupervised freedom of adult life. As we have noted, the words of baptism that slip from his mouth as he drowns Bishop at first seem inconsequential, their significance all but negated by the murder. Had the novel ended here, the echoes of *Huckleberry Finn* would be complete, with both boys boldly acting out their rejections of any authority other than their own (Huck's "All right, then, I'll *go* to hell" might just as well be Tarwater's) and heading out into the wilderness and unbridled freedom.[12]

Tarwater's story continues, however, and in this final section of the novel the supposed American bildungsroman falls apart. The narrator quickly makes it clear that Tarwater's murder of Bishop has not resolved his crisis but instead has intensified it. Tarwater's mysterious hunger for the bread of life torments him as never before, and he is

12. Mark Twain, *The Adventures of Huckleberry Finn* (1884; rpr. New York, 1985), 235.

fearfully haunted by his drowning of Bishop—by both the murder and the baptism. Rather than a crafty, independent Huck figure able to rise above any situation, Tarwater after the drowning is vulnerable, even helpless. His encounters with the various people he meets as he works his way back to Powderhead—the truck driver, the black child, the woman at the store, the homosexual—reveal his lost powers. Even though Tarwater continues to say he has been able to put his past behind him, he clearly has not: Bishop's drowning, the initiation rite that should have set Tarwater free if this were an American bildungs-roman, has only bound the boy tighter to the troubling spirit of his great-uncle.

Adding to the unraveling of the bildungsroman illusion is the downfall of Tarwater's "friend," the voice of the stranger, whose advice Tarwater has followed ever since his great-uncle's death. Tarwater burned the farmhouse when he left Powderhead for the city because his friend whispered that this was the way to beat the old man, and he drowned Bishop for the same reason. But following the advice of this mysterious yet familiar voice has failed to free Tarwater from his religious obsessions. The failure of this friendly counselor is particularly unsettling for the modern reader, because his voice appeared to be the wisest and least crazy in the novel. The other voices belong to characters with whom the reader has trouble identifying: a backwoods moonshiner and self-proclaimed prophet, an idiot child, an unstable schoolteacher beset by strange obsessions. Even Tarwater is too intense and unusual for the reader to feel terribly close to. But the unattached voice, counseling personal independence and taking care of number one, says to Tarwater what the modern reader might like to say and appears to be simply the voice of Tarwater's common sense, his better self trying to rise above the confusion implanted in him by his strange upbringing.

After inviting the reader to share in, and identify with, the wisdom of Tarwater's friendly voice, the narrator here at the end, in a shocking turnaround, reveals the voice's true nature when its unmistakable embodiment, the violet-eyed homosexual, drugs and then rapes Tarwater. The stranger, it becomes agonizingly clear, is no friend at all; he is in fact a representative of the forces of demonism whose fondest dream is to ravish the faithful. His—and the reader's—commonsense vision, a vision valorizing the individual self and denying the divine, the narrator shows, is a wisdom borne straight out of hell. As Tarwater is shocked into a larger Christian vision by his rape, so too does the narrator hope readers will be by their own shocking ravishment that reveals the blindness and demonism of their own intellectualism. Both Tarwater and the readers, utterly chastened, are now prepared for the divine vision that closes the novel.

In the end *The Violent Bear It Away* does turn out to be a bildungsroman, but one of an altogether different sort from that which the reader had anticipated. Rather than being a classic American apprenticeship novel affirming the efforts of a boy to escape the bondage of his past and the constricting society of conformists, *The Violent Bear It Away* is the apprenticeship novel of a prophet sent to warn the people of the terrible speed of God's mercy. Moreover, from another perspective, it is another kind of bildungsroman: that of the prophetic reader. For as O'Connor admitted, all aspects of this novel are distorted and exaggerated in order to make the reader *see*—to see not merely the here and now in all its clarity but also the mysteries to which the here and now open. From this perspective the motion of the novel is as much the reader's as Tarwater's, with the narrator's setting up the secular readers to interpret the novel in one way only, and then delivering a shocking upbraiding meant to reveal to the readers their limited vision. By the end of the novel, the narrator hopes, the secular reader through this chastening shock will be willing to look deeper into life and will become, as O'Connor said those of prophetic insight were, "a realist of distances." The divine vision granted to Tarwater at the end can thus be seen as emblematic of the vision so granted the reader—if the reader has responded to the novel, opening the monologic self to a larger vision of things, the "added dimension" O'Connor liked to speak of (*MM*, 179, 150).

In both "A Good Man Is Hard to Find" and *The Violent Bear It Away* the narrator's basic strategy in communicating with the reader is one of guile and deceit centering on a violent reversal that subverts almost everything that has come before. The reader, returning to O'Connor's vivid word for it, is clobbered. The two works differ, however, in the ultimate vision to which they point. In the novel we find less presence of the dialogic and charitable Catholic vision that O'Connor herself ultimately embraced and that, as I have argued, in "A Good Man Is Hard to Find" is embodied in the grandmother's reaching out to The Misfit before her death. As I suggested in the previous discussion of the novel, O'Connor as author here seems given to the fundamentalism of the narrator; there are only traces of this larger charitable vision in the novel, primarily in the kindness of Buford Munson and in the suggestion—and it is only that—that Tarwater's fanaticism is too extreme, entailing an out-and-out rejection of all reasoning and rationality. But so strong is the narrative voice here that its power fends off all challenges and keeps its fundamentalist vision from coming undone—as often happens in O'Connor's work—so that the novel ends with a strong affirmation of the narrator's vision.

Such an affirmation, in contrast to what we find in "A Good Man Is Hard to Find" and other works, suggests that, like her interactions with her narrators and characters, O'Connor's authorial stance in her relationships with her readers is not consistent from work to work. Pressured herself from a number of forces and voices, including those of her readers, O'Connor changed and adapted her position. It seems she was driven primarily by two powerful—and frequently conflicting—urges toward the readers: a monologic rage, rooted in a severe fundamentalism, to lash out at the readers and so destroy their secularism; and a desire to proceed further after this lashing, to goad the readers to open up to a larger dialogic vision rooted in Christian charity. "A Good Man Is Hard to Find," I suggest, embodies these intentions in an uneasy balance, with O'Connor's fundamentalism and her Catholicism in a charged tension. *The Violent Bear It Away*, in contrast, shows her fundamentalist rage in ascendance, the force and drive of the novel being focused almost entirely on chastening the secular reader and celebrating the fundamentalist vision of the narrator and Tarwater.

Although I have focused almost exclusively in this chapter on how the reader is pressured by O'Connor and her fiction, I want to close by suggesting that O'Connor's relationships with her readers were important, too, for her own dialogic growth. This assertion may at first glance seem odd, given that most of O'Connor's interactions with her audience are refracted through a fundamentalist narrator who acts violently to change the readers' ways. And yet, as in her dealings with her characters, O'Connor saw the secular readers she wrote to, even those she saw resisting her to the end, as aspects of herself, and she said as much in "Writing Short Stories" (*MM*, 95). Thus, in envisioning her readers, in keeping them in mind when she wrote, and in shaping her fiction for them, O'Connor on one level entered into a profound interplay with aspects of herself usually suppressed by her ruling Catholicism. In engaging these voices from within as voices from without, O'Connor brought the Catholic vision under pressure and challenge, placing it in alien contexts. In this sense the secular voice of her readers penetrated her Catholic vision; as O'Connor admitted, she expressed her vision always with the reader in mind, always in ways that would account for how the reader would respond to it. Just as significantly, O'Connor, as her letters in particular indicate, continually envisioned herself as she thought her secular readers would—and, by extension, as her secular self would. Such freeing of herself from her predominant conception of herself opened the way to new perspectives and understanding.

O'Connor's relationship with her readers, then, finally is another expression of the dialogic vision that I have been arguing she possessed. In not closing herself off from the variety of voices of her self and the world, particularly those of her southern homeland—from her raging fundamentalist narrators to the rich assortment of her characters to her hard-nosed intellectual readers—O'Connor deepened her faith and her art. Through her dialogic interplay with these other voices, these other selves, O'Connor resisted the temptation of the monologic and isolated self and grew in stature as the profound thinker and artist we have come to know.

Bibliography

Aiken, David. "Flannery O'Connor's Portrait of the Artist as a Young Failure." *Arizona Quarterly*, XXXII (1976), 245–59.

Allen, Rodney. "The Cage of Matter: The World as Zoo in Flannery O'Connor's *Wise Blood*." *American Literature*, LVIII (1986), 256–70.

Asals, Frederick. *Flannery O'Connor: The Imagination of Extremity*. Athens, Ga., 1982.

Atkins, G. Douglas. *Reading Deconstruction, Deconstructive Reading*. Lexington, Ky., 1983.

Augustine. *The Confessions*. Translated by F. J. Sheed. New York, 1943.

Bakhtin, Mikhail. *The Dialogic Imagination: Four Essays*. Edited by Michael Holquist. Translated by Caryl Emerson and Michael Holquist. Austin, 1981.

———. *Problems of Dostoevsky's Poetics*. Edited and translated by Caryl Emerson. Minneapolis, 1984.

———. *Rabelais and His World*. Translated by Helene Iswolsky. Bloomington, 1984.

———. *Speech Genres and Other Late Essays*. Edited by Caryl Emerson and Michael Holquist. Translated by Vern W. McGee. Austin, 1986.

Brinkmeyer, Robert H., Jr. "A Closer Walk with Thee: Flannery O'Connor and Southern Fundamentalists." *Southern Literary Journal*, XVIII (Spring, 1986), 3–13.

———. *Three Catholic Writers of the Modern South*. Jackson, Miss., 1985.

Burns, Stuart L. "The Evolution of *Wise Blood*." *Modern Fiction Studies*, XVI (1970), 147–62.

Cash, W. J. *The Mind of the South*. New York, 1941.

Cheney, Brainard. "Flannery O'Connor's Campaign for Her Country." *Sewanee Review*, LXXII (1964), 555–58.

Desmond, John F. *Risen Sons: Flannery O'Connor's Vision of History*. Athens, Ga., 1987.

Driskell, Leon V., and Joan T. Brittain. *The Eternal Crossroads: The Art of Flannery O'Connor*. Lexington, Ky., 1971.

Eggenschwiler, David. *The Christian Humanism of Flannery O'Connor.* Detroit, 1972.

Faricy, Robert L. *Teilhard de Chardin's Theology of the Christian in the World.* New York, 1967.

Feeley, Kathleen. *Flannery O'Connor: Voice of the Peacock.* New Brunswick, N.J., 1972.

Feeley, Margaret Peller. "Flannery O'Connor's *Wise Blood*: The Negative Way." *Southern Quarterly*, XVII (1979), 104–22.

Friedman, Melvin J., and Beverly Lyon Clark, eds. *Critical Essays on Flannery O'Connor.* Boston, 1985.

Friedman, Melvin J., and Lewis A. Lawson, eds. *The Added Dimension: The Art and Mind of Flannery O'Connor.* New York, 1966.

Gentry, Marshall Bruce. *Flannery O'Connor's Religion of the Grotesque.* Jackson, Miss., 1986.

Getz, Lorine M. *Flannery O'Connor: Her Life, Library and Book Reviews.* New York, 1980.

Gordon, Caroline. "Flannery O'Connor's *Wise Blood*." *Critique*, II (1958), 3–10.

———. *The Garden of Adonis.* 1937; rpr. New York, 1971.

———. *The Strange Children.* 1951; rpr. New York, 1971.

Gossett, Louise Y. *Violence in Recent Southern Fiction.* Durham, N.C., 1965.

Gray, Richard. *Writing the South: Ideas of an American Region.* Cambridge, England, 1986.

Harpham, Geoffrey Galt. *On the Grotesque: Strategies of Contradiction in Art and Literature.* Princeton, 1982.

Hawkes, John. "Flannery O'Connor's Devil." *Sewanee Review*, LXX (1962), 395–402.

Hawthorne, Nathaniel. *The House of the Seven Gables.* 1851; rpr. Columbus, Ohio, 1965.

Heller, Erich. *The Disinherited Mind: Essays in Modern German Literature and Thought.* Expanded ed. New York, 1975.

Hendin, Josephine. *The World of Flannery O'Connor.* Bloomington, 1970.

Hyman, Stanley Edgar. *Flannery O'Connor.* Minneapolis, 1966.

Joyce, James. *A Portrait of the Artist as a Young Man.* 1916; rpr. New York, 1964.

Katz, Claire. "Flannery O'Connor's Rage of Vision." *American Literature*, XLVI (1974), 54–67.

Kessler, Edward. *Flannery O'Connor and the Language of the Apocalypse.* Princeton, 1986.

Kinney, Arthur F. *Flannery O'Connor's Library: Resources of Being.* Athens, Ga., 1985.

Lawson, Lewis A. *Another Generation: Southern Fiction Since World War II.* Jackson, Miss., 1984.

Lee, Maryat. "Flannery, 1957." *Flannery O'Connor Bulletin*, V (1976), 39–60.

Littlefield, Daniel R., Jr. "Flannery O'Connor's *Wise Blood*." *Mississippi Quarterly*, XXIII (1970), 121–33.

Longstreet, Augustus Baldwin. *Georgia Scenes*. New York, 1897.

Magee, Rosemary M., ed. *Conversations with Flannery O'Connor*. Jackson, Miss., 1987.

Maritain, Jacques. *Art and Scholasticism*. Translated by J. F. Scanlan. London, 1930.

———. *The Dream of Descartes*. Translated by Mabelle L. Andison. New York, 1944.

Martin, Carter W. *The True Country: Themes in the Fiction of Flannery O'Connor*. Nashville, 1969.

May, John R. *The Pruning Word: The Parables of Flannery O'Connor*. Notre Dame, Ind., 1976.

Milder, Robert. "The Protestantism of Flannery O'Connor." *Southern Review*, n.s., XI (1975), 802–19.

Miller, J. Hillis. *The Disappearance of God: Five Nineteenth-Century Writers*. Cambridge, Mass., 1963.

———. *Poets of Reality: Six Twentieth-Century Writers*. Cambridge, Mass., 1965.

Montgomery, Marion, *Possum and Other Receits for the Recovery of "Southern" Being*. Athens, Ga., 1987.

———. *Why Flannery O'Connor Stayed Home*. La Salle, Ill., 1981. Vol. I of Montgomery, *The Prophetic Poet and the Spirit of the Age*. 3 vols.

Morson, Gary Saul, ed. *Bakhtin: Essays and Dialogues on His Work*. Chicago, 1986.

Mounier, Emmanuel. *The Character of Man*. Translated by Cynthia Rowland. New York, 1956.

———. *Personalism*. Translated by Philip Mauret. London, 1952.

Muller, Gilbert H. *Nightmares and Visions: Flannery O'Connor and the Catholic Grotesque*. Athens, Ga., 1972.

O'Connor, Flannery. *The Complete Stories*. New York, 1971.

———. *The Habit of Being: Letters*. Edited by Sally Fitzgerald. New York, 1969.

———. *Mystery and Manners: Occasional Prose*. Edited by Sally Fitzgerald and Robert Fitzgerald. New York, 1969.

———. *The Violent Bear It Away*. New York, 1960.

———. *Wise Blood*. 2d ed. New York, 1962.

Orvell, Miles. *Invisible Parade: The Fiction of Flannery O'Connor*. Philadelphia, 1972.

Park, Clara Claiborne. "Crippled Laughter: Toward Understanding Flannery O'Connor." *American Scholar*, LI (1982), 249–57.

Pegis, Anton C., ed. *Introduction to St. Thomas Aquinas*. New York, 1948.

Percy, Walker. *The Message in the Bottle: How Queer Man Is, How Queer Language Is, and What One Has to Do with the Other.* New York, 1975.

Reiter, Robert, ed. *Flannery O'Connor.* St. Louis, 1968.

Rubin, Louis D., Jr. *A Gallery of Southerners.* Baton Rouge, 1982.

————, ed. *The Comic Imagination in American Literature.* New Brunswick, N.J., 1973.

Schneidau, Herbert N. *Sacred Discontent: The Bible and Western Tradition.* Baton Rouge, 1976.

Shloss, Carol. *Flannery O'Connor's Dark Comedies: The Limits of Inference.* Baton Rouge, 1980.

Simpson, Lewis P. *The Brazen Face of History: Studies in the Literary Consciousness in America.* Baton Rouge, 1980.

————. *The Dispossessed Garden: Pastoral and History in Southern Literature.* 1975; rpr. Baton Rouge, 1983.

Singal, Daniel Joseph. *The War Within: From Victorian to Modernist Thought in the South, 1919–1945.* Chapel Hill, 1982.

Stephens, C. Ralph, ed. *The Correspondence of Flannery O'Connor and the Brainard Cheneys.* Jackson, Miss., 1986.

Stephens, Martha. *The Question of Flannery O'Connor.* Baton Rouge, 1973.

Sullivan, Walter. *Death by Melancholy: Essays on Modern Southern Fiction.* Baton Rouge, 1972.

————. *A Requiem for the Renascence.* Athens, Ga., 1976.

Tate, Allen. *Collected Poems, 1919–1976.* New York, 1977.

————. *Essays of Four Decades.* Chicago, 1968.

————. *Memoirs and Opinions, 1926–1974.* Chicago, 1975.

————. *Mere Literature and the Lost Traveller.* Nashville, 1969.

————. "One Escape from the Dilemma." *Fugitive,* III (April, 1924), 34–36.

Teilhard de Chardin, Pierre. *The Divine Milieu: An Essay on the Interior Life.* Translated by Bernard Wall. New York, 1960.

————. *The Phenomenon of Man.* Translated by Bernard Wall. New York, 1960.

Todorov, Tzvetan. *Mikhail Bakhtin: The Dialogical Principle.* Translated by Wlad Godzich. Minneapolis, 1984.

Twain, Mark. *The Adventures of Huckleberry Finn.* 1884; rpr. New York, 1985.

Welty, Eudora. *The Eye of the Story: Selected Essays and Reviews.* New York, 1978.

Westling, Louise. *Sacred Groves and Ravaged Gardens: The Fiction of Eudora Welty, Carson McCullers, and Flannery O'Connor.* Athens, Ga., 1985.

White, Hayden. *Tropics of Discourse: Essays in Cultural Criticism.* Baltimore, 1978.

Zuber, Leo J., comp. *The Presence of Grace and Other Book Reviews by Flannery O'Connor.* Edited by Carter W. Martin. Athens, Ga., 1983.

Index